Dark Chains

LaTasha "Tacha B." Braxton

Dark Chains is the story of my childhood and my life as I remember it and as it's been told to me. I have striven to tell the truth, the whole truth, and nothing but the truth, so help me God; but I do understand that the following pages are told from my perspective. And, as with any other story, there is always another perspective or perspectives to consider. As such, and to protect the innocent and not-so-innocent, I've changed the names of many friends, family members and other people who came into my life.

Copyright © 2018 by LaTasha Braxton
All rights reserved. This book or any portion thereof
may not be reproduced or used in any manner whatsoever
without the express written permission of the publisher
except for the use of brief quotations in a book review.

Printed in the United States of America
First Printing, 2018

ISBN-13: 978-1986599351
ISBN-10: 1986599353

www.tachab.com

Born Into Dysfunction

I was born in May of 1986 as a high yellow, bushy eye-browed baby with the nickname "Buttons," which my dad gave me. This was in Hampton, Virginia, where my father and his family had grown up on farms around good food, animals, shotguns, love and just straight-to-the-point country living.

By the time I made my appearance, I already had a sensitive and timid sister who was 10 years old, a "rough around the edges," country bad boy for a father, and a cold manipulative mother who held nothing but pain and hatred for the ones who tried loving her the most. My mother was a jealous woman who made enemies of all the good people she'd encountered. Before I was conceived, she and my older sister, Latanya, made their way from their hometown of Washington, D.C., to the fields of Hampton, Virginia. Latanya's father was a womanizer who regularly cheated on my mother. The last straw was when he had drunken sex with another woman at a house party on top of a huge pile of coats for everyone to see. So I guess my mother ran away in hopes of leaving her heartbreak behind.

She and my sister were homeless at first, so they stayed with women my mother met along the way. During that stint, my mother decided to paint this new town red and go to a party, where it just so happened that my father and Uncle Ivan happened to be. It was my father's brother who spotted her right away and thought she was a "brick house," so the two of them exchanged numbers and continued partying.

Some nights passed before my mother decided to use that number. But when she did, instead of wanting to talk to Ivan, she wanted to talk to my father. She told Ivan that she had her eyes fixated on his brother, and wanted to talk to him instead. Taking his rejection like a grown man, he passed the phone right along, and that was the beginning of my parents' relationship.

Not much time passed before my father realized that my mother and sister had no place to call home. Worse yet, the woman they were staying with wanted them out. So my father asked his parents if the two of them could move in with the family; he expressed the feelings he had for my mother, along with the concern he had for her and my sister's well being. My future grandparents agreed, and just like that, my mother and sister had a new place they could call home.

For him, it was love at first sight. I mean, my mother was beautiful. It's understandable that, in his mind, my father thought he had quite a catch. But for her, all she had was a survival strategy. It wouldn't be long at all before my mother became pregnant with me, and what came with me was an ultimatum for my father: "Marry me, or we'll be out of your life for good."

My father loved her and my sister, so it seemed like an easy choice. He was excited to have a new baby on the way and to be starting a family of his own. My father had two other daughters with two other women, one from a previous relationship, and one from a one-night stand. Influenced by my mother's beauty and survival methods, he became more eager by the day to make this situation work.

The first problem with my parents' relationship is that they were moving way too fast. They were both traveling down a road together for all the wrong reasons. He was one naive country boy tricked by the lust of one cold-hearted opportunistic city girl. They were two strangers creating a family. And there I was about to be born in the middle of it all.

Father Dear

My dad and his family didn't have much money growing up, but what they did have a lot of was love. My dad and his three siblings grew up with the kind of parents who showed love and spoke love; they were tough and always gave 100% when it came to their family. They were Christians who grew up on the Word of God and shared his words and ways as often as they could with their children and others in their town. My grandfather was a man of peace and morals, and my grandmother was a short, yet feisty country woman who was a natural nurturer and the glue that held the family together.

Out of all his siblings, my dad was the wild one of the bunch. He would make his share of mistakes, breaking a few laws along the way. He drank a lot, and would turn into the Tasmanian devil, willing to destroy whatever he didn't like standing in his path. He learned as he lived, allowing his mistakes to teach him the lessons he was too stubborn to learn from his parents.

He was a hard-headed handsome fella, filled with country charm. A real ladies' man at his core no matter how he didn't mean to be. In women's eyes, my father was the country Fabio, making women go completely insane over him with no efforts on his part at all. Women just loved caressing the manly hairs on his arms while stroking his ego with comments of how handsome and strong he was. They loved his bad boy persona, and found his need for adrenaline and danger to be alluring.

My dad worked as a fisherman on a Skylark boat, such a perfect job for such a thrill-seeking wild boy. He found excitement in the deadly storms, giant whales, squids, and the rescues of his shipmates almost falling overboard. A true adrenaline junkie who literally swam with the sharks whenever he felt like taking a cool dip, despite the meat-eating creatures that lurked below. And what excited him the most was the one hundred thousand dollar annual salary he made by doing it.

Just like his father, my dad was a self-taught man and a tinkerer to boot. Anything that needed fixing, he could take care of, including cars, which he loved driving and racing too.

Although he was rowdy, he had the Word of God embedded in him at an early age by his parents. He was humane, and showed it by knocking bullies upside their heads for people who couldn't defend themselves. He carried a conscience, though at times, he ignored it. Nonetheless, it was there. And despite how tough he was, family was always the key to his heart. He was just a free-spirited man, with an effortless sense of humor, making jokes about things most people wouldn't dare joke about, and saying things most people would be too reluctant to say. Just a neck bone-loving man who grew up in a small town where disputes were solved by beating the moonshine out of one another.

Mother Dear

My mother came from a broken and dysfunctional past, where her heart had been broken at a young age.

Her own mother left her when she was about seven years old. On the night she left, she crept into my mother's room, sat on the edge of her bed, said, "I love you," and kissed her goodbye. My mother never saw her again. She was then left with her father, who hustled and ran the streets too often to take care of her.

My mother was flat-out neglected. Her health, her wellbeing and her emotional state were all at stake. After she almost died of pneumonia, her God-fearing grandmother took her in, nurturing her back to good health and teaching her the kind of skills she herself had acquired from her days as a nurse.

It would have been nice if that situation could have lasted. But her grandmother fell ill to the point where she couldn't effectively take care of my mother anymore, unintentionally traumatizing my mother that much more. After hearing this news, her father's sister, Aunt Lia, stepped in and adopted my mother with open arms. Aunt Lia already had three other children, two boys and one girl. But she had always wanted another daughter, and she found that in my mother.

In Aunt Lia's eyes, my mother was truly a blessing. She tried her best to give her a loving home with family that just wanted to accept and love her; she wanted to teach her right from wrong and all about God and a moral living.

But by the time that adoption took place, my mother's heart was already far too damaged to openly accept those heartfelt offerings.

Young, scared, confused and hurt, she allowed her pain to influence her into rejecting the beautiful new gift she was offered. My mother's heart was so broken from being abandoned by her parents and then passed from house to house that even when love was right there, ready to wrap its warm arms around her, she couldn't allow herself to embrace it. The potential fallout was too horrifying to risk, and so she worked hard to protect herself from ever feeling abandoned again by not letting anyone else in.

The significance of love wasn't yet instilled in her.

Still so young, she was scared. Scared that another person would hurt her. Scared that another person would say "I love you," and then leave her abandoned and stranded. Scared that if she accepted her Aunt's love, she'd be left vulnerable. Again. In her young mind, she'd come to associate love for weakness. The way she saw it, the more you loved, the more susceptible you were to getting hurt.

I wish someone could have made her see how destructive that way of thinking was to her mind, body and soul. Because the truth is, love is strength.

When you love, you have the power to heal not only yourself, but others. When you love, you are mentally and spiritually protected from evil and vindictiveness. When you love, nothing and no one can trap you in a paralyzed state of misery and hate.

When you love, you are closer to God, and what greater protection is there than that? When you love God, you are then able to appreciate and love yourself. Love is the creator of a positive environment.

Yet hurt, pain and abandonment had allowed my young mother to believe the opposite. She didn't know love because she refused it. In this case, she didn't even give it a chance. She didn't know what it felt like or looked like. My mother was a lost soul – probably a lost soul with all the potential in the world. But a person's greatness can't manifest itself if that individual doesn't love and let God in to help.

My Existence

I have mixed feelings about how I came into existence.

In my eyes, I was born for the wrong reasons, a life conceived by a lie and ulterior motives. Once my mother became pregnant, she told my Dad her birth control failed due to the antibiotics she was also taking. But my dad had been keeping track of my mother's birth control and found out she hadn't been taking them at all.

In fact, he had accumulated tons of information about my mother, including her shenanigans, in the short amount of time he'd known her. He'd make mental notes of her lies and bad behavior, and so he knew she was far from perfect.

But there's something about being in love that can distort the truth and disrupt your common sense. Serious character flaws don't seem half as bad while waltzing on a cloud of adoration. We may even feel as though the objects of our affections have the possibility to change overtime.

The problem is, if their minds and souls aren't with God, and if they're not seeing their issues clearly enough to want to change, then we could be waiting on better days and breakthroughs for a lifetime. In Dad's particular case, he knew of my mother's ways. But because he was in love, his optimism triumphed over his reality.

When I was swimming in Mom's belly, my father's mother embraced her because of how much her son loved her. My Dad was happy about growing his family; and to my grandmother, his happiness was all that mattered. All the same, she knew my mother was a selfish woman; and she did warn him about it. She saw right through my mother's motives, quickly realizing that my mother was a survivalist who would do whatever it took to get by – even if that meant tricking a man out of his pockets with a pregnancy.

My mother saw a naive country boy who made a lot of money, and in the 80's, 100k was considered a jackpot. This was a country boy whose kindness she misconstrued for weakness; she was taking advantage of a man who was hooked on her line like a Yellow fin tuna. And my dad was a man whose kindness quickly faded when he hit the whisky bottle too hard. It was a toxic combination that was never going to end well.

From the time my parents met until my mother's third trimester, she went from being this sweet, concerned, nurturing woman who any man would be happy to marry to a hateful, spiteful and vindictive creature that was filled with pain and was far too prone toward hurtful behavior. She slowly uncloaked her true nature, her true inner image, and made her reintroduction to the man she had just married.

She had sealed the deal. She was now married to a man who made a very decent living, and one with whom she shared an unborn child.

After that was taken care of, my mother switched personalities so fast that my dad thought he was the one going crazy at first. He felt tricked - bamboozled. Confused by the sudden switch-up, and not at all sure what to think or believe at times, it seemed like the more he tried to love her, the more dismissive she became.

Then, on May 15th, I arrived. An innocent little being who instinctually wanted to rely on my parents' knowledge, love and wisdom for everything I needed. But when I arrived, I only had one parent to rely on; my dad was passed out drunk somewhere and missed my birth. This would be the first time out of many important moments he'd miss because of his addiction to alcohol. However, despite his shortcomings, I was immediately my father's pride and joy, and he took me everywhere with him. Only select people were allowed to hold me; even his own sisters had to wait their turn. He wanted me all to himself.

I'm sure my arrival distracted him from his new, and unfortunately, transformed bride as well. And my 10-year-old half-sister, Latanya, saw me as an exciting addition as well. She finally could play the role of big sibling while also having someone to spend time with. I guess I gave her a beautiful distraction from having an emotionless mother and a drunken step-father, a situation which must have been really hard for her to deal with. So I created some happy moments for my family right after I was born, but just not enough to overshadow the dysfunction that plagued our home.

A few months went by when my mother no longer wanted us to live with my Dad's family. She grew tired of the drinking and physical altercations that regularly occurred amongst him and his siblings. The last straw was when my Dad threw his sister through a closed window during one of their drunken arguments. So my dad asked for a five hundred thousand dollar loan through the company he was working for, and when he was approved, left my mother in charge of finding us a new home. Desperate to move-out, she decided to put her signature on a home that was ready for immediate move-in. And when it came time for my Dad to see what his wife had purchased, he was furious to learn she had chosen a double-wide trailer.

Questioning my mother's logic, he wanted to know why on earth she chose a trailer, considering the amount of the loan he secured and how much he earned each year. The thoughts of what kind of home we could have had pissed him off, which led to more tension and more arguments between the two of them. But we had no choice; my mother's signature closed the deal, and this trailer became our new home.

My Dad never could see clear enough to understand why my mother made the poor decision she made. An aggressive and violent environment was the norm for him, but not for her. He was inconsiderate to what scared his wife, and continued with his thoughtlessness when it came to her feelings.

Trailer Park Drama

In our new trailer was where my Dad discovered my mother's love for cocaine, something else she hid from him until they got married.

He began to see my mother take a small glass tube out of her purse at parties; she would swiftly hold it up to her nose, and snort into the tube. This country man knew nothing about cocaine. The only things he was familiar with were ganja and liquor. And he had avoided the ganja like the plague ever since jumping out of his brother's truck head first down a hill in a panic because he got too high.

But one day, my mother managed to get him to try the stuff. She convinced him with basic peer pressure, pitching the euphoria effects the drug gave. After a while, my Dad was hooked on cocaine too; it became a recurring experience that both of my parents shared together. They began putting Latanya, Monae, who was my Dad's other daughter from his previous relationship, and me in the back bedroom to play, while the both of them snorted lines in the living room.

And when my mother wasn't getting high in the living room with Dad, she would go out partying, leaving him to watch us.

She loved the nightlife; I guess it was her means of escape. She would get drunk and flirt with any and every man that happened to notice her, sitting on their laps and stroking their egos right in front of everyone. She didn't care who seen her indiscretions; she didn't even care when my father's sister walked into the same party once, catching her red-handed, seated on the lap of some gentleman at the bar. As small as the town of Hampton was, it was as if my mother wanted to intentionally get caught. Soon, everyone in town except my father knew his wife enjoyed getting drunk and entertaining other men. And for a while, my Dad stayed clueless to my mother's sin, wondering why people in the town would join ears to whisper every time he came around. Until one night, his sister decided to knock on our door to tell him what his wife had been doing every time she went out to these parties. Luckily, my mother wasn't home, because after my Dad caught an earful, he was livid. He even took out his anger on his own sister, yelling and screaming irrational thoughts triggered by the pain he felt in his heart. And when Dad got angry, Latanya knew to grab Monae, me, and our pet cat, and take us back into our bedroom and lock the door.

On this same night, when my mother came home, Dad was waiting up for her in the living room. He wasted no time confronting her about what his sister had told him. The more accusations he spoke, the more she denied them ever happening, and the more antagonizing she became.

She knew she was disrespecting her marriage; it was her way of retaliating against my Dad for his drunken behavior and lack of compassion. These two had poor communication skills, where they each contributed ill behavior to their marriage. But my Dad couldn't see his fault in this situation; all he could see was my mother's. All he could see was his wife disrespecting his marriage by lusting over men who lived in the same town. All he could think about was all of his paychecks he had handed over to my mother, and all of the embarrassment he would have to face when walking down the street or going to the store.

My Dad's pain continued to build with each unpleasant vision, and suddenly he snapped, striking her across her face, launching the smirk my mother carried from all her lying straight across the room. As my puzzled mother held her cheek in her hand, my Dad began to scream at her, reminding her that he was the breadwinner of the family and because of that, he demanded the utmost respect.

Because of mother's unaddressed pain and subsequent behavior, my father began to drink and drug his pain away more often than before. He became an angry drunk, and in return, my mother became more cold and vindictive than she was before. The manipulation, the lies and uncaring behavior began to grow in my mother as if it wasn't bad enough before. Both of my parents were affected by pain and a lack of compassion for one another. It was a situation of two toxic people feeding off of each other's negative traits, blocking any positivity from ever blossoming within their hearts.

My mother was already an abandoned soul, a misguided young woman who would subconsciously put herself into situations that starved her soul. The worst feeling in the world is to love someone who cannot love you back, to care about someone who can only care about themselves. Both of my parents felt this about each other, without recognizing that neither one of them knew how to love the other.

We children were suffering the most, having to constantly hear the yelling and bad language influenced by drugs and alcohol through our locked bedroom door. We dealt with the trauma our mother felt from having a gun put to her face by my father. We dealt with the fear after my father threw a big concrete block through their bedroom window, shattering glass everywhere, with the brick barely missing my tiny head as I innocently slept in my mother's arms. We were succumbing to this dysfunctional curse that would negatively impact too many generations to come.

As We Suffered

As the dysfunction continued, so did my mother's vindictive behavior. My father viewed Latanya as his own; in his eyes, she was his daughter. But my mother, however, felt differently about our blended family. Every time Dad would bring Monae over to the house, mother would treat her like little Orphan Annie after the riches were gone. She would fix dinner and give less food to Monae, while giving her own children bigger portions. Each time she did this, it would hurt my father, making him even more angry. He demanded that she treat all of us equally, with the same level of love he gave to Latanya.

But she didn't want to listen and continued treating Monae like an outsider.

This reassured my father that love for him had no place in my mother's heart; I don't think it ever did. You can't claim to love someone while handling that same person's innocent child with no love at all. At this point, considering how their relationship was failing, the possibility of my mother loving him at all was less than slim. He began to realize how he could count on one hand how many times she had told him she loved him.

The more that set in, the more it hurt him; the more it hurt him, the more drinking and drugging he did. Anger set in more frequently and more permanently as he continued to use alcohol and drugs to cope. Alcoholism was already an established problem in my father's family. So were anxiety and depression. So my mother's lack of love exposed him to his pre-established genetic vulnerability. Again, very unreceptive of his contribution to this dysfunctional marriage, my father began to fixate on what he wanted the most. He wanted a loving, respectful wife and a happy family.

So many toxic people want the happy family with the white picket fence and the playful pet dog, as if this setting is the antidote for their dysfunctional negative life, not realizing that the rearranging of the mind is the only medicine strong enough to break down and dissolve their flawed universe. You can't allow your mind to operate off of fumes of pain, hate and negativity and then wonder why your life sucks. And you can't want respect in a marriage when you fail to give it up yourself. Both of my parents were selfish, wanting the world without wanting to compromise. Wanting love, without wanting to love. So we all stayed suffering.

Young Girls

Young girls mostly learn their motherly nurturing skills by observing their mothers interact with their own children and husband. These little women-in-the-making are supposed to watch their mothers fight for and cherish their families, and then tap into that energy as well. They're supposed to see that love come out, but also feel it and practice it in turn.

A girl's mother is her first female superhero, and with good reason when she sees her mother do everything for her family, yet stay so strong. She'll witness her mother's resilience, poise and love. And when she gets older and becomes her own woman, she'll be properly equipped to be the same way. She'll be conditioned to being magnificent for the simple reason that she's acquired that same ability after witnessing her mother for so long.

She will be beautiful from the inside out. She'll be strong. And she'll be respected, because she refuses to take anything less. A young girl should be taught how to respect herself and everything she owns, including her mind, emotions, body, and soul. Through example and guidance, she's supposed to learn the value of independence, self-worth and self-love.

She should be reassured that she's a princess that will one day rise and become a queen in her own right who will one day carry the responsibilities of her own family. Young girls need strong, wise women with deep morals in their lives to instill the skills and principles that they need to grow into women who deserve to be:

Admired – not abused.

Respected – not used.

Loved – not lied to.

Now, young girls also learn from their fathers' actions as well. How they think they're supposed to be treated by men mostly depends on the lessons they intentionally or unintentionally provide.

A good father will teach his daughter that a man is supposed to cherish and respect her. He'll teach her about the kinds of guys to stay away from, so that, when this little girl gets older, she'll be able to rule out the men who just want to take advantage of her. And she'll be able to identify that one special guy who genuinely wants to spend the rest of his life with her because he truly loves every single nook and cranny that makes her who she is.

This special guy will respect her and love her just as her father does because, as a little girl, she had a great teacher about what respect and love look like. For better or worse, women usually choose mates who share similar characteristics to their fathers, because that's what they're used to and that's what they crave - a father's love.

But what happens to the girl with no positive parental examples? What happens to the girl with the cold mother who conditioned herself to bury her emotions? And what happens to the girl with the father who is an example of who not to marry?

My mother couldn't be a positive example to us, through no fault of her own. When her parents abandoned her, they took those important life lessons right along with them. So there she was, all grown up, in a marriage, with a family, not knowing how to love. And there was my father, leading his family of females with violence and poor judgment.

Feelings

My sister, Latanya, was an emotional child who didn't say much; she would observe all the pain our parents created, then go into our bedroom and bottle up her own. Ignoring your feelings can make them even more powerful. Feelings naturally want to be expressed and acknowledged. They want out. And when they don't get that release, they begin to fester and turn into anger and resentment. My sister was becoming angry with our mother, and she began hating her stepfather. Her feelings went unacknowledged, because our mother and my father were too busy being cruel to one another.

No one sat her down to talk to her about how she felt. No one cared about how their behavior could affect this little girl, or even me for that matter. Healing of the heart wasn't an example given to us by our parents. With each day that passed, Latanya harbored more ill feelings toward the very two people who were supposed to care for her the most.

At just ten years old, Latanya began to write these little notes to herself explaining how much she hated our mother and wished for bad things to happen to her. It was as if she was mad at our mother for putting us into this dysfunctional situation in the first place. She would then hide those letters inside her little toy wooden piano for no one to see. Hurt and emotionally neglected at such a young age, she began to strongly resent our mother, and continued to hate her step-father.

One evening, my father was drawn to that piano, and decided to look inside, finding all my sisters bottled up hate and anger. In something of a panic, he took those letters and immediately showed them to our mother, who reacted with nonchalant dismissal. She seemed to not be bothered by the notes at all.

Either she didn't care, or she was trying her hardest to make it look that way. One way or the other, my mother's response was alarming, and Latanya's feelings continued to go untended.

A few weeks later, my sister's Aunt Tracy, on her dad's side, however, had heard about the dysfunction that plagued our home. Tracy told my mother that she was coming to get Latanya – with or without her permission. I guess my sister couldn't take our environment anymore and decided to reach out to a family member who she knew would care about her well-being.

And she was right, because her aunt didn't hesitate to rescue her niece from the fighting, drugs and hate to which she had been subjected.

Tracy must have sensed the hurt in her little niece's voice when they spoke on the phone. And so, just like that, Latanya was gone, swept back to D.C. where she was born and raised.

With my sister gone, my father began to notice just how cold and selfish my mother could really become. The fact that my mother seemed undisturbed by her daughter's absence was noticeably alarming in itself. It was like the inside of her heart was as hollow as that cheap chocolate bunny kids receive on Easter morning.

Hopes and Delusions

My father was raised to believe that a man never abandons his marriage. And so he took his vows seriously and passionately, no matter how ill-mannered he was. Divorce just wasn't an option for him; whatever problems arose, you were supposed to continue loving one another and trying your hardest to fix things. This is what he learned from observing his parents' relationship growing up. But how can you overcome a hump in a marriage when you aren't aware that you are a big part of the problem?

My parents easily recognized the flaws within each other, but failed to see the imperfections within themselves. The first step in solving issues with a loved one is to confront your imperfections within yourself first, and think about how your behavior could affect the feelings of the other. Try to understand where their reactions come from.

That first "conversation" gives you the opportunity to be more understanding and strategic when you go on to seek resolution. It allows you to take the other person's background, previous pain and personality into consideration.

You must be willing to listen without judgment, you must remain patient, and become selfless. Some couples may need additional assistance to recognize their hurtful behavior. People are products of their environment. If you were raised in dysfunction, the toxic behavior you've acquired from it may be deemed harmless in your eyes, and hurtful in others.

It would have been great if my parents reached out to a therapist or counselor, a loving, conscious and spiritually-connected person who would have been able to help mentally guide them in the right direction. My mother and father needed help relocating their spirits to where it was initially destined to be. They lived in anger without understanding how to care for it.

Everyone gets angry. Everyone feels that emotion. It isn't a question of whether you get angry or not. What's important is what you do with that anger when it begins to surface. How do you let it not control you? What can you do to turn your anger into a positive response or solution? Because impulsive actions that stem from anger solve nothing when something clearly needs to be solved.

A real, mutual solution is one that results in both parties being happy and peacefully existing with each other. But again, you're not going to achieve that if you don't first come to an understanding with yourself that allows you to have these feelings in a healthy manner. Once you get to that personal point, then you're ready to talk to the person who hurt you. You've been observant with yourself, and so you'll be able to be more observant with them as well, noticing their feelings, body language and facial expressions – signs to help you know what to say and what not to say in order to bring about the positive changes you're craving.

You're also able to see the level of pain that person is going through. We hear all the time how "hurt people hurt people." It's become something of a cliché by now. Yet the fact that it's so frequently stated doesn't make it any less true.

My mother was a product of her environment - a product of pain. She had already lied, manipulated and hurt my father throughout most of their short-lived marriage. And my father hurt her with his abuse, drunken behavior, and lack of concern for his wife's feelings. They were both selfish.

Actions are powerful, but it's important to acknowledge that so are emotions. Emotional abuse can be the most painful thing a person can endure because it's abuse of your soul and mind.

A soul and mind are very powerful parts of a person, yet they're also very sensitive. That's why it's so important to be careful about what you subject your mind and body to. If you don't take good care of these elements, you can lose the person you were meant to become. You could become bitter from all of the pain, anger and resentment you feel. And bitter spirits find joy in the misery of others. They find joy in sucking all the light and positive energy from another's aura. They thrive off of bad spirits that live off of destruction.

You become a person who hurts people because someone hurt you. You become part of the problem in this world, spreading pain and tainting hearts. And this ping-pong effect can go on and on if something isn't done to break that bitter cycle.

Yet it can be broken. All it takes is one person to stop that pain in its tracks and say, "No, I will not be a vindictive spirit and I will not retaliate in pain." It just takes one person to be mindful and attempt to resolve the conflict - to heal, talk, understand, and listen.

If you find yourself understanding my parents' story all too well, try this out: Tap into your empathy and sympathy in order to seek a resolution. Become a counselor for the two of you.

In so doing, understand that there's a difference between protecting yourself and retaliation, going out of your way to make sure someone else feels as bad as you do. There's a strategy for everything in life, and it's up to you to come up with the best approach.

Ask yourself:

- Will this heal the situation or hurt it further?
- Am I acting out on my pain, or am I speaking and thinking mindfully?
- Am I acknowledging their pain as well as my own?

My father's judgment was impaired by alcohol and drugs, and my mother was an unguided woman. If your body shows signs of a vitamin D deficiency, you would add vitamin D into your diet to fix and heal your body. Healing unguided people works the same way. If they're unguided, their body and soul lack love. So that's what you would give them in order to heal - love.

Deep down inside, my mother was still that traumatized little girl who was scared of the world and didn't know any better. She emotionally hurt my father because she didn't trust him with anything, especially her feelings.

In any relationship, trust is the first thing that should be created. Without that, any effort toward anything good will be close to impossible. Nothing will be genuine, doubts will be created, and hurt will eventually happen.

You simply can't show true love without trust. If you think you can, then you're living a lie.

By this point in their marriage, neither of my parents trusted each other. My mother couldn't emotionally trust my father, and he couldn't trust her words or actions. This was a disaster, and we all suffered the consequences.

Trust occurs with friendship. It takes place when two or more people genuinely take their precious time and use it to get to know each other. That's something my parents didn't do. They didn't take the time to create a trustworthy bond. They met fast, got into a relationship fast, had a baby fast, then got married fast.

But it's too late for these two to develop a genuine friendship now. They had already destroyed each other too early in their marriage. All my mother sought now was revenge for how my father treated her; she couldn't have cared less about creating a bond.

Vanished

The night before Latanya left to go back to DC with her aunt, our mother played a little game with all of us. In order to get my father on board with it, she claimed it would be fun, exciting and cool.

According to her, she had learned how to read a person's future and character from their handwriting. So she got a blank piece of paper and told my dad and my sister to sign their signatures at the very bottom. And since I couldn't write yet, my mother took my tiny little hand and signed my name for me, then proceeded to "interpret" them.

At the time, Dad thought a family game was a little strange, considering how thick the air was from all of their fighting and hurtful behavior. But he continued to play along for the sake of us kids anyway.

Within weeks, my mother had added content to the top of that very same paper, where she wrote that her husband had relinquished all his custody rights and signed them over to her.

She took the document to court, filed the papers to get full custody of me and set her plans into motion. So when my father came home one day after work, there wasn't a soul there. The furniture, our pet cat, our clothes - nothing remained there but emptiness. My mother didn't even leave the curtains.

This broke him down even further than he already was, and he turned to drink more heavily than ever, along with drugs, negativity and depression. He would go to work on that dangerous Skylark boat in the middle of the sea with nothing but his family on his mind. Not knowing where we were made him far too distracted. He would be on that boat surrounded by danger and influenced by liquor, wanting to end it all.

His family, co-workers and friends began to worry about his mental state as he continued to fall deeper into depression. This is when reality set in, when his flaws began to surface and flood his mind, allowing him to see how horrible of a husband and father he was to us.

At the final custody court hearing, he told the judge to give my mother whatever she wanted; he was just too broken to fight and too depressed to speak. After a few months of depression and self-medicating, he began making attempts to find out where we were. My father started his search by calling Aunt Lia, the woman who had taken my mother in and raised her as her own. And after having a conversation with her, he quickly learned that that's where we had been staying. He also learned that since we were in a safe and stable environment, Latanya had come back to live with us.

My father kept in communication with Aunt Lia and her daughter Valerie, who was living there too, to see how we were doing. Since Aunt Lia was the first person who actually knew of my mother's cold behavior and immoral ways, Dad would console himself by regularly talking to her in an attempt to heal his heart and mind. He even began confiding in Aunt Lia, venting about all the pain he caused his family.

He wanted to know how my sister and I were doing, worrying about us constantly and wanting to know every changing moment in our lives. He would ask about my mother, hoping that one day she would change her mind and return to Hampton with my sister and me by her side.

He couldn't see us or touch us, but just knowing where we were kept him from falling off the deep end altogether. My dad appreciated the kind of person my Aunt Lia was, a compassionate soul who could and would heal so many hearts. She was a great listener, a natural nurturer and a compassionate speaker who had been raised in church by a very religious Christian mother who was active in her community. So it only made sense that he could pour his heart out to her on the phone, knowing that she would comfort his worries.

In a way, she reminded him of his own mother, tough, yet loving and gentle. She was nurturing and compassionate, knowledgeable and wise. My aunt had morals, and my father felt the warmth and safety of her aura, making it comfortable for him to express the pain and feelings he was experiencing.

Time went on, and I had just turned three years old. My father kept in contact with Aunt Lia through the years, but the form of communication had changed. He was writing letters from jail. It seemed as soon as he would be released, he would go right back in for something else he'd done. I remember the first set of letters he wrote to me. I was still learning to read, so my Aunt Lia or Aunt Valerie would help me make sense of the letters. It was a weird feeling, as if my Dad was in the same category as the Tooth Fairy and Santa Claus. I believed he existed only because that's what I was told. I was confused, and wondered why I couldn't see him, speak to him, or touch him.

Attached to these letters would be pictures of him and his family, I would sit at the dining room table and stare at the photos. Attempting to spot any physical resemblance between me and these strangers called family.

First feelings of love

My sister and I loved it at our aunt's home; we felt protected and loved by both Aunt Lia and Valerie. It felt different in a good kind of way. There was structure, positive discipline, respect, and morals – the perfect setting for children, especially those who were used to nothing but dysfunction. Instead of being around chaos and anger, we spent our days with two women who not only said they loved us, but showed it, so we knew what love actually was.

I honestly never felt sadness there, and neither did Latanya. One of my favorite things to do would be running into Aunt Valerie's room in the morning and putting on all of her bracelets, then running around the house with her camera pretending to be her. She would then wake up and laugh at the cuteness, positively affected by my bubbly, loving innocence.

As for Aunt Lia, she was an old-fashioned, beautifully poised woman. Everything she did was feminine and alluring, from how she spoke to how she walked. Even how she loved others was beautiful. She quickly became more like a grandmother to my sister and me, setting a good example of how to be kind and ladylike.

She also had such a wonderful sense of humor and could dress better than the *Vogue* models I'd see on the cover. She was just as, or even more, beautiful than them too.

After her own mother passed away, Aunt Lia became the glue that kept the entire family together. If you were having a tough time, she would open her heart and home to you. If you needed a shoulder to cry on, my aunt was there to listen and help you get through all your pain and sadness. Even plants responded well to her. Aunt Lia had a natural green thumb and used the same skills on her garden as she used to nurture people.

So it only made sense that she had the most beautiful patch in the neighborhood.

I loved sitting in the living room looking out of the big window that overlooked her garden, watching her tend to each flower and plant with the most gentleness, love, and care. I used to be amazed at how she always stayed beautiful, neat, and well-dressed while doing so.

My love for flowers and living things started there, watching Aunt Lia grow the most beautiful and exotic-looking flowers I'd ever seen. I never saw a sick or dying plant in her care. Ever. She just had that touch.

All put together, I looked up to her, respecting her warmth, love, intelligence, spunk and character. And as I began to age, I began to realize how much this woman meant to me. I was a visual learner, and this was one of the greatest lessons I had ever seen.

I would sit back and watch Aunt Lia, hoping that one day, I could be just as charming, confident, and poised as she was. And as I got a wee bit older, it seemed like I had a chance of it, turning into this good-spirited, cute little girl that loved to say hi to everyone.

Unfortunately, I don't recall much of my mother during this time. Aunt Valerie, in particular, would take me on trips to see and do new and exciting things. Knowing how I was a visual learner, she did so much to expand my mind so that I could create my identity and come up with my own perspectives about life.

I went everywhere with my Aunt Valerie; I was her hanging partner on all of our wonderful and mentally-fulfilling adventures to the beach, museums, festivals, light shows, concerts, bike rides, vacations. You name it - we went there.

Just for fun, we'd take the train or bus sometimes to get to one of our adventures, and I would yell out "Hi!" to every single person on the bus or train, touching hearts and making their days.

I began to love loving people. Though I was a complex little girl I was extremely loving and sincere, which my aunt loved about me. While she loved all her little nieces and nephews to pieces, it was the two of us who would sometimes dress up alike to go out.

I should mention that my mother was around. But it was Aunt Valerie who took the time to really get to know me as a human being. It was Aunt Valerie who took time to introduce me to new and exciting things. She was the one who taught and led me through one example after another, including what being a woman was all about.

Aunt Valerie was a teacher at my elementary school, which I also loved. She would pop in my class to see how I was doing, and every time, I could barely hold my excitement. Sometimes my aunt would bring cupcakes or doughnuts for me, my teacher and the rest of the class.

She was just all-around good with children – helping them, teaching them, guiding them. I can recall my sister, some of our cousins and even some kids from school joining us on some of our adventures. For my part, those outings allowed me to love and appreciate the wonders and beauty of nature. I began to recognize how the birds and squirrels fought, played and communicated, the different kind of trees and flowers, and how they made me feel, and the calming beauty of nature that made me feel at peace.

It was also Aunt Valerie who educated me about my African-American roots. As a young girl, I'd portray the white Barbie dolls as beautiful and show disregard to the black dolls. The power of marketing and commercials can do this to young children, manipulating them into thinking that they want or need a particular kind of toy. And so I didn't see beauty in the African-American Barbie dolls until my aunt introduced me to them.

We would go to the toy store, where she'd only allow me to pick out African-American dolls. I was disappointed at first until I began to realize how attractive they really are.

They were gorgeous, with their dark, supple-looking skin and big, thick, jet-black hair. They were very different from their Caucasian counterparts, but in such a lovely way.

Aunt Valerie had introduced me to another side of beauty, an eccentric beauty that resembled me instead of as a rigid color in a rigid way.

But it wasn't until she began introducing me to the carnivals in D.C., that I really started looking at beauty more realistically. I would see these beautiful beings of color, gorgeous women who came in all shades of brown. They were curvy and feminine yet strong and powerful. They had this alluring muscle tone covering every inch of their bodies. They smiled with confidence with their high cheekbones and glanced at the crowd with their big, beautiful flirtatious eyes. Each woman seemed to have their own unique color that glowed and covered their bodies in rich copper, bronze, gold, red bronze, and dark rich silky brown tones. And they wore colorful garments that made their beautifully rich skin color pop out even more. They danced as if they were celebrating the beautiful curves God gave them, and swayed their unique hairstyles of braids and beads, or full thick curly locs melodically with the high tempo beat of the Caribbean music that echoed amongst the city streets. I had never seen anything like them before.

It was at that moment I was proud to call myself a black girl and proud to have some sort of relation to the beauty on display in front of me.

Of course, I experienced beauty across many different spectrums: Beautiful and delicious foods. Beautiful music. Beautiful people.

I was overwhelmed with beauty and diversity in the most positive ways possible. I didn't know it then, but this was my aunt's way of teaching me about my own value, as well as other's. She wanted me to see for myself what it meant to be a person and a woman of color. She showed me something I never would have been able to see on some overly priced commercial.

She showed me substance. She showed me reality. And she did it all in direct response to that first day in the toy store, when I thought I wanted a white Barbie doll instead of a black one.

Aunt Valerie came right out and asked me, "Why do you think the white one is more acceptable and beautiful than the black one?" And she recognized how very advertisement-influenced my answer was when I said, "Because they're just beautiful, and they have pretty clothes and pretty hair."

The carnival experience was her response. She didn't sit me down and lecture me; she did something a million times better – she showed me and, in so doing, allowed me to see for myself and make my own decisions.

My aunts were the best thing that ever happened to me.

As my stay with Aunt Lia and Aunt Valerie continued, Aunt Valerie continued to be the mother I needed, and Aunt Lia continued to be the grandmother I always wanted. My actual mother, for whatever reason, never took the time to do anything remotely similar. I'm not saying she didn't care about us. She probably did. But for whatever reason, she just wasn't concerned with developing us into the strong, knowledgeable, respectful, moral young ladies we ought to be. Her focus was elsewhere.

The way I see it now, both of my aunts were fully aware of that deficiency. So they stepped in and showed us the love we deserved.

These two amazing individuals were my first female role models. And it was because of them that I realized that women can be strong, beautiful and intelligent all at the same time.

The Coldest Day

Throughout all of this, Aunt Lia kept trying to reach through to my mother, the physically grown-up version of that hurt little girl she had once taken in and cared for. But it didn't matter what she did or said; my mother continued to reject the skills she needed to be conscious and aware. She resented any attempts to correct her parenting. She didn't want to hear about it when she did something wrong. She never wanted to listen to those people who were more aware, more knowledgeable, and more skillful than she was, not even for the sake of my sister and me.

Instead, my mother took Lia's guidance and love, and turned it into something negative. All my aunt's advice was born out of sincere love. Yet it still didn't go over well.

My mother began to label my Aunt Lia as a bad person, and viewed her as a controlling nag. She misinterpreted everything Aunt Lia did. If it didn't bring instant gratification to my mother's ears, she labeled it as disrespect. And in so doing, she completely ignored how her daughters were making such necessary physical, emotional and spiritual advancements.

As the saying goes, nothing really lasts forever.

The stalemate between my mother and Aunt Lia got to the point where she threatened to move out and take her daughters with her. When I heard that, Latanya and I were devastated and so were my aunts. None of us could understand why she couldn't see what was good for us – her own children. It seemed to be all about her, not us.

My mother made good on that threat too. I remember fighting back tears the day we left; how I so desperately wanted to grab onto my aunts and never let go, to grab onto them so hard that my mother, even with all her strength, couldn't pry me off.

Even then though, I knew that would never happen. I didn't have the courage to cry, nor to express how much I didn't want to go. Leaving my aunt's home was the first time I really felt true sadness. For the first time, I was heartbroken and devastated. And in the back of my mind, as I prepared to live with my mother but without my two aunts, I knew it wouldn't be the last I experienced those tragic emotions.

When we moved out, it was into someone else's house, not a new one of our own. My mother had begun dating this man, and so it was to his place we moved. He was a nice Caucasian man – a bit naive to what kind of person my mother was, but still nice. You could tell he really wanted a family and really wanted to help my mother, sister, and me. He welcomed us in with open arms, even helping me to build my first snowman at one point.

Yet he wasn't the same as my aunts. Not even close.

Latanya and I had to share a room together, and it was during this time that my sister became more like my caretaker than my sibling. As before, I barely remembered my mother being around. I do remember excitedly running to the balcony whenever I would see her, ready to greet her as she walked into the apartment building. But that didn't happen very often since she worked a lot or just went out a lot. So I would sit back and play with my toys while Latanya cooked our meals, cleaned and slaved in the apartment all day trying to take care of me. My mother's boyfriend worked all day, so it was just the two of us, all day, every day, doing the same things.

It's no surprise that Latanya sadly grew up to be even more timid and emotionally fragile. For years, my mother verbally assaulted her and disregarded who she was trying to be as a human being. All she cared about was what Latanya could do for her, which was take care of me. As a result, my sister never got to experience a normal teenage life.

Instead, this little girl who had so much potential essentially became the modern-day Cinderella.

Just like that mistreated princess, Latanya sacrificed her youth to gain my mother's love and approval. In her young, hope-filled mind, she thought that if she worked hard, our mother would eventually come to show her love and affection. But the more my sister did for her, the more my mother demanded. And the more my sister met every request and demand, the more unappreciative my mother became.

I observed all of that, even at such a very early age. Something inside of me knew her actions weren't right even while another part of me tried so hard to fight that thought. I didn't want to believe my mother was that selfish. The idea that a mother could or would behave so damagingly to her child was so difficult to accept. I didn't want to believe it.

But deep down, I knew better. I still had all of those good examples from my two aunts resting in my head and heart. So I was properly equipped to recognize my mother's right actions from her wrong ones. And, in this case, how my mother treated my sister was wrong.

Consequently, both Latanya and I were miserable and confused. Our newest situation was nothing compared to what we had with our aunts. I missed them very much, and I just didn't understand why we couldn't live there anymore or why I couldn't see them.

My child's mind just couldn't comprehend why someone would want to leave love. Why would you ever want to run away from something as healthy and satisfying as that?

Our house, But Not a Home

We lived with my mother's boyfriend for several months before my mother received her housing assistance voucher. As soon as she did, she picked out a home, and just like that, the relationship she had with that nice man who took us in was over.

She used him, got everything she wanted from him, and then ditched him like an old, worn-out pair of socks. So there I was again, so very young, yet witnessing another one of my mother's horrible traits - taking advantage of the weakness and kindness of others.

She took advantage of my Aunt Lia, of my father, of my sister, and now this nice man who probably truly fell in love with her fraudulent wife-like character.

A single woman again, my mother chose a townhouse to rent that happened to be about ten minutes away from my aunts' home, and mother allowed us to go see them again. That alone cheered me up quite a bit. It felt like a lifetime since I had seen them, but Aunt Valerie and I picked up right where we'd left off, exploring, learning, and having fun. It was such a relief going back to visit the house I'd once called home to spend time with Aunt Lia as well.

I missed them both so much, and they knew it. It showed. And they missed me immensely as well.

At this new place, the only fun my sister and I really had was when my mother decided to entertain guests; she would throw house parties and invite our relatives who had kids our age. We always had a kids' room to ourselves, where we would play games, watch movies, eat snacks, and occasionally sneak downstairs to peep in at what the adults were up to. Those were fun times, but after a while the parties stopped, and my sister and me would have to go back living in our dysfunctional reality.

This new house brought another series of visits about – these ones completely new and, at first, frightening. This was when I began to see things I knew weren't physically there.

While in bed, I would spy two women peeping in my room from the side of the doorway. They would come and visit me every night, just staring at me while my sister and I slept. It scared me enough that I sometimes ran into my mother's room to sleep with her instead, despite how Latanya was right there in the bunk beneath me.

Perhaps the oddest thing about these apparitions was how they resembled my mother, my sister and me. Their features weren't entirely there, and their faces were sort of shadowy. But I could make out a few characteristics nonetheless, and those reminded me of what I looked at every day in the faces of my tiny, fractured family. From what I could see, these creatures could have been related to us, what with their heart-shaped faces, similar eye shapes and high cheekbones.

One was shorter than the other, too, as I recall.

I began to expect them. Their presence at night was that consistent, and so I gradually became less afraid of what they might do. In fact, they started feeling familiar – even calming – as if I'd known them before.

One day, I gathered up the nerve to ask my mother if there was anyone else who came into the house at night. I already knew what the answer would be, but I just wanted to make sure before telling her about the visitors.

Sure enough, she said no. It was just the three of us.

Undaunted, I told her about the women who would visit my bedroom doorway every night. I went on and on about what they looked like and what they did. And then I told her my theory, that they might be spirits because of how they looked.

Of course, my mother laughed it off as if it was nothing. There were no questions following what I told her - no care or concern. Nothing but negativity and judgment by the end of the conversation. Her final response was to tell me I was seeing the spirits because of the bad things I did, like going outside and playing when I wasn't supposed to.

Since that didn't make any sense to me, I didn't believe her one bit.

I wanted to have real answers. I wanted her to think it over and offer me truth. Yet neither happened, which was why I kept the continuing nightly calls to myself after that. Because they did keep happening. There was even a third spirit who came to call shortly after the two others began to make their presences known.

On that occasion, I was in my bed while my mother was in the other room sleeping, when right on the hallway wall, big as day, was a bright gold figure.

It had no face at all and no distinct features - just a silhouette of a person with a long robe-like gown that was outlined in the brightest gold light I'd ever seen. He did, however, have long hair and hands. His one palm was extended out as if he was waiting for something to be given to him. Just waiting. He didn't move; he simply stood there.

And that light around him! It brightened up the entire hallway.

Panicking at the sight, I jumped up and ran as fast as I could past the bright gold figure and into my mother's room, waking her up in the process. When she asked me what was wrong, I was still out of breath, but I managed to tell her that I thought I'd "seen an angel."

In fact, I was convinced of it. Though I'd never seen one before, there was no other possible explanation in my mind.

Unimpressed, my mother responded with, "If it was an angel, what are you afraid for?" Then she went back to sleep, leaving me lying there in her bed, staring at the ceiling with all sorts of questions and feelings running through me.

Bewildered by her comment and taken aback by her attitude, I was left even more confused about what I'd seen. Why was this happening to me? I wanted to know. Why was I seeing such impossible things? What did it mean? Did other children see angels too?

There I was, a little girl who had just seen something remarkable and shocking. And there my mother was, once again, being dismissive.

Latanya, meanwhile, was stewing in her own emotions, and none of them were pleasant. Day by day, she was growing more tired with how she was being treated. I would eavesdrop on her phone conversations with her friends, as she would cry and explain how unfair our mother treated her.

And I couldn't agree more; she was being treated horribly. Our mother would yell at her, acting more like her high school bully than her parental figure. I watched her belittle and antagonize Latanya, verbally attacking her more and more the weaker she became and the more hurt she appeared. I heard our mother yell things at her just to get a certain reaction. And I would sit there watching my sister cry, not knowing what to do to cheer her up.

If Latanya questioned or didn't comply with any of the demands put on her head, she was purposely, intentionally hurt as a result. It was as if my mother fed off of her tears, as if it gave her some kind of sick and twisted energy to hurt again.

That's why, the older my sister got, the more her relationship with our mother dissipated. The only thing this teenager wanted was a mother who knew how to love. She wanted a loving mother who would allow her to be a teenager. She wanted to enjoy life instead of being cooped up in the house like some sort of slave. She wanted a mother who acted like an actual mother.

Latanya never got a "thank you" from our mother, a show of gratitude or any form of appreciation for the work she did. Mother never told her what a good job she was doing or told her, "Thank you for all you do for us."

Living in those kinds of conditions, it's no wonder how Latanya felt unimportant, underappreciated and used. Not only was she babysitting me for free, but she was also babysitting other kids without proper payment. She had taken on the additional tasks as a way to make some extra spending money, expecting to be allowed to keep what she earned. But before long, my mother demanded that little bit of personal income, and Latanya obeyed. She continued to babysit, just to come home and hand over her money.

On top of that, she wasn't allowed to go to any of her friends' parties. She could barely even go to school functions. It became too much for her, understandably so, until she finally couldn't take it anymore. And one day, Latanya went into our mother's room with a face full of tears, and asked if she could go back to living at our aunt's house. And there I stood, in front of our mother's door, with my heart feeling like it had sunken into the pits of my stomach, praying to God that my mother wouldn't let her go.

After what felt like the longest pause of my life, my mother's reply to her request was a cold nonchalant "fine, if you want to go, then go." I saw my sister's pain all over her face that day; she felt as if she'd been carelessly thrown away. Here she was a girl who lived to gain our mother's approval and love through labor, just to be tossed aside as if she was never useful at all. My mother didn't even allow Latanya to use the house phone to call Aunt Valerie to pick her up; instead she made her walk down a long road in the middle of the night to use a payphone. I watched in disbelief as my sister frantically tried to find spare change to make that call. Realizing that if our mother hadn't taken all of Latanya's hard earned babysitting money, she wouldn't have been so frantic in her search.

And just like that, my sister left me again. I was heartbroken and felt empty; I had lost my protector, my caretaker, the one who made me laugh and the only one who understood the pain our mother caused.

As soon as Latanya left, my mother had to stop working for a short period of time because she no longer had a babysitter for me. And because of that, mother showed resentment towards her. She felt wounded and betrayed, and she didn't help her with a single aspect of the move nor did she ever send my aunt's money to help take care of her. Instead of my mother acknowledging that it was her mistreatment that forced Latanya to run away from her, she decided to be vindictive instead.

I would only see my sister when I visited my aunts, and the sudden change continued to sadden me because I missed my sister dearly. But Latanya seemed really happy to be back in such a loving environment, with two wonderful role models. In a way, I was jealous, because I wanted to move back there too, but I knew that was something my mother would never allow to happen.

It turned into just my inattentive mother and me, and being in the house with her all day allowed me to realize more and more things about her, how she never showed any signs of sadness, pain or vulnerability. She never even showed love or joy unless she was getting something out of it. And she never could admit or acknowledge what she had done to damage the people who cared for her.

I've never seen anyone else hurt so many people, all who loved her.

She went about life as if these people created their pain themselves, and she was just the poor little victim to all their finger-pointing. If my sister or I would show any signs of emotion to the chaos she caused, she would antagonize and belittle us for it, deliberately making us feel weak and inferior, just plain old unimportant at times because we always felt like a bother to her.

That's why, even if I felt like I was dying inside from all the teasing and bullying I'd have to experience from other kids for being different, I would show her nothing. Since I no longer had my sister to protect me from cruel kids, I'd just walk home, go to my room, and cry my heart out alone in the closet I once shared with her. I knew if I went to my mother with my tears, she would dismiss me with her carelessness, unconcern, and selfish responses as she always did.

I was emotionally lost - an emotional girl too scared to let her emotions loose.

Too young to challenge my mother's techniques when it came to how she was raising her children, I would sit in my room, on the floor, by my windowsill, wishing someone was there to help me make sense of life. I wanted her to teach me about why I was getting teased by other girls. I wanted her to understand who I was so she could be aware of why I was struggling with social skills. I just wanted her to know me instead of assuming she knew me. I needed her to just talk to me, do things with me, and make me feel like a joy in her life rather than a burden.

Since I had so many needs that weren't being met, I slowly turned into a child who didn't dare speak about her problems or feelings to anyone. With my feelings being ignored as much as they were, I figured they didn't matter. Not them, not my pain, not my troubles. That was how my mother made me feel, and so that's the way I looked at the world.

I shut down.

There were so many times I witnessed her go to extremes to protect herself from any and everyone, even the people who would never dare to hurt her. She couldn't tell the difference between a good person who wanted to love her and a bad person who wanted to harm her, so she would end up pushing away all the good people who could have given her what she needed the most.

Subsequently, the words "I love you" rarely passed her lips. I can count on two hands how many times she ever said "I love you" to me.

Imagine living with a mother who couldn't tell you that.

Imagine what it feels like to never hear it or see it from her.

Latanya's departure meant I was six years old with no babysitter and no older sibling to rely on. The loss left me wondering who would be the one to take care of me when my mother started working again. Who was going to give me a bath, cook my food, protect me, watch me and play with me?

The thought of being alone disturbed my psyche and plagued my mind.

I used to go to church every Sunday with my sister, but when she moved out, I had no choice but to go without her. Fortunately, we did have a type of carpool that went there, where I was the last child to be picked up on the route. Those church kids were very nice to me. I was an eccentric kid, yet they didn't treat me badly for being different or liking different things. Maybe they realized that we all had special traits about ourselves, so we were all unique in our own little way.

I found their behavior refreshing, and looked forward to seeing them every weekend. We would go to Sunday School together, then walk to church service to sit in the same benches, exchanging pieces of paper filled with tic-tac-toe and hangman. Until, of course, we got caught by an adult and had them snatched away.

I loved how accepted I felt there. I loved how much the adults not only cared for their own children, but cared for the others as well. We were a unit. There were many Sundays when I was asked from fellow church members where my sister was, and how come she didn't attend church anymore. I would hold back tears as I told them that she moved. And I would see the look of concern and confusion on their faces, as they stopped themselves from asking about the situation further.

My mother never attended church with us. She would fix me breakfast and go back to watching TV while I waited at the front door for the carpool. And when I came home, she would be doing the same exact thing - watching TV.

I always tried to invite her to church, but she always rejected the offer, saying that she was content sitting home and watching the church programs from her bed.

I sincerely believe that might be where she got her notions on how and when to discipline your child. The truth was that she rarely lectured me or gave me guidance, but she would punish me by telling me I couldn't go outside to play if I disobeyed any of her commands. I would even get belt whoopings every now and then, but more significantly, I never got educated on morals. I never understood why things were wrong and what effect they could have on me as I grew up.

My mother never took the time to enforce any kind of structure or integrity in me. She never told me when I was wrong; she never corrected me. She never gave me tips on how to improve my behavior or how to make friends. She never attempted to give me the necessary lessons to help me grow up into a fully functional adult with morals, sympathy, empathy, integrity and consciousness.

And whenever my mother actually did whoop me, she smirked a lot, as if she was trying really hard to contain an urge to burst out laughing. It was as if her form of discipline was a joke even to her, leaving me confused on whether or not I had actually done something wrong.

I had no emotional connection or reaction from her disciplinary tactics; she never really made me want to sit down and think about what I'd done wrong. I didn't even have an emotional connection with her, I always felt as though my mother was a stranger I knew nothing about.

You can tell the difference between a parent who disciplines their children out of love and one who tries it out because they think it's what's expected of them. Usually, when parents enact this kind of punishment, it's because they don't want their children growing up into immoral human beings. They correct them because they want their kids to grow up understanding and knowing right from wrong. They're trying to instill integrity and a healthy worldview in their offspring to spare them from living toxic lives. Discipline creates healthy characters. But I don't think my mother really understood that.

Lonely

The day came when my mother returned to work, and without my sister there to watch me, my mother had me stay home by myself. And when she was home, all she really did was watch TV in her room and eat snacks. She even ate her dinner in her room; we never ate together like a family. I never had the pleasure to get asked "how was your day" over a hot meal. So I spent most of the time alone, again, feeling as if my mother didn't want to be bothered by me.

After school, I would walk myself home, fix something to eat, do my homework and watch a bunch of cartoons on TV. With all the time I spent alone and bored, I found my imagination to be my greatest ally. I would daydream a lot, acting out roles from my favorite television programs.

And during the summertime, one of my mother's rules was that I couldn't leave the house. I would be cooped up the whole time, watching the other kids frolic around outside from my mother's bedroom window, wishing I could go outside and do some frolicking of my own.

I found it unfair. Why couldn't I go outside and play? Why couldn't I go to the pool, ride my bike, rollerblade, and just be a kid? Or why couldn't my mother at least get me a babysitter so I could enjoy being a kid in my spare time?

I needed those kid experiences; I needed to gain the social skills I knew I lacked. I found it hard to make friends, and difficult to relate to other kids my age.

So I tried to ask my mother for a babysitter a few times, and every time I'd ask, she'd tell me no because a sitter was too expensive. She would then proceed to warn me that if I told anyone I was being left at home alone, Child Protective Services would take me away. They would lock me up in a home, where I wouldn't be able to see any of my family, and eventually, I'd have to go live with strangers. So for so long, I kept quiet.

Another rule was that I was only allowed to answer the phone for my mother and no one else. I wasn't even allowed to tell my aunts about how I was cooped up all day with no permission to go out and play. I couldn't even open certain snacks in the house unless she had previously opened them. This everyday lockdown led me to explore things I shouldn't have, playing with fire, knives, cleaning products, household paint, and even my mother's pepper spray which I choked on a few times. I even began tasting some of the liquor that my mother had in her unlocked liquor cabinet.

My mind never got the stimulation it should have, so I guess this was my way at doing so.

This continued for as long as I could take it.

The truth was that I desperately wanted to make friends and to talk to someone else. One day, I just got so lonely that I called these twins I was friends with from school even though I knew they were on vacation. I called so obsessively that their mom ended up calling mine because of all the voicemails I left.

My mother told me to stop calling them, without even realizing that I was just a lonely kid. Talking to a voicemail was better than nothing.

And this is why, during one of my depressing days at home, I decided to finally answer Aunt Valerie's call despite my very strict instructions not to; I just wanted to hear her voice.

I fought with myself before I picked up, thinking about being taken away and forced to live with someone else. Yet my loneliness and unhappiness won out, and it felt as though my heart had hit the floor when I murmured "hello."

And when I did, Aunt Valerie was shocked that I answered, but I was just delighted to hear her voice, basking in her questions about how I was and what I was doing. We spoke for a bit before she asked me where my mother was. Being maybe seven years old by then, I wasn't old enough to be alone all day or take care of myself properly, which my aunt knew very well.

I could hear her disgust and concern when I answered her truthfully, not only about that question but also concerning how long I'd been staying at home by myself. It scared me, making me wonder what was going to happen next and what my mother would say when she found out.

The rest of the day, I nervously anticipated my mother's keys clicking against the front door. When she did come in, I watched her carefully while she went about her usual routine.

After cautious consideration, I had just decided that she didn't know what I'd done. Yet as soon as my insides started to settle, the phone rang again.

It was Aunt Lia and Aunt Valerie calling to confront her. Expressing their honest and understandable concerns, Aunt Lia told my mother that I needed a babysitter. And if she left me home alone again, she would, indeed, call Child Protective Services.

After that, my mom had a whole string of negative and hurtful things to say about the two aunts who always showed me the love I needed. She especially had bad things to say about aunt Aunt Lia. She attempted to manipulate me into believing that Aunt Lia was bad and trying to hurt me.

Sitting there, listening to her attempt to poison my mind, I knew she was lying. Aunt Lia was a loving and caring person. Nobody had to tell me that when I had seen it plainly and clearly for myself. I knew the difference between someone raising me because they had to and someone raising me because they loved me. My mother was a walking shell, and my aunts were the very opposite.

Honestly, my mother bashing my aunts left me in some state of disbelief.

Children may not always understand the words you choose, but they do always understand your feelings. It's a natural-born instinct. Throughout the stages in the womb, feelings are a baby's first social skill. It's learned behavior. Those little ones feel the connection between themselves and their mothers, which then allows them to communicate through emotions and actions that may also affect the emotions and actions of the mother.

According to scientific studies, unborn children are able to feel the distress, sadness, happiness and anxiety their mother may be experiencing at the time. They sense the kind of person their mother is before they take their first breath of air. Human beings recognize emotions before we so much as know what emotions are. Before we know what physical light feels like, we become masters of sentiment.

But in my circumstance; my mother lacked proper emotions, and so she lacked an identity in my eyes. I continued to feel as though I never knew who she really was, and she didn't know who I was.

Why would I then believe this stranger over such known identities as my aunts with their honest emotions?

My mother didn't seek proper care for me, and so I was still being left home alone until Aunt Valerie stepped in to do something about it. She began to pick me up more, taking me with her on her errand runs, and to the beach along with other outside fun activities. And when we were worn out by all the fun, we would go back to my aunt's home, have dinner together like a family, and then enjoy each other's company some more until my mother returned home from work. And because Aunt Valerie was a teacher, she was off every summer break, and I loved it!

Both of my aunts made sure I at least had a fun summer instead of feeling hopeless and lonely. And Aunt Lia never did call Child Protective Services. I honestly think she just wanted to give my mother a reality check in hopes that she would start making better decisions when it came to my wellbeing.

And in a way, it kind of worked, since my mother began dating again. The only time she ever dated a man or kept him around was when she needed to use one. In my mind I had already came to the conclusion that this new boyfriend could end up being my new sitter.

His name was Dan, and I remember seeing him at a few of my mother's house parties. They went to high school together, so he was already familiar with my family.

He was a likeable guy, very calm and intelligent. He was kind and loved children, and most importantly, he didn't mind babysitting me or the kids in his family. But he never really had a voice; he never challenged my mother's wrongs, even though he was quite aware of them. And he never held a 9-to-5 job; instead, he would take home improvement jobs every so often whenever he needed a few extra dollars.

I saw my mother pay for everything for him, treating him like he was one of her children because of it. He would come to our house and ask my mother for five dollars so that he could buy cigarettes. He became my mother's puppet. Anything she demanded of him, he did. Consequently, I never really saw any real growth between them. At that very young age, I developed a bad perception of how a man is supposed to conduct himself in a relationship. The way it was portrayed to me, it was acceptable for a man to be submissive and not provide for his family.

I used to sit down and just stare at him, wondering why he allowed my mother to do the things and say the things she did. But I supposed that's just how it was. And who was I to challenge the way two grownups behaved?

The only strength I ever saw him display was the knowledge he kept seeking out.

Although he was a pushover, he was very book-smart, constantly reading up on different subjects. Researching for fun, I think knowledge was what kept him thirsty for life. It was a trait that felt like a breath of fresh air to me. Here was someone, finally, who could answer all the out-of-the-box questions I'd been yearning to figure out.

Sure enough, as I got comfortable with Dan being around, I began to ask him all my oddest questions. And he always found it a joy and challenge to engage with me. I'd ask him questions about spirits, space, animals, history, inventions, and philosophical topics, just to name a few; and began to look up to him. He slowly became my favorite male figure to look up and relate to.

Dan treated me with respect and genuinely listened to me, which I was so hungry for due to my lack of success in making friends at school and at home. Moreover, you could tell he loved to teach, and how wonderful he found it that I was so inquisitive about so much.

In my eyes, he slowly began to turn into the dad I never had, not because he was a great father figure, but because I really just wanted a father. I would see other kids interact with their dads and wished I had the same. On a few occasions, I'd even see my sister with her father and immediately would feel sad.

Dan quickly began to realize the kind of relationship my mom had with her two daughters. He felt bad for my sister and me, especially me. Recognizing my love for art and picking up on my eccentricities, he knew I was different from most kids and would wonder why my mother didn't care to do much about it. Since she never bothered to challenge my mind and teach me more, he took it upon himself to develop my mind so I could at least increase my chances at life.

Freedom

I continued to feel like I was being punished for my mother's decisions until I got sick of it. I wanted to go outside and play. I wanted to at least try to enjoy life and make some friends. I thought it was just unfair for her to expect me to spend my childhood in the house, all because she didn't want to pay for a babysitter.

With that mindset firmly in place, I disregarded her rules one day and went outside to play while she was at work. I took my bike and began to ride it around the neighborhood, and it felt great! For once, I felt like a free kid. Like an uncaged bird, I explored my neighborhood, finding pathways and hidden areas that I treated like my little special place of tranquility. I loved nature, so I would explore the woods in my neighborhood with a big walking stick and a backpack filled with my lunch and books. Amongst nature, I felt as if I was finding myself again and figuring out who I really was. Exploring the different kinds of animals and trees and flowers stimulated my mind and senses.

I also began to go to the pool. Starting in three feet of water, I taught myself how to swim until I could reach the deep end. I knew my mother came home every day at around six-thirty. So I would keep my watch handy or check the clock at the pool continuously to make sure I had enough time to run home before she got off the bus.

There were many times when I just didn't care about the time because of all the fun I was having. So she would catch me running in the house after her.

At first, I was scared of being punished. But then I really thought it over. How could I be punished when she was never home? She would yell at me about her rules, but the more she did, the more I didn't care. She would put disciplinary restrictions on me every time she caught me outside playing – just for me to go right back out there the next day.

I wanted to have fun and explore what it was like to be a kid. In my world, that was much more important than her unfair rules. As a result, I got "punished" just for trying to be a kid - not that it affected me one bit.

Because I had so much time to myself – more than I would have liked – I had more time to realize who I was and who I was becoming. It was at that stage in life that I truly began to notice how much different I was from the other kids in the area.

My imagination was different. My speech was different. The things I found interesting were different. And I suppose my character simply seemed unfamiliar to most children my age.

I had questions. I wanted to know why things were the way they were. And how did they become that way? And even though I had my mother's boyfriend to answer my most eccentric questions, I assumed other kids would be interested in the topics I liked too. Yet, as I was beginning to realize, I wanted explanations to things that other children may have found silly. Because of that, I was un-relatable, which was why I always had a hard time fitting in with others.

In some ways, I was too mature for them; in others, too immature. The combination, at least in their minds, resulted in a task they found too exhausting. Figuring me out just wasn't worth it to them, I suppose.

During this time when I continued to be programmed to show no emotion from my mother, while finding my newly found freedom of play, I began to make a friend. She was older and lived a few houses down from ours. She never judged me, and encouraged me to come out and play with her friends. Her name was Sammi, and she would always knock on the door with a crowd full of other kids to see if I wanted to join them in all the fun they were planning to have. She included me in everything they did. In a way, Sammi knew I was different; she knew more things about me before I had even come to the realization of it for myself. My newfound friend was observant, and saw how I would tense up around strangers or large crowds. She knew I was shy and hesitant to talk or even sometimes respond correctly due to my nerves. Sometimes, Sammi would tell the kids to go wait around the corner away from my door so that I could be comfortable coming out to play.

By and by though, I did find another girl who was nice to me, a friend who embraced my eccentric ways and challenges, and because of that, others began to as well.

Because she was older than most of us in the neighborhood, her peers highly respected her. So when Sammi encouraged the other children to be kind to me, they listened. She treated me like her little sister, which was comforting since I felt like I'd just lost my own.

Then, just as I began to actually like my childhood and enjoy the wonders of friends and outdoor fun, I found out that Sammi and her family were moving away. I spent her last day in the neighborhood on her front porch with her. My words couldn't express how sad I was. Admittedly, I was never good at expressing my feelings. My mother never made my sister or me feel as though it was the right thing to do, which meant I was used to bottling everything inside.

But this friend of mine? She knew. She knew I couldn't tell her how sad I was to see her go, but she saw it all over my face. I was fighting back tears the entire time we sat there, and I kept counting each second of each minute that led up to her departure.

I watched as Sammi's family packed up the rest of their belongings into the car. She gave me a hug and told me to be good. And as they drove off, I just sat there on her front stoop. Sitting and sitting and sitting. I must have sat there for an hour, imagining how great it would be if they came back and decided to stay after all.

But I knew that wasn't going to happen. I wanted it to so badly, but I knew it wouldn't.

Walking home, I went to my room; and that's when the tears began to surface. Once they did, it felt like I cried for hours all by myself until I couldn't take the solitaire heartache any longer.

As is natural for any hurt and lost little girl, I went into my mother's room, craving a hug – wanting some words to make me feel better, or to show me what to do next. Looking back today, I realized it was never going to happen. But at the time, I was suffering enough to think there might be a chance.

There my mother was, lying on her bed, laughing loudly at one of her sitcoms while Dan was on the floor next to her reading the paper. I stood at the foot of her bed, waiting for my mother to notice her daughter standing there sulking with a face full of tears - all while being hesitant to interrupt her beloved television show. And as soon as her eyes broke free from her TV to look at me, I cried out, "Sammie moved away, and I'm never going to see her again!"

And in return, all I got was a dismissive tone with actions to match. She pretty much told me to "get over it" and said that I'd make new friends one day. After hearing that, I went back to my room for the rest of the day and evening, where I cried some more. Dan checked on me a few times after that to see if I was okay, but of course, my mother never did.

When my friend moved away, it felt as though my childhood moved right along with her. And in some ways, all the other kids Sammi would bring together felt the same. Some of them stopped playing with one another, some eventually moved away and some just found their own cliques to join.

In the middle of that reorganization, there I was, left to play alone and be alone, except when I was being picked on by kids who thought I was too weird to be liked and accepted. And more and more, I got bullied constantly by groups of them, and it hurt a lot when all I ever wanted to do was make friends. But instead, I got teased for every little thing I did. It didn't matter what I did or did not do; I was ridiculed for it.

What I wore. What I liked to do. What I liked to talk about. What I thought about. Every single element that made up me seemed to get picked apart and tossed away from my own peers. Yet there were still times I was so desperate for friends that I even tried to befriend the children I knew would end up hurting me or my feelings at the end of the day, including this set of three siblings.

I allowed them to use me and treat me badly - the price to pay for human interaction. On many occasions, I invited them over to play with me when I was left home alone. Instead of them trying to get to know me though, they ate my mother's food up and stole her things, including her jewelry. During these events is when my mother began making Dan stay over at the house more while she was at work so he could keep an eye on her things, and I suppose, me as well. I didn't mind it at all, I quickly realized that when Dan was around, these kids never bullied me, but when he left, they would go right back to being cruel. In a way, these kids liked and respected him; they didn't have a father around, so I guess they used my mother's boyfriend to fill their void too. But either way, I was still being used, and still being bullied. I would literally feel as though these kids were slowly, brutally pulling my heart out. With each and every tease, with every mean comment, and with every mistreatment, I felt as though I was dying inside.

During this time, I gathered up the nerve to invite my bullies to go to church with me. At first, they didn't take my invitation seriously. But after much convincing, they agreed and became the new additions to the carpool.

The way I figured it, if these kids saw how we treated each other at church, they may want to start treating me and other people that way too. But the experience had very little effect on them as far as I could tell. They always ended up being the children who got disciplined the most in church, something they needed anyway. But after church ended, they were still bullies.

All the while, my mother would yell at me, punish me, and even whoop me for some of the things they did whenever I invited them over to play. At times, I'd go as far as covering for them to avoid being teased and treated badly for telling on them.

The bullying was a constant thing, and it was made that much more heartbreaking after I told my mom about it. At first, she pretty much told me to go handle that situation myself. Then she turned around and befriended the kids who bullied me. I would be walking home with my mother, coming back from somewhere, when we would run into them. And then I'd have to listen to the sweet and pleasant conversations she'd make with the kids who would just enjoy bullying me the very next day.

Afterward, I questioned her on why she was being so nice and welcoming to children who were mean to me all of the time. Her answer was, "They did nothing to me. Why should I dislike them just because they dislike you?"

Hearing that from my own mother just reassured me that I was destined to feel alone and unimportant for a very long time.

I remember running back home one day, away from a group of girls who thought it would be fun to beat on me first thing in the morning. When I was supposed to be leaving on the bus to go to school, I found that I just couldn't take it anymore. The bullying and the hate from the other kids just got too much for my spirit to handle, and I ran home with a face full of tears because of it.

My mother was staying home from work that day, and as always, she dismissed me. In fact, she was downright angry that I had "acted like a coward," running home instead of facing my bullies.

What she couldn't see was that I was facing them every single day, and I had grown tired. I was sad and depressed, and I had no more fight left in me that day.

Kids were mean to me just to see my reactions – or lack thereof – to the pain and embarrassment they inflicted. On some days, I laughed with them. Other times, I showed no signs of emotion, not a single little hair of it. You could hit me as hard as you wanted, and I wouldn't show a fraction of what I felt. Because that was how I was taught.

To my mother, emotions were for the weak. She considered tears to be a trait for losers, and I guess my bullies found those inflected lessons in me amusing.

After a certain point, I guess I just got used to being rejected. It was going to happen whether I liked it or not, so I tried my hardest to avoid it by playing by myself all over again. At least I still had my bike riding and swimming and nature hikes to comfort me when I felt discouraged or lonely. And I tried to have as much fun as I could on my own.

But with every activity I enjoyed, I couldn't help but wonder how it would feel to be able to experience them with other children.

It made me wonder whether I was really that weird to love. Was I doing something wrong?

There were so many times I wanted to tell my aunts everything that was going on at home. But I was too afraid to for a number of reasons; I was too scared to get my feelings hurt any more than they already were. I was also afraid that when I did finally get a moment to express myself to them, it would hurt too much for me to bear, as if releasing it would feel like shards of glass piercing through my soul and out of my skin.

Even when I cried to myself in my bedroom closet with the door closed, I was still holding back emotions, because I was afraid my mother would hear me crying and scold me for it.

The whole thing was embarrassing. I felt full of shame that these children treated me the way they did and then my mother did too. And so

I worried that my aunts would think something was wrong with me and wouldn't like me anymore if they knew.

It's tragic, but true.

During another Sunday at church, some of the kids got in trouble for taking all the candy out of the dish in the women's bathroom, something that happened more often than it should. I just so happened to decide to join them this time, and of course, that was the time we got caught by Mrs. Maggie, the wife of the man who carpooled us there each Sunday.

Finding us guilty as anything, with our fingers actually in the bowl, she slapped our hands so that we let the candy go reflexively. After that, we had to sit beside Mrs. Maggie the entire church service, as we watched in envy at the other children who got to sit together and enjoy a few rounds of tic-tac-toe and hangman.

That was the first time I ever understood why I was being disciplined. It was the first time I ever felt anything behind the punishment. It was love and compassion; however, I was too young and inexperienced to fully grasp and appreciate it.

Mrs. Maggie was a strong, older black woman who did the right thing and disciplined the younger generation. This was someone who corrected us so that we wouldn't grow up to be greedy, selfish thieves. She wanted all of us to walk and act with dignity and respect - to walk and act as God would.

She was trying to instill Him within us. But instead of accepting it that way, I sulked about it instead.

Like any kid would be, I was mad. I went home after church that day with nothing but Mrs. Maggie and her discipline on my mind. I actually stewed about it for a few days before I told my mother what had happened, taking those days to contemplate whether or not I should speak to her about it at all.

But, there I went again, foolishly walking into her room, hoping that this time she would be the mother I need. Wondering if this time she would care more about my problems than one of her TV shows. As soon as I reached her room, she immediately told me to stay quiet until the commercials came on, and so I waited patiently. And when the time came for my words to reach her ears, her laughter reached mine.

Her only real response was to tell me that I shouldn't have taken the candy. Then she asked me if I still wanted to go to church with them or not, and If I wanted to stop, then I would have to call Mrs. Maggie myself and explain why.

My mother gave my immature mind an option when she shouldn't have.

Church was something I needed. And right then, I also needed a parent to tell me as much. I was prepared to make a terrible mistake, and my mother was going to sit on her bed with her TV on and allow me to do it.

It only made sense that I was scared to make a decision when I shouldn't have had to make one in the first place. Yet that's what I was being told to do with no guidance or moral instruction whatsoever.

I chose the wrong decision.

I called Mrs. Maggie that evening and told her I didn't want to go to church anymore. It felt wrong, and I felt guilty. I had been going there for years, and speaking the necessary words to leave all that made me feel horrible.

You could just hear the disappointment in Mrs. Maggie's voice too. It hurt to hear, and at that moment, I was very sure I had made the wrong decision. Yet those awful words were out of my mouth, and it felt like it was already too late to take them back. So I didn't.

For a long time after that, I was angry with myself. Angry with myself and angry with my mother too for letting it happen. I became more and more aware each day that I couldn't trust her – not her advice and definitely not her love.

With each weekend that passed, I missed my church family more and more. I missed Sunday school. I missed the tic-tac-toe and hangman games. I missed the kids that didn't bully me, I missed the entire experience, and I wanted to go back. I missed it so much that I tried more than once to work up the nerve to reach out to Mrs. Maggie. But something always held me back. So instead, I would block my number and ring through just to hear her voice in hopes that she would automatically know it was me and invite me back to church.

I was terrible at confrontation. It made me nervous.

But avoiding that confrontation didn't keep me from feeling completely lost and stupid. Church had been the only place I was accepted, and I ruined it by being a brat and not accepting my faults and consequences. I wanted so badly to tell Mrs. Maggie how sorry I was and beg her to accept me back. I cried so many times just thinking of them all.

As young as I was, I still recognized that I needed guidance, lectures and examples - that I needed to be molded into my full potential. And I clearly wasn't going to get it from my mother. Because again, I don't think she cared.

What's Wrong With Me?

A short period of time went by with no positive changes. Latanya was on her way to college to begin her new chapter in life. I didn't want her to go; it was bad enough that I didn't see her everyday like I used to, now I felt as though I may not see much of her at all. Once again, here was a moment when I desperately wanted to express my feelings for someone I love, but couldn't because fear wouldn't let me. As I watched my sister pack her belongings, all I could do was bathe in the pain I felt from holding in my tears.

And when she left, I was reminded of my emptiness.

I began to resent myself for not being able to communicate my feelings, wondering what could be wrong with me to make me unable to do this. I felt like a wasted vessel for human life. I soon began experiencing many other psychological difficulties.

I started to sit in front of my TV for hours and hours at a time, rocking back in fourth, counting each syllable and phrase that every single person said. These shows became my introduction to some mental problems I found too embarrassing to tell anyone about.

Experiencing my first signs of Obsessive-Compulsive Disorder, or OCD, I became obsessed with counting, patterns, phrases and syllables. Then I began to count the words and phrases of the people I spoke to or simply interacted with; when they weren't looking, I'd move my head up and down while mumbling the words I heard in a melodic tone in order to keep an accurate track of my counting.

I would count syllables, phrases, sentences, speeches and paragraphs. It didn't matter in what form these letters or words were in. If they were words, I felt obligated to count each and every single one.

I hid my obsession from everyone who mattered. Plus, it was only at home where I, ironically, felt comfortable enough to display my issues fully. When I was out in public among crowds, I hid the severity of my problem by counting solely in my head. But behind closed doors, I counted out loud with repetitive head movements and nods. Sometimes I even blinked my eyes along with each syllable I counted.

At home, my mother most likely saw my actions, but quickly or ultimately dismissed them.

But I did notice Dan introducing me to activities that could help develop my mind. I didn't know it then, but Dan began to introduce me to occupational therapy-type activities. He would play these games with me that required me to think fast before executing a sequence of movements with my hands and fingers. I would have to either mimic his hand movements, or find ways to quickly catch his fingers before he made them disappear into his hand. Dan was trying to help my mind develop, after knowing for sure that my mother didn't have it in her to do it herself. And all this time, I just figured his efforts were just games he would play with me when he thought I was bored.

But as always, Dan never confronted my mother about it, as if it was a lost cause trying to get my mother's attention to care. So my struggles continued to be left in the dark by everyone except him.

At a young age, I was convinced that I was losing my mind for sure. First I was seeing spirits, and then this repetitive ritual that seemed to be controlling my mind and everything I did. I began to feel as though these were the real reasons why I couldn't make friends.

Anxious and obsessed, depressed and worried, deep down inside, I really wanted more adults to notice what I was doing. I wanted to get caught in my OCD episodes so that someone could intervene and ask me if I was okay. I wanted someone to actually bring my challenges to light.

But no one ever did.

I felt more alone than ever; it was just me and my thoughts.

Over time, my OCD began to grow into an uncontrollable nightmare. If I didn't count as many words, syllables, and things as I could, I was sure something terrible would happen to me. It felt as though my only options in life were to count or die.

There was no room for anything else. I didn't care about activities or trying to make friends anymore, because I was too obsessed and occupied with counting. Every single day, I took the same chair and placed it in the same place right in front of my TV. I would sit there so many times and for so long that the chair made permanent indents on my bedroom carpet from where I would perfectly place it. So not only was I obsessed with counting, but I was obsessed with the placement of objects too.

That indent on that floor? If I didn't place the chair exactly where those carpet marks were each day, I'd have to repeat the act over and over again until I got it no less than perfect.

I also began to wash my hands more frequently. Even in my traumatized young mind back then, I knew that wasn't normal. I would wash my hands and still feel the soap on my skin, even though I knew there was no soap left. Yet until my mind assured me that the soap was completely washed off, I would rinse my hands repeatedly until I could accept that fact.

It wasn't uncommon for me to stand over the sink for thirty minutes at a time, washing my hands until they felt clean enough for my mind to be at ease. I began to develop these mentally controlling rituals all around the house, and still, my mother didn't care to notice.

I would think, if I had been living with my aunts, they would have cared enough to notice and do something about it.

I think that was when I really, fully began to realize that I was emotionally and mentally on my own. Sometimes, you want something so badly that it takes multiple painful lessons to teach you that it's not going to work out. In those situations, hopefully, you learn something new each time until you can finally accept the truth. This is how I felt with my mother. Why would I continue in confiding in a woman, who shows me time after time again she just isn't interested? Not interested in my feelings, my thoughts, or who I am or could grow up to be.

It was that full acceptance that allowed me start handling my OCD in a more constructive manner. I didn't want to have it anymore. I wanted to be able to control it. So I woke up one day and decided enough was enough. The counting and obsessive behavior simply needed to stop.

And to make that happen, I started trying out new things. I started taking electronics apart in an attempt to see how they worked, then putting them back together again. I used my OCD habits to remember where the parts went and how, and I didn't stop studying until I knew each piece's location by memory.

That helped. A lot.

I also took off all the doorknobs in the house and switched them around to different doors, repeating those alterations until I felt as though I got them perfect. I even began to time myself to see how fast I could take one off and put another one back on – to beautiful results.

My brain felt alive and capable of doing anything. I felt empowered and optimistic about myself, my potential, and who I was. I was growing happier and stronger.

My obsession started with science and engineering, and quickly moved to the arts. Listening to music, I rehearsed the melodies until I got them perfect. The same went for the music and lyrics, which I taught myself over and over again until my brain was satisfied with the outcome. I became a perfectionist, creating my own renditions of amazing yet challenging radio songs, and I got good at counting the rhythms, melodies, and patterns of each and every sound of a song.

Within three to five seconds, I could identify what direction a song would take. In the same way some people counted cards, I counted music, remembering every instrument and every pitch. I stored information and sounds in my mind like a mini laptop with a huge hard drive.

That's how I came to fall in love with music. It was such a broad form of art with so many elements that anyone could explore. I was never bored with it; my mind was always stimulated and ready for the challenge.

My mind wanted more of art - more of creating. I had opened the door to an entire gateway my brain couldn't get enough of. I began to love music so much that I built my own recording studio in my mother's bathroom. I honestly had no idea what I was making; all I knew was that I wanted to make songs in there.

To that end, I gathered about four recorders and recorded a hook on the one. The second one, I used for a harmony; and the third was for the main vocals.

As for the fourth, that, I saved to capture my hook, harmony, main vocals, and myself, singing adlibs and filling up any additional needed sounds.

I would be in that bathroom for hours upon hours, making sure I had the perfect song, arranging everything just so until I got them just right. With care and courage, my OCD had made me a creative perfectionist so that I no longer resented or was afraid of my psyche's form of coping. I embraced it, realizing that when I applied it to art, tinkering, and creating, the possibilities were endless.

As I began to truly appreciate it, I could create spectacular things with my talent and mind, which chased away my loneliness and depression. Art made me feel as though I belonged to something. And I wanted to feel more of it.

As long as I had my creative mind working alongside my OCD, I didn't care.

Next up, I decided to literally try my hand at drawing. Whether it was something around the house or the nature outside my window, I wanted to sketch it. At times, I even drew what was in my head, since there were always lots of exciting things going on in there.

First, it was stick figures that were motionless and simple. But I wasn't pleased with those; I wanted more. So I began to study the human body, paying attention to the movements and details of the human anatomy. I knew my rough depictions weren't close to being realistic enough, and I couldn't rest until I made them look as close to reality as possible. So I started adding extra lines to the legs and then the arms, and more details to the eyes. Slowly but surely, they began to take form.

Magazines, photos and even that once-problematic TV became resources I drew on while perfecting my craft. I'd go through packs of computer paper in a day, practicing non-stop until the people I drew began to look like they were really dancing, walking, singing and flipping their hair.

While I was obsessed with drawing any and everything I could see, my favorite thing to sketch was powerful women. Women in leadership roles appeared beautiful, smart and authoritative just like my two aunts.

These drawings became my friends. Each woman, each person in general I captured, had a story, complete with a name and persona. Since I didn't have many friends, I created my own within the characters of my drawings.

Thanks to my OCD, I began identifying myself as a self-learner. Something that started out as a negative in my life had become a fulfilling, inspiring asset – a challenging, amazing comfort. OCD became my superpower. It taught me how to tie my shoe, spell, sing, draw, and cook - my secret weapon no one else knew about.

The days of me sitting in front of my TV counting syllables were finally over. Caught up in the creative arts, I began to dabble in acting without really putting much effort or thought into what it actually was. I had no name for it; I just knew that, on my spare time, I enjoyed mocking certain commercials I'd catch. And because I was so good at memorizing the words along with the facial expressions and movements, I got them down pretty quickly.

Similarly, music videos became my study guides to dance. After memorizing those moves or commercial lines; I would go and stand in front of a mirror to perform them. My emotions and words were always perfectly on cue.

Next up, I began to realize how strong of an empath I was becoming, despite or perhaps because of the parental neglect I'd been subjected to. I was very familiar with other people's emotions and had a lot of time to observe behaviors, even my mother's and the children who rejected me or bullied me. Thanks to my lack of friends, I spent a lot of time sitting on my front stoop, watching the kids who didn't want to play with me. And in doing that, I began to notice things about them that they didn't want others to see or maybe didn't even fully recognize themselves, pain in their eyes and hardships expressed through their body language.

I knew when someone was sad, mad, embarrassed, lying, or just uncomfortable. Looking back now, I suppose I was far ahead of my time – a young girl with an old soul, trying to manage her broad mind. And although I was great at identifying the unspoken emotions of others, I continued to struggle with identifying my own. My emotions confused me; whereas, the emotions of others were easily clear. And as I continued to ponder about the lack of regard I had for my own feelings, things became much more clear. It's not that I couldn't identify my emotions; I just fought hard not to. The thought of my true emotions scared me, as if I could lose every bit of my self control if I allowed myself to recognize them for what they are. I was turning into a person who could mask their true nature, while effectively reading through the true nature of others. I was a ninja in training, hiding upon high grounds, and blanketed amongst the darkness.

Now She Sees Me

Since my mother's neglectful behavior was something I was used to by this point, I learned to rely on my OCD, my aunts, my mother's boyfriend and myself, to mold and raise me. Yet, as it turned out, she still could surprise me.

After discovering my newfound talents, my mother finally started to pay attention to me. Catching glimpses of her daughter dancing, drawing, singing and acting, I guess she couldn't help herself but to notice my skills. She began to pay attention to my talents, eavesdropping on me when I was practicing my acting, singing and dancing. After I finished performing a commercial I had memorized, or a song I had written, I would turn around to catch my mother peeping through the small space of my cracked bedroom or bathroom door, grinning from ear to ear, in a newfound expression of amazement. She began to do this more often, paying attention to my talents, while continuing to neglect me as a person.

Up until this time, I just thought she was incapable of showing me – or anyone else – love and attention. But my perspectives about her started to change. I now recognized that if she wanted to pay attention to me, she could have. I guess she only paid attention to what she found interesting or beneficial.

Maybe being her daughter wasn't good enough to gain her love, affection and attention.

Maybe I never excited her well enough to want to get to know me better as a person.

As soon as she realized I possessed interesting talents though, she became the loving, friendly and warm mother I'd always wished I had – for her own benefit, of course. She saw an opportunity in me. How I'd acquired my talents, she didn't know or care to know. All she knew was that she now had a daughter who could possibly change her lifestyle.

It didn't take my mother much time at all to confront me about turning my talents into a career, where we could live happily ever after for the rest of our lives. She made it sound fun and appealing, and had me thinking I could live my life utilizing my skills and producing things I could be proud of.

The way she explained it, it sounded like such a golden opportunity to my ears. I could buy a house and car when I grew up, and go to work every day creating and doing what I loved.

It was a thought that got me excited. So when she asked me if I wanted to be an actress and singer, I said yes.

As soon as I did, she began looking out for me.

My mother wasted no time finding an agent to sign me. I'd never seen her in this way before. Working so hard. For me.

The agency she found told her that, in order for me to be signed, I would have to audition - a word I didn't understand. But she reassured me that everything would be fine and that I would do great, then went about ensuring exactly that. She started searching for these acting skits called monologues, instructing me to memorize at least three different ones in order to pass.

And then she helped me with them.

She helped me memorize each and every skit. She helped me with everything from my tone of voice to my facial expressions. She helped me line by line.

Every day, multiple times a day, my mother helped me with my monologues. This task came before homework, since all that mattered was my performance and whatever results she could glean from them.

My OCD had made me good at memorizing, so that part came quickly enough to me. It was everything else, I was told, that needed to be analyzed and tweaked. And so I performed in front of my mother over and over again, who would then critique me on my hand movements, my expressions and my body language so that my monologues would be nothing less than perfect.

It was surprising how good she was at coaching and teaching. Bit by instructive bit, my mother was there molding me into a packaged deal for an industry I had no clue about. There was just one detail she left out, and that was on purpose. It wasn't until we were almost up to audition day that she told me I'd have to recite and perform these monologues in front of people.

That revelation made me so very nervous. Up until then, art had always been a personal thing I did alone for no one to see or hear. I'd never performed in front of anyone before, and that was precisely what I told her, that I was scared. And believe me, I was.

But she told me I'd be just fine. Once again, she brushed my concerns off as if they didn't matter to her. Because, of course, they didn't. Dismissing my feelings, she went right back to making sure I memorized my monologues correctly.

I found myself rehearsing these monologues in my head all day, going over them in my sleep, in the shower, while I ate dinner, at school – I rehearsed them any and everywhere. To some degree, that made sense considering that's how my brain was conditioned to work, reviewing something until I was confident I had it right was my norm.

Yet there was an edge to my obsession this time that had never been there before. There was a major difference. I wasn't performing or creating for my own pleasure anymore. This would be for my mother, and in front of strangers.

I was doing it to gain something. And that made me want to explode inside.

The pressure was incredible when I was finally feeling accepted and important to her. I felt as if she loved me. As if she wanted me to succeed. As if she cared. She was acting like a real mom, and I didn't want it to end, no matter how much of a facade it was.

Whenever I memorized a monologue to her standards, she would tell me how proud she was. Then she would add how happy she'd be if I was accepted to the talent agency. In other words, it was a bribe - a deliberate manipulation.

If I did every single thing she wanted me to do, she would be mother of the year.

I had to be about eight or nine when I first stepped out on stage for my first audition. Nervous and anxious as anything, knowing full well how disappointed my mother would be if I didn't do it right, I recited my lines just as she'd told me to. The whole time going into it, I thought about how attentive and caring she had been toward me recently, and how much I didn't want it to end.

Yet when I went into that room filled with cameras and lights and adults, it felt as if my own mother had thrown me into a cave of wolves – the hungriest ones available. These adults were serious and stern; utterly by the book and looking emotionless. They treated all the kids there like cattle, calling names one by one and then dismissing each selection without a shred of encouragement, always in a rush to get to the next one.

I went into that room feeling as if I wanted to lie down on the floor and just die. The audition itself was one of the hardest things I ever did up to that point. And while I got the contract, it wasn't without a price. I cannot describe how mentally and emotionally exhausted I was from trying to keep it all together.

When my mother heard the news that I'd passed, she was naturally excited. Extremely so. She even gave me a kiss on the cheek, something she hadn't done since I was a toddler.

It was such a relief. I honestly thought the worst was over, expecting to go right to the next stage of happily living my dream with a loving parent by my side. I was young, yes, but I'd also been encouraged to believe nothing less than that huge, heartbreaking lie.

My mother had made it seem as if all the hard work would be over once I got the contract. I could just start having fun with what I was good at after that. No pressure - just art and fun.

It didn't take long for that illusion to shatter to pieces though. My agency was all about money, rejection and pressure; they quickly told my mother that I needed to build up my resume further. The more skills a child or talent has, the more jobs they could get. And the more jobs they could get, the higher their chances were at being chosen at auditions.

After hearing that, my mother enrolled me in as many classes and lessons as she could. Dance classes, art classes, martial arts classes, modeling classes, singing lessons. The list went on, and my education took a backseat.

School was no longer important. Landing jobs and gigs were.

The more appealing I became to casting directors and producers, the more my childhood disintegrated even further. A rising prospect, my agency began to send me on audition after audition until I was seriously second-guessing my feelings for what I'd gotten myself into. It wasn't long at all before I realized that I was going to have to face those horrible anxious, nervous, and fearful sensations I'd experienced that first day on a regular basis.

Feeling bamboozled by my mother, I knew I was trapped. My life of play turned into a life of work almost overnight. I practiced so much. So very, very much: memorizing and rehearsing for jobs all day every day. And when I didn't have lines or monologues to practice, I was busy attending three, four or five classes a week, with more lessons on the weekends to perfect my craft.

We took the bus or train in the rain, sleet, storm or snow to get to wherever my mother decided I needed to go. Whatever weather Mother Nature prepared, it was no match for this human parent of mine. I never got a break.

Before those exhausting days, art had been the hideaway I dwelled in when my mind got too much for my tiny body. Art had been my professor and my peace, but now it was just one more torment.

My agency would send me a script the evening before my audition, and my mother would make me memorize and rehearse it the entire night long, then rehearse it non-stop on the way to the trial. And I wouldn't stop rehearsing until the casting director called my name and it was my turn to perform.

Walking into each new room, I always felt the other children's discomfort and anxiety on top of my own, which made me stress out even more. It was like a mental battleground at those auditions, with low, murmured lines from apprehensive little ones, and whispered critiques from greedy parents everywhere you turned.

My mother always seemed to be the most pushy and overbearing one of them all, forcing me to rehearse no matter how mentally exhausted I became. She'd give me these short breaks, then push me right back into rehearsing again. It was so intense that not even my OCD appreciated the effort.

Yet that wasn't the worst part of the process. Nor was it the actual performance, although I had come to recognize how very shy I was. Only comfortable responding to people, I realized that, under pressure, I internally lost it no matter how poised I might come across to everyone outside my head.

Even so, the worst part always came after all that – waiting for the callback.

Sometimes the agency called to let me know I got the job or that I'd been selected for round two. If the agency didn't call at all though, then I simply hadn't gotten the part.

It was utterly nerve-racking. My brain would go into a state of second-guessing, wondering whether or not I'd made the right impression, making me wish I'd done my lines this way instead of that way.

The first time my agency called me to let me know I had the job, you would have thought my mother hit the lottery for millions. I never saw her so happy before, especially not with me. She treated me like I was the most special, most important person in the world after that phone call.

It felt nice, I admit. But I did wonder why. And what was still to come?

They reached out again a few days later with the details, explaining what I should wear and bring, how my hair should be, and what additional scripts I should memorize. My mother proceeded to bombard me with her advice and critiques, which I did my best to process.

The day of the job, we were greeted by some of the staff, who gave us instructions, and told my mother where she could sit while I worked – which I definitely did. I was on set all day for this commercial about Shark Week, acting my heart out in exhaustion, in a constant state of pressure by the producers and my mother.

Throughout the process, I hoped it would be the last time I had to do any such thing. I always hoped it would be the last. But it never ever was.

My life turned into a never-ending cycle - a schedule of classes, lessons, and school that went on for years. My mother would give me the script, I would rehearse it, and then it would be off to the audition we'd go.

When I got the job, she'd be the happiest most loving parent a girl could ever have. When I didn't or if I messed up at the audition though, she wouldn't even look at me, much less speak to me. I'd be left to stare at the disgust and disappointment she made sure would cover her face. It was like I was a bad dog that had gone into her closet and chewed up all her designer shoes.

Back from an audition I didn't do so well at, I would walk with her to catch the next bus or train, and she would intentionally walk too fast until it was close to impossible for me to keep up. If I turned my head for just one second, I would have lost her.

One day, getting the mail for her, I found an envelope with my name on it from my agency. That got me curious enough to open it, where I just so happened to find a check inside for about six-hundred dollars. And when I confronted my mother about it, she could barely look into my eyes as she grinned in guilt.

Naturally, it was a check for the previous job I had done. But since I simply hadn't understood the way things worked up until then, the revelation hit me hard.

This entire time, when I'd been rehearsing, and auditioning, and staying up late studying lines, going to all those classes, it had all been for my mother to get a check. All that fear and pressure was to put money in her pocket.

In a cruel moment, everything began to make sense. I used to wonder so hard why she treated me so horribly when I didn't get a job. And now I knew. It was because of money - money she didn't even tell me we were getting.

Up until then, my mother had made it seem as if those jobs were opportunities - stepping stones toward my big break. That's all I knew, and I never questioned her.

After that revelation, my mother still took the check, only this time with a sad explanation that it was going toward taking care of me. And, she added, just because my name was on a piece of mail didn't mean it belonged to me.

"I want some of that money," I responded. "I worked so hard for it, so I deserve a piece."

A look of disbelief came over her face, as if I was shockingly wrong for wanting something tangible to hold from my blood, sweat and tears.

I think she gave me about fifty dollars to keep me quiet. She did that every now and then. But most of the time, I never received anything, often with the excuse that whatever performance I'd successfully completed was "an unpaid gig."

I never believed it.

As the days passed into weeks that amassed into months, I grew oh-so-tired of having to be so perfect all the time.

There was this one audition, where I had to perform on a big stage with hundreds of people in the audience. Before it, I was mainly used to being in small- to medium-sized rooms with small groups of people. So this audition with this big stage and all those focused eyes made me panicky – much more so than usual.

Dan was present that time, and while I kept my nervousness to myself as I usually tried to do, I had a feeling that he knew just how scared I really was. Whenever I looked at him, he had this "you'll do just fine" expression on his face, mixed in with an "I know you don't like doing this" look. Perhaps he'd known all along, or perhaps my stage fright was just that intensely obvious this time around.

When my name was called and I proceeded to the stage, I looked into that crowd and forgot every line I'd worked so hard to memorize. Every last word was gone as I stared outward, frozen in fear other than the trembling that had taken over me. It didn't help at all that I knew my mother was livid. I could see her out there, and her anger and disgust seemed to rise further with each terrible second that passed. I don't know how long I stood there until the audience, most of them parents, began to shout out words of encouragement to me.

And just like that, I was able to go through my performance.

There were two parts to it that day, a monologue and a song, the latter of which I did a particularly great job on. I know that because those same kind adults came up to me after I left the stage and told me so, adding in that it was okay to make mistakes, as I had when I froze on stage. They said things like, "as long as you tried your best" and "you sung beautifully." They even agreed that, despite my little hiccup, my acting skills were great.

I'd never met them before, yet they cared enough to encourage me, which was enough to make me start understanding that imperfection could be acceptable – contrary to what my mother had conveyed to me in so many ways.

Walking back to her in that room, I knew I'd embarrassed and infuriated her. But I didn't want all the good comments I now had stored in my brain to be erased, so I made sure to focus on Dan instead. As we left, he put his hand on top of my head and told me, "You'll be okay, Boop. You didn't do bad at all. You just got a little nervous is all."

So I told him about the positive things those adults had said to me, and it was a lovely conversation while my mother walked fast in front of us. I guess that she quite simply couldn't take it after a certain point though, because she whirled on him soon enough.

"Don't you lie to her!" she snapped. "She did horribly! I don't care what those people said." Then she turned to me. "Those people didn't say you did good in your acting; they just liked your singing. You messed up, and you did bad!"

As usual, Dan went silent in response to her inner ugliness on display. It was a quality she continued to showcase that entire week, as she ignored me and treated me like I meant nothing. My feelings were hurt, but not to the same degree thanks to the loving, positive words I had stored in my head.

They were my companions every day. And the more I thought about them, the more I began to realize my worth. Whenever I felt as though my mother's nasty and heartless comments were effecting me, I'd break out my secret weapon of encouragement and replay those lines – my lines – over and over again in my head, determining how I wasn't going to feel bad for being human anymore.

In addition, I started to figure out that I related to adults better than my own peers – a natural result of working like a grown woman. The further into acting I got, the more I got used to being around grownups. Sometimes my jobs would last for weeks at a time, leading me to build little relationships with the people around me, talking to them about older topics like they were the only ones to discuss. Since my childhood was so abnormal, talking with kids about kid stuff just didn't seem realistic to me, and I had no interest in doing so.

During school hours, being tired was something I was all-too familiar with. With all the gigs I pulled in for my agency and mother, it wasn't uncommon for me to be out until midnight, just to get up early again the very next day for school. Part of this was because my mother hated to drive, so we would have to be on public transportation for hours at a time, and then walk additional miles and miles to get to where she wanted me to go.

I still wanted love and acceptance, from her especially. Otherwise, I would have stopped. I was definitely in the industry for all the wrong reasons, which took its toll on me beyond the physical too. Between my mother pushing me into it – constantly pushing me – and some of the people on set or behind the cameras, I began to think that love was something that could be snatched back whenever time permitted. Why not when I witnessed people pretending to like children just to keep their steady jobs when it was so obvious they couldn't stand our pesky behinds?

Around this time was when my sister started visiting home from college, I only got to visit her one time since she went away, so I missed her immensely. Latanya's and my mother's relationship was still shaky, but despite the tension, the three of us went on a few outings together anyway. During this one particular outing to the mall, my mother offered to buy us a few winter outfits. Filled with excitement, Latanya and I went into the same store to browse as our mother waited on the bench across from us. I had two pairs of boots I chose in my hand, and so did my sister. And when the time came for our mother to pay for our things, she turned to Latanya and said, "you're only allowed to get one pair".

And when my sister pointed out to our mother how unfair it was for me to be able to get two pairs of boots, while she only got one, my mother turned to her and said, "Your sister can get more stuff because she's still in school, and you dropped out." This was the first time I learned Latanya had quit school; I honestly thought she was home visiting temporarily. I stayed silent, while thinking about how our mother never helped her financially when she was in school. I thought, my sister dropped out of school because she couldn't afford it, and now our mother was chastising her for it.

For the rest of our outing, my sister sulked, as she witnessed our mother buy only me the clothes I wanted. And situations like this began to happen often, as my mother showed more favoritism towards me than she did her other daughter. After a while, my sister stopped coming around our mother altogether, and continued to find a mother in our Aunt Valerie. Latanya had her fair share of life's struggles as she tried to support herself and find the next step towards her next journey. She was just as lost as I was, trying to depend on the little bit of knowledge she had provided for herself over the years. But soon, she became pregnant by a man who didn't care enough to be around. And although the thought of my very first nephew excited me, it saddened me to watch her go through this pregnancy without the support and help of the father. Fortunately, she had the love of our aunts, Valerie and Lia, along with aunts from her dad's side of the family to keep her going.

As I continued acting for my agency, I quickly learned that the way to my mother's heart was based off of what I could do for her. She was never interested in things she couldn't benefit from. As my sister's belly grew, my mother's distaste for her decision-making grew right along with it, as if my mother had no influence at all in why my sister ended up on the path she did.

The more things I realized about my mother, the more attentive I grew towards other mothers around me. Like on the subway, at an audition, or just in the neighborhood where I lived, I observed other mothers with their kids. They were vigilant, concerned, soft, loving, nurturing and selfless. And if their children were in the throes of an asthma attack, and begged them to call 9-1-1, they would have.

I had been recently diagnosed with that breathing condition, and it could get bad, to the point where my inhaler didn't even stop it and I would feel as though I might stop breathing altogether and die at any given moment. An inhaler, my mother's home remedies: Nothing seemed to work for me, and I missed entire days and more of school as a result. Instead of sitting at my desk, I would be in bed, hot and sweating, unable to sleep or lay down all the way, struggling to take in just a subtle amount of air.

Those attacks would last for a week or two, and I would plead with my mother to take me to the hospital, barely managing to murmur 9-1-1. But she refused me every time, saying that calling the ambulance would cost her too much money. So I would just have to fight through it even though fighting felt so impossible.

Struggling to breathe frightened me and triggered my anxiety, which would make it that much worse. I would lay there in a sweaty, light-headed panic while my mother tried to shove hot chicken broth down my throat despite how I knew full well that wasn't going to help. She would also try dabbing my forehead and chest with a wet washcloth instead of calling for the medics or asking one of my aunts to come take me to the hospital. I constantly questioned my mother's judgment; I could have died, many times. For the longest time, my mother made me think that asthma attacks that lasted for weeks at a time were normal. And she continued jeopardizing my well being to save herself from having to pay anymore bills.

Jealousy

When I wasn't almost dying from asphyxiation, or at school, or at auditions, or at a job, I was still spending time with Aunt Valerie. We would still explore different places, food and events together. And many times, my younger cousin Omar would accompany us on our journeys as well. I loved it. Being with them would always make me forget about the sadness that resided in my heart. I would sometimes just stare at her, wanting to let it all out - my mother's manipulation, the mistreatment, the neglect. I wanted to open my mouth and tell her everything that was going on and how I was feeling.

But as always, I never could. I continued to keep silent and act as if nothing was the matter.

My mother must have noticed a difference in me all the same when I was with my aunt verses when I was with her, and not to mention, my sister preferring our aunts' love over her lack of love any day. The more we hung out, the more jealous she became until she decided to put an end to it altogether.

Coming into my room one day, she told me I wasn't allowed to see Aunt Valerie anymore - just out of the blue.

Crushed, I demanded to know why, even though I already knew the reason. My mother had made no attempt to hide her hatred for months. Yet she refused to give me a legitimate answer, since she didn't have one good enough to give. She looked so guilty standing in my doorway, attempting to take someone away who genuinely loved me - all because she couldn't love me herself.

"Aunt Valerie is like a second mother to me," I tried to explain, which was true but didn't help me out one bit.

"That woman isn't your second mother!" she snapped. "Does she buy you clothes or give us money? Does she put food on the table?"

She continued along those lines, yelling about materialistic things. Not once did she stray from that focus.

The fact that, yes, Aunt Valerie actually did buy me things crossed my mind. And there was also the very valid argument to be made that she looked out for my feelings and mind and self, treating me like a human being, like a child who needed to be nurtured, loved and valued.

I didn't get to say any of that, however. All I could do was sit there and cry. I cried so hard I felt light-headed while my mother kept screaming at me for labeling my aunt as a second mother, and then ridiculed me for crying. According to her, there was no reason I should be crying like a baby.

But there was. I was crushed and heartbroken, and words couldn't describe the emptiness I felt.

My mother seemed utterly set on snatching away every person who ever loved me, and I know my aunt felt the same way. We were both torn and confused, wondering why she could do such a thing. But she took pleasure in the effects of her wicked ways. She was vindictive with no good reason at all. She created negativity where there wasn't any present.

This latest proof of her character left me sick to my stomach for a while, and I felt like I'd lost a piece of me while my resentment toward her grew stronger by the day. I might have been too complicatedly broken to understand it at the time, but it was happening nonetheless.

Forced away from my aunt, I was becoming more and more isolated and dependent on my mother, who continued giving me surges of valuation and devaluation as suited her moods. With every acting job I got, I was the best thing that happened to her. And whenever an audition didn't go well, I was a disgrace. I began to feel like nothing more than a mechanical object or doll that was required to use my emotions for acting jobs alone. It was shameful to show them anywhere else.

Feeling unloved ninety percent of the time, I took to roaming the woods. The trees, grass and creeks never pushed me away or misunderstood me. Out in the middle of nature, I could be vulnerable and cry and speak up about things I wished I could bring up at home.

I thought a lot about my father during those times, wondering about what kind of person he was, wondering if what my mother said about him for all those years were true. Would my life have been any different if I was raised by him and his family? Most of the time, I wished I had the money and means to just up and run away to try to find him. Overall, I just wanted to leave. I fantasized about it plenty of times.

Meanwhile, on my mother's end, reality was starting to set in. Almost all the help she'd once had was gone. She no longer had my sister's live-in nanny services. She no longer had my Aunt Valerie, who would pick me up and watch me. The only person left was Dan, a man with no nine-to-five.

Admittedly, he did everything she asked, no matter how ridiculous, and after my aunt was kicked out of the picture, I saw a lot more of him. My mother had him babysit me more, and even take me to classes and auditions when his sister's car was available. Really, he was slowly taking my sister's position and being treated like her too - a fact he recognized. There were many times when the two of us would share a look when my mother was being mean or selfish.

We both knew what kind of person she was. We just got used to being silent about it.

Sometimes, I would stare at my mother, trying to find just one thing to admire. It was easy enough with other people I knew. Aunt Lia and Valerie had dozens of wonderful qualities. My sister always loved and took care of me no matter how stressed-out she got under the demands imposed on her. I even admired Dan for his book knowledge and his open-mindedness despite his many flaws.

But when it came to my mother, the only thing I could come up with was that she provided a good example of what not to be.

This forced break from my aunt lasted for many months, until one day, my mother came into my room to tell me I could see my Aunt Valerie again. I knew her reason was because she needed her. And I'm pretty sure my aunt was aware of that as well. But it didn't matter to either one of us. We were happy to be reunited back together again. And just like that, my aunt and I picked up right where we left off.

Right From Wrong

Middle school brought about a whole range of changes in my life, whether I wanted them or not.

My mother began to get me sex-education books, including ones about masturbation, from the library instead of sitting me down to talk about it with me herself. I'd take the books, skim through them and throw them aside, knowing full-well how ridiculous it was that she couldn't teach me about the topic one-on-one.

I remember when I was younger, listening to her and my sister attempting to have the dreaded sex talk. It was so forced – a waste of time for both of them. They sat there arguing over the spelling of the word rather than discussing the definition. Because, back then, even though my sister was a high school student, she thought it was spelled "sax." That goes to show how attentive our mother was with our education and the life lessons we needed, especially as young women.

Within my first year of middle school, I got my period for the first time. I was so embarrassed. I had always taken it upon myself to carry pads in my book bag just in case this moment happened to me at school. All I knew was that you put a pad on. As for when to change it, what kinds to use, and what to expect concerning cramps, fatigue, bloating and nausea, I knew nothing about these aspects.

The pads I carried with me and used were overnight pads; they were big, thick and bulky. They were uncomfortable and I felt humiliated. I felt as if everyone noticed I was wearing them. Most likely, they did.

When I came home from school that day, I sat down on the couch, waiting for my mother to come home from work so I could get some help on what to do. When she walked through the door and into the living room, I wasted no time telling her that I had my period at school. And she responded with, "Okay. Hurry up. We're going to be late for dance class."

I wasn't in shock, or in disbelief.

I was prepared for her to give me exactly what she gave - nothing.

So as I always had done, I learned what I needed to know elsewhere.

I ended up finding out how to wear pads properly and what kinds to use through girls in my school, who, naturally, had learned from their nurturing and caring mothers.

In the locker rooms after gym class was where I learned all about sex, grooming and other teenage girl-related tips. This is when I noticed I was a late bloomer; I had no breasts and no curves like the other girls my age. I would always look at them, and then stare at myself in the mirror and wonder why I didn't look the same. For a while there, I actually thought something was wrong with me since I wasn't developing fast enough. I even began to stuff my bra in a desperate attempt to fit in, since nobody had told me that every girl develops at her own pace.

It was such an awkward time for me, and I could have really used an interactive mother to tell me about these things. I needed a mother to tell me the importance about respecting myself so that boys wouldn't take advantage of me. I needed a mother who would have encouraged my transition into young womanhood, one who would have taught me how to do my hair, paint my nails, and how to dress. Instead, I struggled with every inch of growing up. I went through my ugly duckling phase alone, and I got teased about my appearance every single day. The only time my mother put effort into making me look decent, was when I had an audition or a job coming up.

Academically speaking, I was doing okay, but I could have been doing much better. And whenever that became too obvious, my mother would punish me even though she was still making me put acting and modeling first. The more that continued, the more I felt like she should have been punished instead of me.

In growing aversion to everything she stood for, my tolerance for her drastically dropped. I began to speak up and speak out against her wrongdoings, confidently telling her when I disagreed or when her actions bothered me.

I began to tell her when she was wrong, or when she said something ridiculous.

Not surprisingly, that led to many – many – arguments between us. In a lot of ways, I found myself being treated like my older sister had been before me. It seemed as though she got joy out of verbally hurting me, all while daring me to respect her with silent submission. When I would lash right back, my mother informed me that I was a loser. That I was stupid and dumb. That I would never amount to anything, and that I'd be stuck living with her forever because of how much I needed her.

She even told me I'd end up just like my father.

That pushed me beyond mere sadness to flat-out fury.

Fed up with how wrong she was all the time, with the neglect and manipulation, the antagonizing and hurtful words, and what my life had become thanks to her parenting and lack of love, I continued to speak up. Every time she verbally attacked me, I would verbally attack her right back.

If I was stupid, then so was she!

If I was a loser, then so was she!

I was her truth, her mirror, reflecting everything she'd done in an attempt to make her see and feel every wrong thing she had done to my sister and me. I told her how cold she was and mean she was, and how stupid her rules were.

The more I spoke up to defend myself, the more insults she threw right back. She called me a demon or the devil every time I stood up and demanded some respect of my own. I was evil, she would say. And then she'd go to her room and watch church programs on TV just as soon as she was done putting me down.

It left me fuming. How could she be so hateful and hurt so many people who loved her, and then turn around and call herself a Christian? How could she call me evil and a demon for sticking up to her abuse, then go watch some television church program?

Here was this woman who took joy out of a child's pain and misery – her own child's pain and misery! Yet she turned around and called herself a moral creature. I was disgusted with her efforts of trying to suppress her guilt with Christianity. It was like she knew she was wrong but thought watching religious services could erase all her sins and hurtful behavior.

That was when I truly began to think she was absolutely crazy. I questioned every single thing about her, and started to see that I barely knew who she was when it came down to it. She was too occupied creating false personas to cover up how horrible she was.

I watched this woman fake-laugh and hold these painted on smiles on her face when she spoke to strangers. It made me sick watching how fraudulently pleasant she could become after saying something hurtful and disgusting to me. And so, witnessing my mother's act first-hand day in and day out, I studied it. I studied her in order to protect myself.

The way I saw it, in order to protect yourself from someone, you had to first know what that someone was capable of. What are their strengths and weaknesses and overall character? How do they react to life's situations and act within life as a situation itself? You must understand them inside and out to maintain your safety and emotional freedom, which is why I went about doing exactly that.

I knew when she was embarrassed and when she lied. I knew when she was manipulating and when she was being spiteful. I knew when she was jealous of another person, and I knew when she was jealous of me for the talents I possessed. I began to learn the character she had created – what she had become – after all those years.

During this analysis process, I remembered how timid my sister used to be when she lived with us – how she didn't vocalize her opinions very often. Latanya was emotional and scared of our mother. No matter how wrong that woman was, Latanya would just bite the bullet and take it. Though that didn't help her at all. I witnessed firsthand how she fed off my sister's fear.

That's why I knew that if I stopped defending myself, my mother would end up treating me even worse than before. So with every hurtful comment she threw at me, I made certain to throw it right back. Every time she called me a demon, I responded with, "No! You're the demon! Only a demon would say something like that to their own child." And whenever she'd yell, "You're just like your father, and you're going to end up just like him," I came back with, "Yes! I'd rather be like him than like a person who hurts other people – like you!"

I barely even knew my father other than the horrible things she would say about him. For a while my mother had my sister and I convinced that my father was this scary abusive monster. She would tell us stories about how he would drag her by her hair, and pull out a loaded gun and shove it in her face. Every last one of her stories depicted her as beauty and my father as the beast.

Life as a Battle

I got used to having to defend myself against my mother on a daily basis. She would smirk while she called me horrible names and said horrible things about me, as if she was getting her kicks by doing so.

School, however, seemed to be getting better for a little while. After auditioning to be a part of the step team, I was accepted and finally started to make some friends on the team. But my grades weren't good enough, and so I eventually got kicked off the team as a result. I remember how, at one particular step show, a judgmental teacher walked passed me as we were performing and said, "I wish your grades were as good as you stepped."

I thought, how dare this Toucan Sam looking mf'r disparage me, as if he knows me, my life and everything I have to go through well enough to make his judgments!

It was another jab to my confidence, as if I didn't have enough coming from my mother. That comment momentarily took my joy away, and made me think of how lost of a kid I was. It made me remember that I didn't have a mother I could rely on, and most likely, I never would. This teacher had interrupted my joy, and I took that hurtful comment and added it to every other malicious comment I had collected over the years.

There was no compassion there, but even while the snide comment seeped into my soul, I wasn't surprised. I didn't think compassion even existed, at least not for me. The way I rationalized it, I was either utterly unlikeable or unworthy of kindness or love, or the world was quite simply a cold, mean and hateful place all around.

Yet, despite that philosophy, I found myself looking at other people's families more and more, and wanting what they had. I wanted the smiles and the silly sibling bickering. The worried mothers who gave out too many kisses looked so tangible and yet so wretchedly unattainable, and the same went for the dads who were the toughest guys in the world, only to completely melt for their daughters and wives.

That kind of life seemed like a fairytale, but I wanted it so badly. Even the most basic aspects of family life, like eating dinner as a family, came across as foreign and exotic. We never did that. Back when Latanya was living with us, it would be the two of us. And ever since, I mostly ate by myself in my room or at the dining room table, while my mother would eat in front of her TV.

I would just sit and think about how different my life would be if I had a family like the ones I saw around me. I wanted love so bad. I needed it badly. I was dying inside.

Children who get their feelings hurt too much develop a hard, harsh outer shell. So if someone had grabbed me, hugged me and told me how much they loved me, I probably wouldn't have known how to take it. It would have been confusing and uncomfortable; it wasn't something I was used to. And there was a good chance I would have broken down in tears from the attention alone.

Maybe someone would have stepped in if I'd told them how bad my mother was truly treating me. I know my aunts would have done something. But I continued to keep it all to myself.

Taking matters into my own jaded little hands, I tried out new things that my mother couldn't influence. These activities were for me. I had picked them, not her.

One of those unpressured ventures was the women's chorus. There was an audition for a lead part, and I got it, practicing on my own and with the other girls until it came time for the school performance. There were actually two showings on two different nights, and my mother and Dan attended the first.

I'll admit I was excited.

As always, I looked into the crowd to see if I could spot my mother. And during my solo performance especially, I kept looking toward her to see if I could read her expression.

I did.

I saw her sitting in the crowd, emotionless and unentertained. She showed no signs of encouragement or excitement at all, as if she didn't want to be there in the first place. It was utterly bewildering how strangers in the audience could look more enthused and supportive of me than my own mother.

Yet she attended the second showing too. Once again, I did my solo part. And once again, I caught her looking as if she didn't want to be there or be bothered. After it was over, all she said to me was, "You did better at the first performance than you did with this one."

After that, my anger toward her and my life in general kept on growing. I harbored so much pain and resentment in my heart and soul that a positive thought just couldn't form in my young mind about anything. I hated it all - acting, modeling, and all those lessons. My existence and everything about me. My mother too. Of course my mother too. But as for myself, I was a little girl who only saw negativity reflected in the mirror, something that wasn't good enough or wasn't worthy enough every time.

My self-esteem lowered each day, in part because of how hard my mother worked to isolate me. In retaliation for standing up to her, she started to call Aunt Valerie and give her one-sided stories. Whatever negativity I had thrown right back at her, my mother would relay without explaining why I'd said it or what she herself had done to warrant such a reaction.

She got on the phone to lie about me constantly, making it seem like I was the most evil and misbehaved child she had ever crossed paths with. I was failing at school, she would tell her. I was being disrespectful, she'd sigh. And because she was so very good at lying, she worked her magic until Aunt Valerie began honestly thinking I was rebelling against my mother's love.

She put more effort into fabricating stories than she ever did into parenting me, much less loving me. With careful manipulation and deceptions, she made it seem like I was the one being abusive, which made her the victim.

My mother did everything in her power to make my aunt view me as someone I wasn't. Aunt Valerie had no idea about the hurtful things my mother was saying and doing to me. She had no idea how I was being treated. She knew nothing of the abusive handling and selfish neglect, or that my mother would tear my self-esteem down every little chance she got. That's why the well-worked lies stuck.

It began to feel as if my mother was trying to manipulate every single adult who loved me into thinking poorly of me in some way, shape or form. It seemed like she wanted nobody to love me at all.

Really though, I believe she was just mad she could no longer control my thoughts about her anymore. So she turned her energy to control other people's thoughts about me. Immediately after every argument we had, she would get on the phone with my aunt and lie about me. And like everything else she did, it started to take its toll, on both my beloved role model and me. As I grew older, I stopped visiting my aunts' home as much, too tired of looking into Aunt Valerie's eyes and seeing what I thought were pained perceptions.

After a while, it was too exhausting to worry about the effect her deceptions were having all around. Caring was beyond my capability when she'd gone so far out of her way and applied herself so forcefully to making sure that no adult wanted to listen to a word I had to say. I was sure she'd manipulated the minds of my family members so well that trying to tell them the truth would be nothing but a waste of time.

If that sounds like I gave up, I did. Then, consider why.

By all appearances, my mother enjoyed herself thoroughly while doing her best to ruin my life and doing a phenomenal job ruining my reputation. She certainly practiced it enough, to the point where she called the police on me for swiping my pointer finger across her chocolate cake.

I just wanted to taste the icing, and I got the police called on me for it.

She lied to the officer who responded too. Of course she did. She told the woman I was out of control and disrespectful. And when I attempted to explain that my mother had called because of a cake, it was too ridiculous of a story to be believed, especially from a youth. Instead, the officer went on telling my mother how she had no tolerance for bad kids. After hearing what yet another judgmental adult had to say about me, I just shut down while fixating on how much I hated my life.

I wasn't a bad kid; I was a damaged kid who was dealing with a heartbreak caused by the woman who was supposed to love me the most. Middle school was when I gave up on acceptance, love and myself.

Getting such positive reinforcement from the policewoman only exacerbated my mother's purposeful insanity. She began to call the cops on me about little frivolous things – so much, that the same officer would often come in order to diffuse the situation. One officer even told me that he knew what she was like, calling them for every little thing. So he did his best to come to our house before any other officers could arrive.

He became someone – the only person – I could open up to about her unfairness and hatred. Everyone else believed her though.

My mother was a liar. A cold-hearted, controlling, manipulating liar. And she was good at what she did.

The result was that the only thing close to a loving family I had was the fictitious ones I would watch on TV. There were plenty of times I'd sit in front of it with tears rolling down my eyes because of how much my own reality was a mess.

I thought a lot about my sister during that time, wondering if I would be the next daughter to leave – the next daughter who just couldn't take it anymore. How had she felt stepping out of the grasp of such an emotionally unavailable woman? What had that been like? How good had it felt?

Misguidance and Thrills

High school was approaching and the only thing I found to be a joy was my new cute-faced nephew. My sister was now a mother, and we were all so happy to have this new little addition to the family. Even my mother was filled with joy. For the first time in my life, I was witnessing my mother become this loving, nurturing and overprotective grandmother almost overnight, a role my sister and I never seen her take on before, especially not with us.

She would be cold towards us one minute, and in seconds, transform into mother goddess as soon as her grandchild entered the room, leaving Latanya and I relieved in knowing she would treat her grandchildren this way, but at the same time, wondering why she could never treat us the same.

As high school began and continued, the more confrontational I became. I grew angry and careless. After so many years of taking care of myself and looking out for myself, I took it a step further and began to do what I wanted when I wanted. Why not live up to the rotten expectations everybody already had of me?

I saw no reason not to earn the reputation I already had.

With that in mind, I stayed out for weeks at a time, only going home to pack a small bag that included makeup, deodorant and clothes. Often enough, I'd be accompanied by men much closer to my mother's age, who would wait outside in their cars while I grabbed my stuff. They took me wherever I needed or wanted to go, and bought me what I needed. My mother would peep out the window whenever we'd come along. So she saw it all, yet she never said anything on the subject. Not to me, anyway.

I never had sex with those men, but sometimes they and I would hang out in my parking lot, drinking liquor and smoking. My mother even caught me smoking once. When I went back into the house, it was to hear her on the phone with Aunt Valerie, gossiping about what she'd seen me doing. "Yeah, she's out there smoking cigarettes," she sighed. "First her sister was, and now her." Then she launched into her typical routine about how bad I was.

If that was true – and part of it was – then why not confront me about it? That was my question. Her daughter, a minor, was behaving in illegal and unhealthy behavior. Yet instead of sitting me down to at least try talking me onto the right track, her first and only thought was to gossip. My mother sounded excited and eager when gossiping, as if she was elated to finally have something true and bad to defame me with. I felt like a fool, thinking about all the years I wanted this woman to help me, thinking about all the wasted moments I sat down fantasizing about how wonderful it would be if she were different. But I was officially done with the fantasies, and in my eyes, my reality was just as grim as my future. I continued with my destructive life, seeking out my own kind of help, the short-term kind that distracted me from the pain I'd otherwise be in. I took what I thought I deserved and what I thought I needed. I took the love of people who knew nothing about the word, only how to use people themselves. Really, I took the love of people who weren't much different from my mom.

It's not surprising that I went on to get involved with the wrong crowd in high school, a circle of other girls who were damaged too. To me, they were my sisters, and we encouraged each other to drink, fight, steal and do drugs. They were compelling because, finally, I had someone to relate to. When they stayed out for weeks at a time, their mothers didn't bother looking for them either. When they eventually came home, their mothers didn't bother to lecture them about the dangers of their behavior, just like my mother didn't bother to.

We were emotionally immature children engaging in mature activities with men who should have been more mature themselves than to entertain a bunch of high school girls. Those men would have sex with my underage friends, and some attempted to have sex with me. But that's one trap I never fell into, mainly because the thought of sex frightened me out of the idea entirely. So I made sure they knew that I considered them to be brothers, and nothing more.

I witnessed all my friends getting taken advantage though. The men would bring them into back rooms and take their turns having sex with them. I was the only virgin in the group, and I kept that information about myself a secret. Guys never really appealed to me, and neither did their intentions. But of course, I was the only one out of my female friends who felt this way, so even though I'd found a group of fellow misguided girls to hang out with, I still felt odd and out of place at times. There were many times when I felt as though I wasn't supposed to be there, with these people, and around similar dysfunction.

Because I truly wasn't. My soul was crying, yearning for something greater, something healthier, and something made from love. I didn't know any better, and the anger and sadness I harbored knew this and took full advantage. I began inflicting pain upon myself just as my mother has done to me for all these years. I had no love to give myself, and had been stripped of all possibilities to acquire it.

My soul lacked guidance and morals like a diabetic lacks insulin. My soul was sick, needing to be healed by love, but I was too young-minded, confused and damaged to do anything about it. How could I have known love was what I needed?

Here I existed, a naturally talented person with unexplained gifts. My soul was never put here to waste those gifts; it was put here to complete its purpose with the gifts it was given.

For years, I was nurturing my soul with art and music and knowledge, subconsciously training myself to be greater, for a greater cause. But for the first time in my life, I was distracted from seeing any of the good I possessed. My mother made me hate who I was meant to be before I even understood who I was.

Like any other child – any other person – I belonged in an atmosphere where people cared about me and paid attention to who I was as a person. I belonged in an atmosphere where people cared enough to see my gifts and helped me better understand them and myself. I was created to expect growth in an environment that produced love and knowledge, not pain and misguidance.

That kind of environment was where I belonged. That was what I needed.

But I was too busy letting pain destroy me to realize this. I was ruining my life and growing up too fast. I should have been in a school classroom, learning and studying for my future. I should have been thinking about where I wanted to be in life and what I wanted to do. I should have been thinking about what my purpose was, and what plans I should make. I should have been listening and speaking to God. Because I shouldn't have left Him in the first place.

And that's the thing. I left Him; He didn't leave me. God would have never given me all these gifts to do something greater than myself, to then just leave me. I just couldn't hear Him because of the fog of pain clouding my senses. I just couldn't understand my heavenly Father when He was trying to show me my way. I not only rebelled against life and against my true nature, but I was rebelling against God too. The one man who had all the love and guidance I needed was there yearning for me all of those years.

I continued to roam around with my senses clouded though, skipping school, drinking and smoking weed, traveling from city to city. Sometimes I would come home at two, three or four in the morning during the school week, drunk and throwing up all over the place. I knew my mother heard me on numerous occasions, stumbling into the house after a night of drinking with thirty- and forty-year-old men.

I'm sure my mother heard me running into things and knocking over any and everything that seemed to be in the path of my drunken and high body, not that she ever did anything about it.

I was among criminals and misguided individuals, all of us feeding off the little bit of love we had left inside ourselves, trying to figure out life without worthwhile instructors. Meanwhile, my ugly duckling phase was officially over, and so I became more vulnerable to the fraudulent love others were too quick to offer. Since my mother failed to teach me what I needed to know about becoming a young lady, and why it was important, I got my knowledge off the streets and from females I should not have been learning from.

The only people who would sit me down and teach me were strippers and men two or three times my age. There were no true morals or integrity involved, just survival skills, and I took what I could get until

I was acting out my mother's lies. All of those stories she told about me year after year were slowly playing out until I was officially a young girl who stayed in the streets and did things she shouldn't do.

Nothing was ideal about any of it, but I acted the way I acted, and it happened the way it happened.

For years, I had built up a basement of negative emotions that I kept under lock and key, scared to let them show. But I found that, when I drank, I got a form of release. That's when some of my emotions got brave enough to escape and experience the world. It was a welcome escape in so many ways – drinking and thinking, and crying hard as a result.

I would drink and get mad at how my life was and wasn't. I would drink to express my inner sadness. Drinking became my ritual. If I was upset, I'd drink. I was a teenager – a minor – able to drink two forty-ounce bottles of malt liquor, back to back, while still staying coherent and aware of everything around me. Sometimes I would get so angry during these escapes that I'd scare people into hiding or walking away. For me though, it felt good to express myself and let it all rush out.

Of course, when that self-prescribed therapy wore off, I was always faced with the next day, hurt and more depressed than I felt before.

Love had slowly and painfully become one of the biggest misconceptions in my life. I began to forget what love felt like, and what it looked and sounded like. What it's supposed to be and what it shouldn't be. In my mind, love was covered and hidden by one big, giant question mark.

As far as acting, my contract would run out as soon as I turned eighteen, since my agency catered to kids. So the older I got, the less jobs I had, and the less and less income I brought in each year. I wasn't at all upset about that situation, considering how I wasn't getting the money anyway, and I definitely wasn't thinking about the puny little twenty- or fifty-dollar bills my mother would toss me while she kept ninety-eight percent of my earnings.

It should have been a relief that my acting hell was coming to an end, except that I knew it wasn't. My mother was already researching adult agencies for me even while she stopped buying me clothes and shoes, or worrying about my appearance. The less I brought in for her, the less she cared. It got to the point where I outgrew everything she ever bought me for this acting career of hers. I had one pair of shoes left that I wore every single day. Until one day, I decided to start stealing my clothes and shoes from department stores from then on forward.

It wasn't like she was destitute either. My mother had money. I took a peek at her tax documents one year, and she was making a little over forty grand a year. It was clear she was saving her money to herself, while leaving me to steal the necessities I needed. Naturally, she made excuses about why she never bought me anything, blaming my behavior and poor grades for her parenting choices.

But it wasn't the lack of material things that cut me so badly. It was the lack of discipline, structure and guidance. It was the fact that nobody was running up to me to say, "I love you. And this behavior stops today!" or "I love you enough to help you pull through this because I believe in you and who you can become."

Here's a truth for any parents reading this: Kids really do appreciate discipline. They might not act like it, but they do when it's part of the very definition of love. A parent who loves their child disciplines them, showing and expressing to them the difference between right and wrong, and the morals they should maintain.

Without discipline, children will hurt themselves and others, acting wrongfully without any thought or feeling behind it at all because they were never taught to have thought or feeling about common decency. Before long, they become what's wrong with the world - a new addition to the pain and stress that plagues society.

I know because I was one of those children without discipline or love. And I didn't consider my actions to be wrong or hurtful to anyone.

I was that girl that no one could really see except to criticize, that young girl who wasn't observed carefully enough. I became the face of every other misunderstood, heartbroken little girl who's too ashamed or naive to open up her mouth and scream for help. I was coming closer to experiencing my own emotional breakdown, as if my feelings and words could no longer be held down by bolts and metal chains alone.

During one of our many arguments, I felt as if I had enough of my mother's antagonizing and her urge of wanting an angry reaction from me. I began to peel back every protective layer I had built to keep me safe from my mother's cruelty. For once, I gave my sadness a stage to speak.

"Mom! what is wrong with you, why can't you just love me! Why are you giving up on me?"

I confronted her with tears covering my face and drowning my eyes. She looked at me and flat-out told me she'd given up on me a long time ago. And as she spoke those words, she chuckled and smirked. It was like the hurt expressions on my face entertained her better than any show she had ever watched could.

The more hurt I became, the more she laughed. The more my eyes turned bloodshot red, the more she antagonized me, while my brain worked hard to vilify and justify her at the same time.

I must have done something especially wrong, right? Maybe I shouldn't have confronted her about how she treated me. She had said she gave up on me because I'm a burden and was just too much to deal with. That was the first time I fully ran away. I grabbed whatever clothes were close to me at the time – all of my stolen garments. And I left.

I didn't know where I was going. All I knew was that I had to get out of there. Away from her.

I walked down the street to the playground about two minutes away from my house. I loved the little area because it was nestled in between two rows of townhouses, with everything hidden by trees and bushes. Even then, nature was something I felt comfortable around. Being surrounded by the beauty of trees felt as though I was being swaddled by Mother Nature herself.

So enveloped, I sat on one of the swings and cried the tears I'd been holding back for years, tears that escaped my soul without the use of alcohol and drugs for once.

I cried so hard I fell front-forward out of the swing and onto my knees, grabbing the closest thing to me, which was the mulch on the ground while I continued to weep and tell myself to toughen up.

My first heartbreak was never a boy or a best friend who found a new best friend. My first heartbreak was my mother.

Despite everything I'd observed and knew about her, I still loved my mother, and I hated it. It was as if the reason for me still loving her and wanting the same in return was more of a biological explanation than anything else. How could I still love such a cruel, cold, selfish creature?

How could I love someone who made me feel worthless?

Like on so many occasions before, I asked myself. Why is this my life? Why is this my mother? Is this how my sister felt right before she left?

It was dark and cold, and there I was alone on the ground of a playground weeping and feeling like a cold punk while doing it.

As strong as I wanted to be, I couldn't control my thoughts this time. In my mind, I had given up on me too. After so many years of neglect, this was the first time I really and truly found no significance in my life. I felt useless and dumb. I felt like a failure.

I wanted so badly to go to my aunts and tell them everything, but I didn't think they'd believe me. For that matter, I couldn't think of anyone who would.

My mother's smirk hung over me, as did those last words: "I been gave up on you a long time ago."

Those words hurt me near to death, because they proved me right. I wanted everything I knew about my mother to be a lie, but she'd proven me right once and for all. There was no coming back from those words.

The reality of it was one of the most devastating moments I had ever encountered in my short-lived life. My mother, a woman from whom I was made and shared a body with for nine months, was a soul-damager. She was a tormentor. And she was very intentional about it.

She did it because she chose to. She did it because it gave her pleasure.

As I sat on that ground in front of that swing in the middle of that night, reflecting and crying, my next realization was how much I regretted allowing my emotions to show in her presence. Every tear that tried to leave my eyes was simply one more reason for her to chuckle and smile. Why had I given her such pleasure? At my expense?

The park was my only real home for about what seemed to be two hours. After that, I got up, gathered myself and walked to a friend's house, where I asked if I could stay – permanently. Surprisingly, they said yes. The mom did tell me I'd have to ask my mother, and I agreed to that stipulation. Though, of course, I didn't ask her right away. I waited a few weeks to go home to speak to her about it.

She said no.

Because I was a minor, she informed me, I wasn't allowed to just go and move out of her house. I found this odd, since she never had a problem with me staying away from home for weeks at a time, doing Lord knows what with who. She then told me if I didn't return home, she would call the police on me - again.

In response, I told her to do whatever she felt she needed to do, as I walked out of her front door for another few weeks.

Honestly, I didn't care about her calling the police. The way I saw it, if I didn't want to be found, I wasn't going to be.

So I continued with life, looking for love in all the wrong places, in the streets with these thugs and degenerates who had lived hard lives just like me, if not harder. Each one had a different struggle that eventually boiled down to a lack of love and compassion, and unfortunately, that was my comfort zone. That's the environment I was familiar with.

I got to see which levels of pain manifested which traits. Many I could completely relate to, and others that I couldn't but still found companionship with. The universe gave me a mother who didn't know how to love, and the streets then gave me the opposite. The love the streets provided was an unhealthy one, but better than what I was getting at home.

Still naive, yet growing colder and bitter every single day.

I didn't trust a soul; I questioned everything, and I began to openly defend myself. I fought back because that's all I was used to. I'd first learned the craft at home, and now I was perfecting it. When strangers or known entities attempted to threaten me, I had no problem handling the issue, because I didn't care. I lacked social skills, but my fists were more than capable. And taking a punch myself was nothing compared to what I'd been through emotionally for all those years.

Once again, I just didn't care.

I was developing a tomboy persona, a tomboy who just happened to be attractive. I had a pretty face and a nice shape, not that I thought much about either. After years of the particular kinds of abuse I received, my self-esteem was really low. I was very humble about my appearance; essentially, I never had the opportunity to be stuck up about my physical appearance and I honestly didn't think how I looked was such a big deal.

It was much more important to just get through life as unscathed as I could possibly be. I know that some girls take the opposite route to survive, but I was too busy trying to cope with what had happened in my life and kept happening in my life to focus on the concept of being attractive to the opposite sex.

Nobody taught me about the group of insecure girls who go around picking on pretty girls because they're jealous. So my one-track mind was focused on immediate, physical self-preservation. And so immediate, physical self-preservation was all I did.

School was barely part of my life's equation. I was failing high school, because I put absolutely no effort toward it. I barely even put effort into going. Whenever my friends and I would actually go, it would be to roam the halls drunk, looking for our next non-academic adventure. So it wasn't shocking when, one by one, all the kids I hung out with were being kicked out of school.

Then, also not surprisingly, it was my turn to be called before the staff and school psychologist.

What did take me aback was that my mother actually showed up for it, that's when I knew it was serious. She had never agreed to meetings with my teachers before. She pretty much would tell them not to bother her about my behavior, that while I was at school, I was their problem.

At the meeting, the staff went around expressing their concerns for my behavior and work ethic, which my mother made excuses for without ever once blaming herself. It was their fault, she implied if not stated, not hers. Sitting there quietly, I wanted to open all her closets and let the skeletons out, but I didn't. Once again, I was afraid to open up and allow my feelings to show.

To their credit, the school did try to press her on those kinds of details, asking her why she allowed such behavior and wondering what was going on at home that might be spurring me on. Her responses were steadfast: The blame belonged elsewhere, and she had the cleanest hands around.

I know it flabbergasted the school staff to hear her explanations, excuses and absolute refusal to consider herself anything other than the victim. Besides, she told them, she had already enrolled me in military school.

That was the first I had heard about it. But it made sense. She didn't raise me properly, and now she wanted to get rid of me so I could really become someone else's problem. It was just more of the same to me; I had lost the desire to care.

Back with her for a few weeks, all I heard was how much of a great opportunity this would be for me and how many positive things would happen once I learned to submit. My mother's words went in one ear and out the other; I no longer trusted her, so her words held no value to me. Then I was off with no protest whatsoever. My mother may have thought she manipulated me into going, but in all actuality, I once again just didn't care.

I still didn't care when I got there to find military sergeants raising their own blood pressure by yelling at each kid who didn't completely follow each rule. It was ridiculous, and to me, unhelpful. It wasn't going to change anything when it simply felt like more of the same abuse I'd already gone through. In her all-governing selfishness, my mother had given me the same kind of reality she'd already helped me create, yet expected me to change from it.

Yes, I was young and immature when it came to my decision-making, but I was confident that I didn't need military school. Being treated badly by strangers was not going to help my heart heal. That much was obvious to me.

Today, the misconceptions people have about hurt children and young adults sickens me. Not every hurt kid is bad, and not every bad kid is hurt. Like everyone else on the planet, they're individuals. And we need to take our time identifying who is who, and what is what, for each and every one of them who appears to be struggling with life.

Along with my mother, the drill sergeants at the military camp misdiagnosed me and gave me the wrong medicine. I needed nurturing, not yelling. I needed to realize I could be great, that I was beautiful inside and out, and that it was never too late to change. So this facility, which doled out discipline, structure, physical and mental torture, verbal abuse and nerve-racking chaos, made me feel worse about myself - if it made any changes at all. The way I saw it, the facilitators were a bunch of people getting paid to appear scary, when I had met way scarier people on the streets or at auditions.

Throughout this time though, someone very specific still hadn't given up on trying to reunite with me. That's why, one day, I received a letter from someone whose handwriting happened to resemble mine quite a bit.

Opening up the envelope, there it lay - a letter from my father. I guess Aunt Lia had given him my new address, and it was perfect timing.

Before then, I had tried to write Dan, but he never once wrote me back - my mother's orders. My father though? After that initial correspondence, he wrote me back every single time I reached out.

I loved him through the paper with the very first sentence I read on that very first precious piece of paper. It was so obvious how much we had in common and how much we could have in common going forward. He too had let my mother create pain in his heart, but he'd overcome it. In his letters, he admitted to his past faults and told me he became a devoted Christian while being incarcerated all of these years. He had set aside his hurt, anger, and bad behavior to become the person he was meant to be.

Compassionate and sincere, he spoke from a place of love and wisdom that I yearned for. On instinct, I knew that this man was someone from whom I could learn. He was a part of me, and he loved me. I could tell within the words he wrote that he did.

It was exactly what I needed, and I immediately opened up to him. About everything too; he was the first person I really told about my mother.

I poured out information about her behavior and how she treated me. I detailed what I had gone through as if we were the very best of friends and I could trust him up, down, back and forth. For some reason, this man - this stranger - didn't feel like a stranger at all.

For the first time in so very, very long, I felt loved. The sensation – the recognition – was so refreshing and restorative, yet nerve-racking at the same time. Because even while I was confiding in him with the same kind of relief a shipwreck survivor would have clinging to a lifesaver, I kept remembering all the horrible things my mother had told me about him. And she had told me so many over so many years. My rational side realized that yes, he used to be abusive, and there was a possibility he still could be. But the perfect image my mother attempted to paint of herself for my recollection, was just as fake as the love she gave when she needed to gain something.

For years, my mother had valued and devalued me, breaking my heart this way and that in the process. So in the back of my mind, I was scared my dad would end up doing the same.

That worry wasn't his fault. My first impression gave me no signs of him being the type of person to do any such thing. It was a wall of my own construction - something I had up just in case he did disappoint me.

I didn't think he would, but what if he did?

I remembered back so very long ago to when I was a happy, thriving little bundle of innocence sitting down with Aunt Valerie and reading Dad's letters, the ones where he would send me pictures of himself so I'd know what he looked like. I remembered staring at his pictures where I marveled about how much he looked like me. I would then think about what our lives would have been like if we never left Hampton.

Now that I was older and seeing pictures of him again, I felt like I was reliving those moments all over. I was back in my childhood, girlishly awed at how much I resembled this man. I finally knew where I got my eyes, full eyebrows, lips, hairline and cheekbones. I got them from him because I was his.

As the communication between us developed, I woke up one day and realized I'd had enough of military school. I was done hopping from one abusive situation to another; I needed to get out. Just like that, it was so clear what I needed, a stable environment and a chance - anything but what I was surrounded by at that moment.

So I decided to get myself kicked out.

The school was full of discipline and structure, yes, but just not the kind I needed. If anything, it just made me more angry. With discipline being the institution's main objective, not education or social skills or constructive criticism, I had nothing to look forward to but my father's letters. And those did more to urge me out than anything else, since they reminded me that I was made for something more.

One day, I stole some cake from the chow hall – a blueberry one, to be exact. I did it on purpose so everyone could see. They deprived us of junk food and juice, so I figured that some jealous person would snitch on me, and that jealous person did.

I was called into the office and told I'd be put into Fourth Platoon for my actions, which was where all of the extra-disobedient cadets were placed. But I respectfully told them to get lost and send me home, which they had no problem doing after I was done ranting. I applied my best acting skills that day and threw an absolute tantrum.

For that Oscar-worthy performance, I got the exact role I wanted, a nice, one-way ticket out of there.

The next morning, my mother and Aunt Valerie came to pick me up. They were both visibly upset, but I honestly didn't care. I was tired of being labeled and tired of letting my so-called parent dictate my life. So I didn't let her choose my next place; I took the initiative to research schools myself after a few weeks went by.

That's when I came across this alternative school located in the middle of nowhere in Baltimore, Maryland. Right off the bat, it sounded like a better alternative than the hellhole my mother had put me in so willingly, but I went about doing my research all the same, with positive results.

From what I could tell, this school was a lot like a college experience. It wasn't marketed for kids with disciplinary issues. It was simply an option. As a young person, you could either go to high school for your diploma, or you could go to the alternative school to get your GED and learn a trade instead. It sounded like the most ideal situation under the circumstances, and I just knew it was the route I wanted to go.

When I told my mother about it, I had to beg her to take me to one of the featured orientations, but she did eventually agree to go. It worked out just about as well as if I had planned it out from start to finish. I was accepted; it was official, and I would be once-again headed on a journey away from home. But this time, it was a journey I actually wanted and needed.

For the first time in a long time, I was optimistic about my future. I was determined to make something of myself, and nothing was going to get in my way. It was a very good thing I had that attitude too, because my first week was just like any other new situation I had experienced. Too many girls decided they didn't like me before they got to know me, and too many boys decided they liked me before they even figured out my name.

That was okay though, since I went into that school with the mentality that I didn't want to make any friends. This wasn't to be closed-off for the sake of being closed-off, and perhaps I came across as snotty in the process. But I understood all too well that this was my last chance at graduating. I couldn't let anything as silly as jealous girls or lustful boys ruin it for me.

I just wanted to work toward getting my GED. Other than that, I wanted to be left alone. Going in, that was the approach I adopted.

They immediately assigned me to a dorm, which was the only aspect about the school I didn't like. Being trapped in close quarters with a bunch of catty girls, most of who secretly or openly hated my guts, was hardly ideal. Then again, what they said and did, and how they behaved, wasn't anything I hadn't experienced already. So I did manage to maintain my mantra and ignore them for the most part.

I'm not a completely cooled cucumber now, and I certainly wasn't back then either. So every once in a while, those girls did get under my skin. And when they did, it was hard to not feel like punching a few of them in their face.

But despite those irritating moments, I thrived.

Every morning we woke up, got dressed in our uniforms, and headed downstairs to breakfast. From there, you attend the classes you need to pass the GED. After passing the GED, you took trade classes until you were finished with the program. Thanks to the structure and feel of the campus, it came across more like a college setting than a high school, even if it was filled with a wide range of ages.

Caught up in this positive environment, I passed my GED the first time I took the test. And I passed it with flying colors too – not bad for a girl who'd spent her entire high school career skipping classes, getting skunk drunk and smoking weed. Admittedly, my mind always picked up on things fast. Still, I found it amazing how well it worked when I was nestled into a place that was both structured and encouraging.

Since I had earned my GED, I had two choices: I could learn about a trade or I could call it a day and go home. Honestly, I didn't care about the former, but I definitely did care about avoiding my mother's house. So I selected retail sales, and started that curriculum.

And in this particular class, there was this one girl who right from the start couldn't stand me.

As far as I know, I never did anything to her. She didn't like me on sight, and so she expressed her distaste for my presence whenever she got the chance, which was often enough. Every day of that first week of trade classes, she made sure to make comments about me. Normally subliminal and indirect in nature, they were quite obvious nonetheless – and intentionally so.

That whole first week, I ignored the insults. But then the second week started, I was assigned to a table with this girl, and the verbal nastiness just kept coming. That's when I finally snapped.

Jumping to my feet, I told her if she had a problem with me, we could handle it out in the hallway or in the bathroom. It was her choice and it didn't matter much to me, but we were going to have it out somewhere one way or the other.

The way I saw it, I had already earned my GED, so this fight I could accept. If I got kicked out for it, then, so be it, I could just take my GED and go home.

In the moment, I guess I didn't much think about how much I wanted to avoid my mother.

I was loud. I was angry. And I was tired of being attacked by people I didn't even know. I fought back because I felt I had to, not because I wanted to, a fact that infuriated me. For a week, I had sat in that classroom listening to this girl antagonize me over and over again just like my mother always did back at home. And while I'd fought so hard to ignore her bullying, I just couldn't hold it in anymore.

I snapped so badly that every single person came out of their classrooms to see what was going on.

That then led to conversations with faculty members, not only about why I'd snapped in that particular instance, but also about the rest of my time there. It was discussed how the girls in my dorm would try to set me up, jump me, lie about me and talk about any little thing they could find wrong about me. That's why they ended up moving me to another dorm altogether, a decision that I didn't mind at all.

This new area was filled with down-to-earth lesbians, which made for much nicer living conditions than what I left behind. I had very few problems at this new dorm, made friends fast and never had any issues with the girls personally. It felt pretty good, in no small part because it made me understand even more that I hadn't done anything wrong. Those other dorm-mates were picking on me because of issues they had, not because of anything I'd done to them.

Switching dorms changed so much for me, and that's when I really began to enjoy my stay. It was when I started to feel like I was part of a community. My new friends had my back, including whenever a girl from the old dorm would try to start something with me.

I loved that about them. They hated bullies just as much as I did, and they stuck by each other no matter what. They had a sister bond. So while they certainly fought at times, they loved even harder. Plus, they were all unique in their own ways and proud of the characteristics they called their own. Their strength was something I admired so much about them.

For so long, I'd been conditioned to be ashamed of the quirks and traits and aspects that made up who I was. But now, I started to come into my own in that regard, learning a lot from these girls.

But of course, being in that environment also made me question my sexuality. Before leaving for school I lost my virginity, though I don't remember losing it.

I didn't even know his name. I was too drunk and high to remember the specifics. What started out as harmless fooling around turned into something I wasn't prepared for. I didn't consent to it; I was too wasted to consent to anything. And when I woke up the next day from that unpleasant experience, I never told anyone.

Back before that day, I always pictured how I would lose my virginity and when. Yet after all those years of being scared of sex and waiting, some guy I barely knew just took it.

It made perfect sense then that I'd question my sexuality. I already knew my bad experience had me thinking sex with a man is not enjoyable. So I attempted to dip into the lady pond and date a girl – with confusing and awkward results. I didn't really get much out of it really, I was too young and didn't know what I was doing.

My thoughts on the subject were intensely confusing. On the one hand, I related more to these girls than I ever did with their straight counterparts. They were strong, vocal, independent and not scared to be themselves, all of which I loved. At the same time though, there was something I found attractive about manly men. So after frolicking in the lady pond for a while, I decided to give dating a guy from my school a try. I didn't know much about relationships at all. I didn't know what to do. What was allowed. How to act. How not to act. What was expected of a girlfriend.

I didn't know a thing.

So I ended up hating it, it was forced and unfamiliar to me.

Which came to no surprise, I never had that good example of what a healthy relationship looked like growing up. And all the older men I hung out with and considered brothers, were flat out dogs.

There was so much I seen them do, that I found disturbing. Through my lens, guys cheated, took advantage, lied, hurt and manipulated as if their intentions are just to rob a woman of all her strength, inner beauty, and common sense.

But my lesbian friends, however, seemed more compassionate and selfless. They were more understanding and honest with their feelings, which pulled me toward them. There were also some cons I saw too though. When they fought, there were no boundaries. I would see my friends fight with their significant others to the point where I thought I was going to have a genuine panic attack just by witnessing the chaos. I used to think, "Oh my gosh! What the hell is this?"

Every time they fought, it was World War II all over again. I learned quickly when to leave a room and find shelter before a massive lesbian quarrel went down.

Resourcefulness

While sorting out all my different perspectives about my own relationship, along with the battle of the sexes. I was getting closer to my one trade teacher. Really, she was like our trade mother, who you could tell had no problem with loving and caring for troubled and misunderstood teens. Authentic and genuine, she had no problem telling us what we needed to hear; we all appreciated her mothering attitude and abilities. Missing an actual mother myself, I know I latched onto her like a magnet on a fridge.

She was strong and knowledgeable, and had a way of letting us know we could do better without tearing our self-esteem into bits and pieces. There were many moments when she would sense the sadness or anger from one of her students, and she would waste no time getting to the root of our problems. She had a way of talking to us that made us comfortable about being ourselves. She made it safe for us to express whichever pains plagued our hearts at the time without judgment. She mended relationships, helped solve our problems, and educated us about real life. She was the real deal, and we all respected her for it. She understood more than anyone else at that school; she knew that troubled kids need compassion and understanding, not hostility and verbal abuse. We're a lot more sensitive than we appear. I know that more often than not, we come off as tough and hard. But in actuality, we're about as soft, scared and fragile as you can get. Our hearts are damaged, and our souls have been compromised. Broken down, we're damaged goods who need help but are too scared to accept it without some significant and genuine effort.

We'll never show you our true selves unless the gestures are coming from true concern and sincerity. It's because we fear that once we reach a vulnerable state with someone, that person will have the power to truly destroy what little of ourselves we've been able to keep.

That's a lot of carefully constructed and carefully maintained walls to get through. But our trade teacher had a way of making us all vulnerable through her genuine kindness and relatability. It was a result that she never abused. The more vulnerable we got, the more she cared.

I wish I could say her influence was enough to keep me completely safe from all bad influences. But it was just a short period of time that went by before I began to get closer to a specific friend from my dorm. She was a stripper, who would tell me tales about the nightlife and how much money she made from it. It sounded so good.

This all came at a time when I had no money of my own, and my mother certainly never sent me anything unless I was doing exactly what she wanted me to do. As I got older, she had begun to bribe me with materialistic things. I could only get clothes and other necessities from her if I did exactly what she said without a question asked or an objection made. No matter how wrong and hurtful she behaved, she didn't want any kind of confrontation from it. So if I told her the truth about how horrible she was acting, she would snatch back everything she did buy for me. If I didn't listen to her every command, she would snatch her gifts back.

That was her leverage. Her control.

So when this friend of mine started telling me all about her fast and easy cash, I wanted in. There was no hesitation at all on my part. In my mind, I needed in.

She told me I could start going with her on the weekends, and I agreed right away. All I could think about was how my life could change for the better with some real money flowing in.

Not once did I think about what I would have to do or what I'd endure to get that kind of cash.

The first time I went to the strip club, was during one of my weekends home away from school, and I was ready. That's what I genuinely thought - that I was ready. She and two of her male friends picked me up from my mother's house, and I didn't get nervous until I hit the club door. Then all I saw were drunk and loud men.

Drunk. Loud. Obnoxious. Disrespectful. Ashamed. Those were the men and the emotions and the actions I found myself facing.

Immediately, there was lust and nakedness everywhere: women giving lap dances, some slowly taking their lingerie off on stage, some sneaking off into the parking lot to have sex for even faster cash. Women would be bent all the way over, while these men literally had their entire faces two inches away from their lady parts, like they were contemplating on jumping in it. I'd never seen anything like it before.

My friend appeared to be a veteran in this lifestyle, so she wasn't nervous at all. But, me? I was a nervous wreck, my normal anxiety levels amplified by a trillion percent and I was sweating so much that I had to pat myself down with baby wipes to cool off, all the while feeling like I would pass out on the floor from fright.

She took me to the back where the changing rooms were located, filled with aggressive and bitter women, every one of them. Everyone had an attitude problem, and from what I could tell that first night, many of them hated being there. It was an addiction though.

Fast cash always is. You hate the job until it gave you a pile of cash to hold in your hand. And then, when the cash was gone, you went right back to hating the job and doing it all over again.

I still had stage fright, so I avoided the stage as much as I could. I would do mostly lap dances, even though I hated every second of it. I had to remain drunk just to tolerate the customers' disgusting behavior.

I'll admit that being a stripper increased my dislike for men, especially black men. They were the ones who willingly encouraged me to see things and do things that were disgusting. They were the ones who treated me like a piece of meat ready to be devoured due to their gluttony. To them, I was just an object with no feelings or brain.

Sadly, once again, I had moved from one abusive situation to the next. Yet that fast cash was oh-so alluring when it gave me a new level of independence from my mother.

Stripping was my opportunity to be free from her control and manipulation. As long as I was able to buy myself what I needed, she had no control over me. It was just that I had to degrade and disrespect myself and my body to accomplish that much. I even got rid of the boyfriend I had throughout school, a guy who didn't provide, yet complained and whined about me stripping to support myself. I was sucked in a life, driven by the need of independence. And anyone who stood in the way of that, had to go.

One weekend, my mother went into my room and went through my bags, where she found some high heels and skimpy stripping clothes, along with a large wad of cash.

She confronted me on, which made me furious.

Yes, I was stripping even though I was still underage. But after how I'd lived these past years, I didn't care how young I was. And why did she?

I wanted to yell at her. I wanted to yell at her so badly.

How dare you take the time to go through my things when you don't ever take the time to guide me through life? You manipulate and try to control me at every chance you get, yet you're surprised it's come to this? You've either neglected me or used me or treated me like a burden instead of as your own daughter my whole entire life! You used and abused my mind, talents and emotions. You gossiped and lied about what I was doing – to family. To Aunt Valerie! – rather than love me and teach me and tell them the damn truth.

I had no guidance from my mother whatsoever, yet she had the audacity to go through my things and question what I was doing. And so I had to question whether she was actually concerned or if she just wanted a cut of my money.

Of course I lied to her. I told her I was a bartender's apprentice, and that I wore sexy tops with jeans and shorts for the tips. And I told her that I didn't care if she believed me or not. Because I truly didn't.

For years, she'd left me with no clothes and one pair of shoes. So if she had a problem with something, it wasn't any of my concern.

I kept dancing for a while after that, even traveling to different strip clubs in other cities after I graduated early from school. I was proud of myself for finishing school, and I was proud of what I'd accomplished there. I had studied, I had applied myself, and I hadn't let anyone get me in trouble or get me kicked out. But I was still dancing to support myself nonetheless, and falling deeper and deeper into this sinful lifestyle.

Spreading Wickedness

During this time, my mother and Dan broke up after she cheated on him because "he didn't want to keep a job."

That was something my mother knew for years though; he didn't work much at all. He only took side jobs when he needed to. At the same time, my mother intentionally used him as a chauffeur and a babysitter whenever she needed either one.

Was he a good role model as a provider? No. Of course not. If we had to depend on what he brought in to live, we would have all been out on the streets.

Was he a good role model of the kind of strength a man should have in a relationship? That would be a no as well.

But he did do a lot for us. And he was the only one who cared to notice and help me with the challenges I faced growing up. He deserved a better parting than what he got.

Tired of how he wasn't providing anything financially, my mother took up with another man and she wasn't very subtle about it either. One day, when Dan used his key to visit, as he always did, he wasn't greeted by my mother and me as expected. He was greeted by dim lights, soft music, and another man, who was snuggled up on the couch with his arms wrapped around his woman.

It was horrible and hurtful to witness. That steaming hurt I felt rise off of his shoulders was the most intense display of feeling I ever witnessed. And seeing him try to hide his emotions from the other man while he walked back up those steps, and toward that front door was the most uncomfortable thing I ever watched.

And I did watch it. I stayed silent, but I observed it all.

Later that night, he came back to the house and ripped the Christmas lights he'd recently put up for my mom right off the front door. He even tossed the trash bin around a few times, leaving a blanket of debris on the front porch. Dan was hurt and he was angry, and I understood why. Normally, he wasn't the type to get mad or allow his anger to get the best of him. Whenever he got mad, he made sure to think it over before he acted.

But not this time.

What he did by ripping off those Christmas lights was rather shocking, I'll admit, but why he did it wasn't at all.

My mother didn't seem bothered a bit by the act of vandalism. When she saw what he'd done, she just laughed and called him crazy for doing it.

I distinctly remember looking at her like she was completely insane. She had just broken a man's heart with no warning, and she was laughing about it, labeling him the bad guy in the process. Her exact words were, "I can't believe he did that." Yet the way I saw it, she was lucky that's all he did.

You don't hurt someone like that. You don't purposely bring some man home just to break it off with another one. Dan, now my mother's ex, was around since I was about six or seven years old. All those years of them being together, and yet she couldn't respect him enough to break up with him a little more gently than that.

Naturally, I was reluctant to speak to him after that. The thought made me nervous, having to make myself vulnerable like that by sharing my emotions with him and asking him to share right back. But I was hurt for him; I felt his pain as well. I felt his despair and embarrassment.

There was also the fact that I'd always considered him to be a father figure, someone to fill the void left by my own dad's absence. Someone I called stepfather. He was someone I asked all of my out-of-the-box questions, who comforted me when my mother was being cruel and cold towards me, and who I'd thought, on more than one occasion, understood me the most.

So I sucked it up and called him.

Perhaps I shouldn't have. Perhaps it was something I needed to do regardless, but it definitely felt like a mistake at the time. Out of hurt, he hurt me as well. He told me I was just another person he knew. That was it. And it broke my heart a little bit more to hear him tell me that. What I'd always taken him for wasn't true any longer. Why hurt me because my mother hurt you?

I tried really hard to cover up my sadness, to act as though he had said nothing at all. With the memories of him never writing me back in military school, I suppose I was able to take this newest heartbreak better than all the others. But I still got off the phone with him that day and told myself I would never speak to him again.

Admittedly, it only took a few weeks for that decision to change though. He called, and I answered, listening to him converse with me like nothing had ever happened and nothing had ever been said.

It was confusing. At first, I honestly didn't know if he felt bad for what he'd said - if he realized that he'd hurt me out of anger and was now trying to fix it? Or if he was just trying to continue a relationship with me as a way of maintaining a connection with my mother.

People do that. They get heartbroken by someone they're still in love with, and then attempt to build or keep a relationship with the person closest to that lost love. I guess it's their way of having the next best thing – as if it's some sort of substituted medicine that will heal them the same way.

Out of all the possibilities, that was my biggest suspicion. And as time went on, I continued to feel that way. He would call me and we would talk about out-of-the-box topics as usual. But then he would sneak in a question like, "What's your mother doing?" or "How is she?" It was strange. Here my mother was semi-dating, and now cheating on the bus driver she cheated on Dan with. Yet he was still asking questions about her, and even coming over to fix things in the house when she wasn't around.

Amongst all of this chaos, my sister had just announced she was having another baby by another man who didn't care to be around. And once again I was excited, but sad to witness my sister go through yet another pregnancy alone. She was now living with her dad's sisters, and only coming around my mother when she needed a babysitter.

This all happened while I was getting ready to go off to college, stripping all the while. Personally, I thought I might want to go for law or business, but my mother had other plans.

She was the one who chose my college and my major, and I didn't put up any real fight about it. In a way, I didn't really care because I wanted away from her, and I just wasn't ready to decide what I wanted to do quite yet.

People expected me to fully know such things right after I graduated, even though I barely knew who I was then, let alone who I wanted to be five years down the road. I had absolutely no clue, and no examples to guide me. The "where do you see yourself in 10 years" question was never presented to me, and so I never thought much about applying it.

For the time being, I was much more concerned about getting out of her house than anything else. And complying with her wishes for a little while longer appeared to be the fastest way toward that goal.

Therefore, I did what she told me to do. I went to the college she wanted me to go to, and I chose the major she wanted me to choose. And in return, I received all the dorm room supplies and clothes I could ever want or need. Whatever I wanted, my mother gave it to me. As long as I was her puppet, it seemed, I could have the world.

She told me that when I graduated and got a decent job, I should take care of her. Because that's what children did when they got older; They took care of their parents just the same way their parents cared for them.

Personally, I agreed and still do. All of that dedication, hard work, guidance and love parents supply their children with should have appreciative results when the child is older and able to contribute. But since my mother never applied any dedication, hard work, guidance and love to me, I figured I owed her nothing.

Since education was never stressed in my house, I didn't really understand the importance of choosing the right major at that time. I didn't even understand the importance of going to college. In my mind, it was just something you did once you're done with high school.

Similarly, credit cards were just something to use. So I had several with large spending amounts on them. Not really knowing the dangers involved if I treated them irresponsibly or understanding that they could ruin my credit and opportunities at independence, I told my mother that I had them. Her reply to that was just to smirk and say, "You may not want to do that, but okay."

That was it.

She knew about finances. But didn't waste her time educating me about any of it. In a way, maybe even a big way, it was like she wanted me to be dependent on her for as long as she wanted or needed me to be.

I, on the other hand, didn't want to be tied to anyone. So I started college with the same mentality I went into the alternative school with - I wasn't there to make friends. I was there to do my bid and get out. I arrived to college with a cold shoulder and my pet kitten that was given to me by Dan's sister before I left; he was the only creature I wanted to be bothered by. My sister had just given birth to my second nephew right before leaving for college, and once again, my mother was just as loving and nurturing as she was when my first nephew arrived. It was now clear to my sister and I that our mother could be motherly after all; she just refused to be that way with us. The only relationship Latanya and my mother continued to have was the kind a mother would have with her babysitter.

For the first few months after school started, I would go straight to my room after I was finished with all my classes. I wanted to be away from people at all times. I didn't want anything to do with people of any sort, including these ones. The teenagers and young adults I grew up with back at home were raw, tough and aggressive. These ones seemed spoiled and over-privileged.

Since I had so little in common with individuals who hadn't seen, fought and survived their fair shares of struggle, I didn't relate to my fellow students at college. And I already figured that, most likely, the girls were going to hate me and the guys were going to try to get in my pants. Already all too familiar with the patterns of people and groups, I wanted no part of any of it or anyone.

Besides, the way I saw it, I had already done and went through everything my fellow female college students were experiencing at this school - probably a dozen times over too. I'd been running the streets and going to clubs since high school. I'd watch as these young women ran around campus acting like bats out of hell, and I wanted no part in their ridiculous behavior. As for the boys, again, I'd been hanging out with men two or three decades older than me for years. So I considered this new collection of males around me to be nothing more than amateur men in training.

Essentially, I didn't have the "my parents aren't here, so I can do whatever I want" syndrome because I hadn't had a real parent practically my whole life, and so I'd already been there and done that.

All the same, a few months in, I found that I couldn't hold to my own rules. I actually had to be social with some of my classmates – engaging with them in social conversations for school projects and homework – which did not make me happy. I still had issues talking to people I didn't know, an act I found both uncomfortable and silly. So every time a professor would announce a group project, I'd get irritated.

Why did I have to associate with anyone when all the someones I'd known before had been so displeasing, disappointing or dangerous? I did recognize what an antisocial character I was becoming, but I didn't care. These people weren't like me. They didn't have the mark of struggle within them. The way I saw it, they'd never been through anything more than a broken nail or bad football game.

Despite my best efforts, one thing led to another until, one day, I found myself sitting at the head of a cafeteria table filled with so-called friends. Friends I didn't even want. Friends I'd tried to avoid. As it turned out, college was different than high school and middle school and elementary school and the streets, at least in that people tended to gravitate to me because I was pretty, aggressive, and didn't want to be bothered. So many kids with that "my parents aren't here" syndrome ended up needing a parent after all and latching onto me like I was their damn stepmother. No matter how much I wished otherwise, they felt protected by me.

I hated it. It was too much pressure, and I just simply hated it. All I wanted was for someone to protect me, not the other way around. I'd been missing protection and security all my life. Why the hell would I want to protect a bunch of scared, spoiled college kids?

Perhaps because of that or perhaps because of everything that had come before, I picked up drinking more heavily again. I mean, liquor was everywhere. Weed was too. So I had access to whatever I wanted to the point where I made alliances and started running a group of girls like a drug cartel family.

On my end, there was no substance with these girls. No real relationship. No emotions. They knew nothing about me, partially because I made sure it happened that way and partially because they didn't take the time out to understand who I was as a person. Yet on their end, they were predictable and I knew everything I needed to know about them. They were simply weak-minded girls who just wanted to feel as though they were older than they really were. They wanted to belong, but they wanted to belong with those individuals they deemed worthwhile.

In other words, they'd hang out with you if you were so-called cool. No thought ever took place in their heads as to who and what people actually were. Then again, in their defense, I guess I could really say that about most of the people I crossed paths with in college. Out of all of them, I only ever considered a very small handful of them to be actual friends.

I'll also admit that I didn't do anything to make them better people. All I knew was survival, and in the environment I used to dabble in, people who couldn't protect themselves got chewed up and spit out faster than that cheap bubblegum from the gumball machine in the grocery store. I was cold, I was ruthless, and I didn't care. So there was nothing positive or influential about my vision, and my followers were following something that was no good for themselves, me, or anyone else.

Unhappy with the whole situation and everyone involved – myself included – my grades started slipping as the semesters passed. They had started out good, but they slowly began to decline.

It started out with math, which was my definite weakness. I failed each math class I took while still passing all my other subjects. But then it got to the point when I was placed on academic probation. The real problem? I didn't take school seriously, but how could I? I lived in a world where making money for my mother was a priority, a world where education wasn't discussed or deemed valuable to my future. Only if my world was different…

No Self-Love

In the past, my self-esteem and confidence weren't great, I know. But I was always able to at least get mentally motivated enough to keep myself moving. Not anymore. There I was, in my twenties, in college and I was mentally and emotionally exhausted. Withered. I felt finished.

I had no motivation to give myself, and I had no one to supply it to me either.

I'd reached the point in my life where I realized I was suffering from my mother's mistakes and behavior. But I hadn't reached the point where I could confidently tell myself that her behavior and what she had and hadn't done for me did not define who I could become or who I was even then. I was mourning my own self, because I felt dead inside. I felt empty, and I had no clue how to achieve my own peace in life.

If I struggled to become who I was meant to be, I'd have to strip so much away of what I'd become that I was afraid there wouldn't be anything left, that the process would be too painful and I'd be left naked and mauled.

That was always a possibility, but that didn't mean it wouldn't have been a worthwhile step for me to take. What would be left after I removed myself from what I thought I was and what I thought I knew? A fresh start, most likely. A sense of awareness. And a quiet room for God to reach the child He'd created who lost her way.

But I had no faith to take those steps. I was merely a hustle without the action. I couldn't see correctly, and I couldn't think straight. And worse yet, I couldn't hear the messages God was trying to give me.

Those feelings I had about myself and about life in general lingered for quite some time. I was depressed and angry without really noticing it since I'd been so used to and so conditioned to feel that way. As a result, I couldn't even recognize the difference between what I was going through and what was considered healthy. I would come home from school on holiday breaks and watch my mother take over the role of projecting who and what I was to the world.

If an adult asked me a question, she would interrupt me and answer it. If anyone attempted to get to know me, my mother would step in like a freelance public relations expert and take complete control of the process. I used to sit back and look at the expressions on other people's faces when they'd realize that my mother simply wouldn't allow me to answer for myself – not one single question.

It was so ridiculous that, on several occasions, other adults would get fed up with her projecting herself onto answers meant for me, and they would start ignoring her on purpose. They'd give me head nods and eye contact necessary to allow me to say my own thoughts and tell my own story.

I realized a lot in college, but unfortunately, I didn't learn enough, and not just in how I continued letting my mother run roughshod over my life. I'm sorry to say that I went from one abusive person to another, including to a new boyfriend of mine who started out as a friend. His name was Vince. He was a deceiver, a guy who seemed nice, and charming in the beginning.

We were together for a while, and everything seemed to go well enough for that time period. But then I got pregnant. It seemed as though, as soon as I was carrying his child, all of his vile colors began to show. Vince went from being a friend to being abusive, manipulative and hateful.

It was never his fault though. That's what he told me. It was never his fault. It didn't matter what wrong he committed; according to him, it was always somehow because of me. It was my fault. He would yell and scream in my face if I made a mistake or had an opinion he didn't care for. He would embarrass me in front of others; then blame me for his actions.

It was always me making him spit in my face.

Or me making him cheat on me.

Or me making him belittle me.

I was stupid, dumb. Vince made sure to let me know that nobody else liked me, and if I left him, no one would deem me good enough to marry.

My response to all of that? I found myself apologizing for things I shouldn't just to stop the fighting and hurt. He would attack everything about me, as if I wasn't good enough for him at all. He was a horrible person, but I was vulnerable to wanting a family I could love and call my own. And that's why I took it all — every bit of disgusting behavior.

He would show me he hated me, then tell me how much he loved me afterward. My self-esteem was already low, thanks to my mother. Now it seemed irreparable as this man tore and broke me down little by little, piece by piece.

Vince was a disgusting individual. Disgusting because he never saw any error in his actions. Disgusting because he treated me horribly with no remorse. Disgusting because he blamed me for the abuse he doled out on me. Despicable because he took pleasure in keeping me and my spirit under the feet of his sick and twisted ego.

My pregnancy was a horrible experience. I was sad the majority of the time, confused and lost, with my hopes at love absolutely shattered. My hopes for that perfect family had been misplaced. And so I went from running my own drug cartel to being that quiet, abused girl with all those bruises and nothing to say about them — nothing to scream back or demand better than what I was getting. I was the girl who felt humiliated every time strangers looked into my eyes, knowing I was a victim of mistreatment and abuse.

I knew what they were thinking all too well. I saw it all over their faces - the look. The look of, "You stupid girl, why don't you get out?" and "Don't you know you're good enough and beautiful enough to find someone who will treat you like the queen you are?"

But the thing was, I didn't know. I considered myself just as worthless and stupid as Vince told me I was. And I wanted love. I was terrified of losing any form of love I could acquire; even if it wasn't love at all, just a sick, twisted façade of it. I was just that desperate. I needed love like a baby needs her mother's milk.

I needed affection, and I turned into a pathetic young girl in order to get it.

When I found out I was pregnant, I was happy. I wanted this baby so much. I wanted a little piece of me that would and could love me back. I just wanted a family, the family I'd dreamt about for years. Besides, being abused had become the norm for me. Though this might seem contradictory, that meant I always had the hope in mind that maybe, one day, things would change and this guy in my life would begin to love me as I loved him – that he would eventually stop verbally, emotionally, and physically harming me. I hoped that one day, I could have my happy ending.

Being young and naïve and so utterly damaged, that's what I truly thought while the father of my unborn child did everything he wanted to me.

He threw a bucket of water on me at one point. Other times, he busted the windows out of my car and spit in my face. He even peed on my car. Then, if I actually did work up the nerve to call the police, he would turn around and file false reports on me to be even more vindictive.

He spread lies about me to his family and to anyone else who would listen. He even threatened to take my unborn child away if I wasn't pleased with how he treated me. This so-called man would jump in my face and scream so loudly that my ears would ring afterward. I got called useless more times than I can count, and there was plenty more emotional abuse where that word came from, all in an attempt to break my spirits, which, most of the time, worked exactly as intended.

He was one way out in public, fooling everyone with his fake, charming demeanor. Thanks to his careful, controlled, yet seemingly carefree act around them, he tricked almost everyone he met into believing that he was a good-hearted and spirited young man who treated me like a woman worth respecting. It was never until after he got behind closed doors that he turned into something obviously and inexcusably nasty and cruel.

The more I tried to protect myself, the more abuse he doled out. It was like he was obsessed with torturing every single fragment of feelings I had left.

My relationship with my mother, of course, wasn't going well either. When I was about four or five months pregnant, I came home from work one day to find all my stuff outside. My mother was kicking me out of the house.

She said it was because I was being disrespectful to her, but I knew it was because I ended up pregnant, shattering her plans to have her daughter take care of her financially someday. My mother's definition of being disrespectful was someone not doing any and everything she wanted them to do. If you even tried to question her order with a thought or action of your own, that was deemed disrespectful and you were deserving of her wrath as punishment.

It was very similar to the person I called boyfriend at the time.

Very similar.

When she kicked me out of the house, my mother didn't even have the decency to toss all of my belongings out onto the lawn. She held onto the things I really used and needed.

She kept my makeup. She kept my bedding, my microwave and the mini-refrigerator she had bought me for college. As if making me homeless wasn't enough, she wanted me to really look it and feel it too.

I knew what being kicked out meant. I understood all the ramifications. It meant I was in an abusive relationship with a horrible man who I was going to have to depend on for a place to stay, which meant I would experience even more abuse. My mother had just thrown me to one very vicious wolf.

Naturally, I had never told her before that he was abusive. But it wasn't hard to notice with the amount of bruises on my arms that might be hidden easily enough out in public but were a lot more difficult to cover in one's own home.

Angry, afraid and hurt at the thought of my well being lying in the hands of Vince, I kicked my window so hard that my leg went right through it. My adrenaline was so high that I walked right through my window, pregnant and all. My right leg went numb right away. Yet where my pain receptors failed to notify me that I was badly hurt, my eyes were able to fill in just fine. Looking down, I could see blood gushing out of my leg like a punctured water hose.

My baby!

That was my first thought, and my first action was to feel my stomach for cuts while my leg kept hemorrhaging. There didn't seem to be any damage done to my abdomen though, which was so exceptionally relieving that it made me light-headed. Or, wait, I really was lightheaded, wasn't I?

Blood was everywhere, covering the carpet below me.

That's when my mother came into the room, calmly called 9-1-1, and tied a rag around my leg to stem the bleeding. As soon as she was off the phone, I remember crying and screaming at her.

"Why?" I demanded. Why was she doing this? And how? How could she kick me out when I was pregnant? Was it because of whose baby I was carrying?

She didn't like him. I knew she didn't like him, though for completely different reasons than she should have. So even though my unborn child's father was so unfathomably cruel, I began to defend him in order to convince my abusive mother to accept him. And all the while, I was begging her not to do this to me.

Judging by the expression of sheer joy that crossed my mother's face, she enjoyed my whimpering and pleading. She took pleasure in my weakened state, and she wanted me to need her - just like Vince wanted me to need him.

Their desire was for me to actually be the very scum they told me I was over and over again. That would, after all, be a great way to control and manipulate and hurt me.

And it worked.

I suppose I was transmitting all of that pain, physical and psychological, into my unborn baby's nerves and senses. Just how I was born into dysfunction, it appeared I was going to do the same thing to this new little life I'd been charged to care for. History was repeating itself, and I didn't have the proper knowledge or powers of God to stop it.

Yet that new little life probably saved me right there. I didn't want to live anymore. I wanted out. And if it weren't for my unborn child, I probably would have proceeded to erase my existence from this world. It would have been so exceptionally easy after that day, when my mother showed me just how little she thought about me. Literally bloodied and broken, I lay there pleading with her to just support me.

All those years of desperately wanting her love came pouring out right along with the blood I was losing from my leg. I asked her to accept me. Accept me for who I was, and help me become someone I could be proud of.

Calm as ever, she shook her head from left to right repeatedly.

She ran her fingers across my head, and with a smirk said, "No."

She said "no" to her own daughter asking to be loved, helped and accepted. She said "no."

She also said, "You weren't supposed to do this. You weren't supposed to get pregnant."

Supporting her grandchild and me was not an option she felt like dealing with. She made that very clear with words and actions.

I guess I had ruined her plans of becoming rich and supporting her in the lifestyle she craved. I'd messed up the plot she'd had running through her head for years - being the mother of a rich actress who got whatever her blackened heart desired.

All my life, I heard her make comments about my sister and me getting older and financially supporting her. She'd even stated on numerous occasions that she wished she'd had boys instead of girls, because she felt as though boys supported their mothers automatically.

But that theory of hers was all wrong; a good mother will always have her children by her side, regardless of whether they're boys or girls. When a woman loves her kids and raises them to the best of her ability and to their full potential, she'll never be alone. Her children will grow each day appreciating her love, knowing how great of a mother she'd been to them through both their good phases and their bad.

My mother will never experience this because she was cruel and cold toward both of her daughters, who might not have been sons, but would have been delighted to show her love nonetheless if she'd ever given them the chance.

When the ambulance came, the police weren't too far behind. I was already outside on the gurney being rolled into the ambulance when the officer arrived. But I still got to hear how upset he was at the fact that my mother would kick out her pregnant daughter.

When he confronted her about it, telling her how wrong and insensitive she was for her actions, she just laughed. She laughed it off as if her actions and the larger situation were nothing than one big joke to her. It was as if nothing was wrong, as if I wasn't pregnant, injured and, finally, homeless.

Out of all the laughs she let out in the face of my pain, that particular one may have stayed in my head the longest. It played on repeat inside me all the way to the hospital and, from there, all the way through my life.

The police officer and EMTs must have felt a fraction of the pain I did. You could see the hurt and disappointment on their own faces, despite how it wasn't their mother laughing in their wounds. My leg was ripped open almost to the bone, and blood and flesh were everywhere, sights I'm sure these emergency professionals had seen before. Yet I noticed how some of them had to fight back tears while they worked hard to keep me calm and alive.

They felt sorry for me. But beyond that, I felt like they recognized me. Out of everyone in my life at that time, those individuals saw right through me for who I was and right through my mother for who she was. They understood that my life was hard, and they knew my mother was the cause of it.

That sincere sympathy and those expressions of emotion they tried so hard to hold back – for my sake, too – were warm and powerful. And right then and there, I think that some of the icicles hanging on my cold and heavy heart began to melt.

Watching them and being with them, I forgot about my injury and the cruelty that plagued my reality. When they opened up their hearts and demonstrated their feelings about my situation, their compassion and concern became an unexpected treasure. Until then, I had no idea people could do any such thing - love a stranger like that. Love and care for someone they didn't even know.

I felt safe and wanted. And, despite my horrible circumstances, I felt loved.

Upon entering the hospital, the nurses, doctors, and staff were just as caring and compassionate. It was like they glowed with love and light. I saw it, I felt it, and for the first time, I knew what it was. I recognized it. It made me want to stay there for as long as I could. For forever, if possible.

I began to cry again, though not because of my injury. It was because I was overwhelmed by these strangers loving me - strangers who took the time to understand and care for me. I was feeling something I had been missing practically my whole life.

What they offered me was more welcoming than I can say, yet it was also that much more shattering because I didn't know where else to find it.

Lying in my hospital bed with a torn Achilles' tendon, everything ran through my mind during my stay. I wondered where I would end up and how my baby was doing through all of this drama. I knew he felt my pain and my heartbreak. I knew he felt my cries, concern and loneliness, in which case, he was hurting too. It was a concept I hated the most out of the long list of traumas on my heart and mind. The last thing I wanted was for him to be suffering because of me.

Lying in my hospital bed, I dreamt of a life with people who were kind to me. A life where I could love without being afraid of the concept. A life where people took me in and loved me so deeply that my heart and perspectives would change in God's image.

The only thing that kept me from falling into a deep depression was the team of nurses, who were compassionate, warm-hearted and exactly what I needed. If it weren't for them, my thoughts would have eaten me alive. Instead, their kindness prompted me to think.

I was concerned with my basic survival, of course, especially since it wasn't just mine I had to be thinking of now. I finally allowed myself to recognize that the guy my child would call his father, wouldn't be much of one to him.

I realized that I had grown tired of the abuse and mistreatment. And that wasn't the only epiphany I had. I also accepted that I just wanted to co-parent with Vince; I no longer wanted a relationship with him. He was just too mean, cruel, angry, selfish and evil. Worse yet, he failed to acknowledge it, just like my mother.

Those who don't acknowledge their negative behavior for what it truly is are the most dangerous kind of people to attempt a relationship with; they're not remorseful, and they're not mindful of other's feelings. These people spread pain and misery like a forest fire, and see no wrong in the wildlife lost along the way. This was my mother and child's father in every way - people who inflicted pain upon another blindly and unknowingly, or uncaringly or purposely. And when it was unknowingly, it was because their inner demons wanted it to be that way. They preferred it to be that way.

That's what the devil wants. He wants that thick, misleading fog in front of your eyes, mouth, nose and ears. He wants your senses compromised and disoriented. He wants his victims in a trance while they do his immoral bidding.

People walk around with inner demons every day. And the only way to rid and release your body from those toxins is to let the love and light of God into your soul and into your life. We all have a piece of God in us; it's just that some of us lose touch with his presence during our journeys. For me, it was during my passage into survival-mode in a harsh world. For my mother, it must have been back when she was that hurt and lost little girl who felt abandoned by everyone and refused to let Aunt Lia's love in. For my child's father, it probably stemmed from his own upbringing as well.

All of that thinking made me conclude that, for all of those reasons, we couldn't be a family at all. We couldn't raise our child together when he was how he was. My dream of having a home with him couldn't work out when he was so willing to hock spit in my face and call me stupid and lazy. When he would push me against cars hard enough to leave bruises. He would pour bottles of wine over my head for daring to speak my mind or have an opinion. When he would threaten to throw me in jail if I left him or tried going to the police for help. When he would cheat on me while I was pregnant and take advantage of the fact that I needed him at my lowest.

It suddenly seemed so clear that he was an abuser, and that trying to love him would only give him the energy to abuse me more. Abusers feed off of vulnerability and fear. They use tactics to keep you afraid to defend yourself against them. They are cowards - afraid to feel the consequences of their own actions. And no, it doesn't matter how hurt they are themselves; you cannot heal them. You cannot save them. You can only help yourself by walking away.

Make no mistake of it either - my child's father was hurt and hurting. His own mother was just as manipulative and cruel as he was thanks to the anger, hatred, abuse and aggression she had been exposed to growing up with her own father.

Really, Vince's parents were trapped in their own worlds, knowing full well that their son had serious problems with judgment and anger, yet they did nothing about it. They recognized it, spoke about it, and saw it with their own eyes. But then they would turn around and teach him how to lie his way out of his resulting court issues. They were enablers.

As a result, Vince never took any responsibility for his actions, because he didn't have to.

Not only did they encourage his deceit and ill-mannered behavior; they financially supported it too. Every time he would break the law or do something horrible to someone, they would pay for his lawyer, even going so far as to manipulate the victims into not defending themselves. I knew of occasions when they went so far as to befriend their son's targets in order to get all the information they needed to defend him in court. After they'd gathered everything they thought they needed to know, they cast the twice-abused person off, leaving them even more weakened and discouraged. And if you failed to fall for their manipulation and stood your ground, they would label you as evil, crazy, and someone worthy of being destroyed.

His mother was the worst of the two, putting all of this stuff in his head about how an African man should be. Most of her theories were downright wrong and abusive. She taught him how he should be superior and dominate over his mate. She pressured him to have the upper hand in situations, no matter how wrong he was. She made him into an unwise bully obsessed with having control, while having none of the logic and morals to handle the responsibilities he craved. She fine-tuned his rage into something even more intense, giving him advice on how to dominate me and make me do what he wanted.

Vince's mother taught him that a woman's opinions meant nothing compared to his.

His father, meanwhile, seemed to be much more like me, or at least who I could turn out to be if I continued to stay in this abusive relationship. He came across as being too afraid and timid to have any voice at all; his wife and son easily manipulated him. He would apologize excessively for things that didn't need an apology at all. He would drink a lot, and attempted to stay to himself most of the time. I honestly didn't blame him. I understood all too well the urge to hide away from abusive, toxic people, all while keeping a drink in one hand.

Vince was the product of a generational curse, another chain formed with a will and a way to tear a family apart. He was one more example of dysfunction being passed down from one generation to another.

Thanks to my own intimately devastating experiences with generational curses, I'm well aware of one when I see it. I feel it; I know it's there. I've had that sixth sense for a long time, and I certainly was familiar with it back when I was lying on that hospital bed. So I only wish that my epiphanies had infiltrated my heart and head sooner. But I guess that a hospital bed with limited television channels will force you to think a little more deeply than you otherwise might.

As such, without any suitable distractions, I wanted to know who would love me when I left. Could anyone? I began to question whether I was lovable outside of a hospital at all, and if I was even deserving of the wonderful things attached with love. Vince never gave the impression that I was. My mother never treated me like that was true.

So, again, could I be loved?

I had many talks with myself, mainly at night, as if I was trying to get a glimpse of who I really was versus what I was conditioned to be. In a way, I felt as though there was something better brewing within my entire existence, as if I was not meant to live in the sad state I'd found myself in, taking so much pain.

I wanted to fight.

I wanted to live.

And I wanted people to respect me. I was tired of allowing disrespect into my life.

There was no way out but up, as I began to see; since I wanted out, I supposed I'd have to go up.

That hospital had a rejuvenating effect on my mind, no matter how frightening the circumstances that landed me there. It made me see that good still existed. I saw that love is very real, and compassion is one of the best qualities a person can have. I felt that staff's concerns so clearly during my stay, from the expressions on nurses' and doctors' faces as they reviewed my circumstances to the words they said. If they could have, I'm quite sure many of them would have helped more.

As it turned out, despite all the abuse it took and the lies it accepted, my soul never lost the ability to be attracted to love. Apparently, my heart wasn't as cold as I'd thought. If anything, it had remained its natural texture and temperature this entire time; it was just covered in a steel-like protective covering that often felt cold. In actuality, it was simply surrounding a warm, beating life force that was patiently, awaiting its healing process.

I do genuinely believe that my healing process began there, but it still had a long way to completion. It would be nice if I could say that my hospital stay changed everything – that all the realizations I had there immediately drove me to do exactly what I needed to do for both myself and my baby. But it wasn't quite that easy.

Aunt Valerie came to see me before I was discharged, and perhaps I was projecting, but to me, she seemed disappointed. So while she offered me a place to stay at her home, all I could dwell on was her perception of me throughout the last several years, of how she'd bought up all of my mother's lies about me. The way I saw it, Aunt Valerie thought the worst of me, and that hurt me like nothing else I could focus on right then and there. How she looked at me hurt; it was a gaze filled with disappointment.

I had and still could disappoint her.

No matter where the emphasis was placed, it hurt each and every way.

I was certain that, in her mind, I was this bad young girl going down the wrong path. And that might very well have been the case. But she couldn't see the truth, and she couldn't see my neglect because I kept quiet and once again protected an abuser by being afraid to speak out.

She couldn't see my pain and struggles because I fought back every emotion to hide them. My decision that day was based off of pain, not good, strong, solid logic. And it was based off of fear.

I was silenced by the fear I had for my mother and what she could do to me next. So far, she had called the police on me, lied about me, and tried to convince everyone, myself included, that I was evil. What more could she do to me if I spoke up and told the truth? I really didn't want to know. What I did know was that I was scared of who she might turn against me next.

I was silenced by the fear that no one would ever believe me because of how well she covered up her own bad behavior.

I was silenced by fear of my child's father, the type of fear my mother had worked so hard to instill in me. I walked in fear because I was used to it. And because of this, I feared staying with my aunt.

So I refused her offer. It felt like it hurt too much to say yes, and so I turned to something much more familiar instead - my abusive boyfriend. After all of my epiphanies, I chose him anyway. Sometimes truly hurt people need to receive a message more than once before they truly accept it. That's what happened to me.

So when it came time to leave the hospital after my surgeries and the first steps of my recovery, I went to live with my abusive boyfriend and his dysfunctional family, who all knew he was an abuser and enabled it anyway.

Knowing the exact situation I was getting myself into, I was heartbroken when I got my discharge papers from the hospital. But I left, right into my boyfriend's parents' toxic house.

That exact stay was short. I was only there for a few weeks before his father and mother moved me in with their other relatives, an aunt and uncle, in order to keep me away from their son. They wanted him to graduate college with no distractions, but I wasn't sure how much of a distraction I really was, taking into account that he never really did much for me to begin with.

Pregnant and with a long-legged cast on that reached my thigh, I couldn't move around without either my crutches or a wheelchair, none of which stopped him from continuing to be selfish, cruel and mean-spirited. He was a bully who liked to take advantage of the weak, and I was at my most vulnerable since he'd met me. The one positive aspect of this living situation was that he was gone at school most of the time. But when he would come home to visit, it felt as though he did so just to treat me horribly or neglect what I needed. He would get mad whenever I'd tell him how alone I felt or when I'd point out how he never helped me. In return, he would say that if I didn't like my situation, I could give him the baby when he was born and just go.

Well, he would scream it. He never just spoke to me.

It got to the point where I just stopped speaking up for myself altogether. It was easier that way. It hurt less. And I very much wanted the pain to stop.

Broken

During this time, I was trying to finish up my college courses online. But then my financial aid ran out, and I couldn't afford to pay the remainder on my own. Plus, my injured Achilles' tendon had to be repaired with nerve-replacement surgery - the reason why I had to wear that long, thick cast that went all the way up to my thigh. It was the most uncomfortable feeling to endure at the time, particularly when I was expected to literally do everything for myself.

If I needed food, I had to go to the grocery store to get it. So I would drive with my left leg while my right was propped up on the passenger's seat. I would struggle into the grocery store, hopping and out of breath at times from using my crutches. I had to be careful not to fall and injure my baby, so I took small, calculated hops, pushing a grocery cart with my left hand while balancing myself on one crutch with my right hand. My other crutch would be placed in the grocery cart with my food as I hopped from aisle to aisle.

Most of the time, I would have to carry out about three to four bags in each hand out of the grocery store. I would fight back tears as I hopped toward my truck, just wanting to fall down on the ground, grocery bags and all. At times, the only thing I wanted to do was just give up and cry.

People would stare and ask if I needed help, but I always said, "No, thank you." Of course they were right; I did need the help. And we all knew it. I didn't say no because I didn't want someone's kind assistance. Lord knows how much I wanted and needed it. I wanted it badly. But in my mind, I just couldn't accept it.

In my mind, I needed to train myself to be able to do these things on my own. I knew I was weakened and broken down from all the abuse. And I knew I needed to get stronger. So this was my way of doing it. The way I looked at it, I was alone and needed to learn how to depend on myself and only myself.

Nonetheless, I remember trembling at the look on people's faces when they saw my struggles - this pregnant girl with her growing belly and heavy bags barely making it to her truck on her crutches. Their sadness and concern was practically tangible, exactly like with the nurses, EMTs and doctors at that hospital. They hurt just looking at me, as if they wanted nothing more than to ignore my assurances that I was just fine, grab my bags and bring them to the truck already.

It was like this everywhere I went.

Yet I really was doing my best to prepare. I knew it would just be my child and me, so I was training myself to gain the strength I needed to do this - to be a single mother. If that meant hopping to my car with my crutches and all of those heavy bags, then so be it. If that meant watching as people's hearts broke watching me have to struggle after I'd bravely refused their help, then so be it.

In some way, I think they knew. They knew what I was doing, and they figured out why I was doing it. Because they wouldn't be there when I got to the apartment building and had to park my truck somewhere that might feel miles away. They couldn't assist me when I had to take the elevator to the 14th floor and walk a long hallway to get to the apartment unit. And they couldn't walk beside me with my additional groceries so that I didn't have to make that walk multiple times in order to get all the grocery bags inside.

It was very nice of them to offer, but the assistance could only go so far. So I figured I was better off just fending for myself altogether, and I got used to saying, "No, thank you."

It was about learning how to be alone. That's why I endured the self-abuse of refusing anyone's help out in public – so that I could endure the abuse when I got to my living space. I had to suffer myself so I could survive. I had to struggle with these groceries. I had to be alone.

Not surprisingly, my anxiety began to worsen, and I constantly dealt with thoughts and images of how I would have to survive. How I would have to live? Would I be able to get through this hard time in my premature life?

Every single negative thought plagued my mind in those moments. I didn't know how much more misery I would have to endure before things got better. How much more could I take? I was already a sitting duck and an injured punching bag with absolutely nothing but the clothes on my back and a truck that was in pretty bad shape.

Most of my time, I was already living out of my truck. Although I technically was living with Vince's family, it just never felt right. Every chance he got, he would threaten to kick me out of his aunt's apartment. So my 1997 Ford Explorer was my second home.

I did a lot in that car, but I mostly cried in it. That was my place to go and get away from it all. That's where I could go and scream, yell, and whimper, knowing that no one else could hear me. My truck was the only place where I felt safe. I would choose a remote and quiet location to drive to, and then I would just sob.

I would sob about my life, thinking about the nice nurses, EMTs, and doctors from the hospital. I would think about why my mother didn't love me. Why people didn't like me. Why the people I loved treated me the way they had. I didn't understand any of it. All I could do was cry.

Really, I spent most of my pregnancy crying. What was supposed to be the happiest and most joyful experience a woman experiences was downright miserable. I should have been bonding with my baby and transmitting calm thoughts, sending happiness and contentment his way, surrounded by people who loved me and were excited for him to enter the world.

Pregnant mothers are meant to spend this time learning from their own mothers and other helpful women who have already gone through the process. They should hear stories about the "terrible-two" stage and what to do for a fussy baby who's teething. Like any other mother, I wanted my pregnancy to be supportive and welcoming, not only for me but also for the little life inside of me. I felt horribly guilty, knowing that I could be hurting him by going through all of this.

To those ends, I would place my hand on my stomach and apologize for how sad I was, explaining why he might be feeling despair and stress so that at least he had some understanding of it. Then I would promise him a better life, assuring my baby that I'd love him like no other. Sitting in my truck like that, I described whatever beautiful things I saw around me, trying to teach him about the kind of joy and happiness I couldn't remember feeling myself.

And then I would cry some more.

I did get stronger and stronger through all that sorrow, but I got angrier too. There was so much to be mad at, starting with me and ending with the world. In my eyes, the world was a cruel and unfair place. And the nicer you were in it, the more it would tear you apart and break you down.

That was the lowest point in my life up until then – when strangers wanted to help me more than my family did. But I just figured that was how my life would have to be. I was neglected and always would be, as far as I could tell.

At some point, I got good at coming up with mental strategies to help cope with neglect before it could even show itself. It was a great survival strategy, but that's all I was doing. Just surviving. I had no more time to think about love or the possibilities of it. I was so busy thinking about hate and how to protect myself that I rather forgot to remember there was anything else out there.

For me, that was it. For others, it seemed like a different story.

Most of my days consisted of watching families and how they interacted with each other. I would see them and imagine how good it must feel to have those kinds of connections with people to talk to and share things with, trust, love, and joke around with - A family I could learn from.

I knew what a healthy family looked like. I witnessed their happy interactions all the time; I loved taking it in. The experience was one I wanted so badly that I would study it whenever I saw it on display. From there, I began to live vicariously through them, feeling their smiles, their laughs, and their giggles. I would even emotionally accept the hugs and warm pats on the back I'd witness a father giving to a son. I felt the love a toddler had for the family dog, and the attachment between mothers and their children.

I guess that was my soul's way of getting whatever I could to survive. Because, otherwise, my heart was withered.

The downside was that I also ended up feeling the negative emotions I saw around me. Anger. Embarrassment. Fear. Sympathy for a person I witnessed getting hurt, knowing too well how devastating painful emotions can be - how they can crush you and kill your spirit.

Perhaps, I considered, my situation would be different if only I had picked the right guy. That was something I pondered a lot, sitting in my truck. If only I could have the same baby I had in my belly, just with a different man. If only I had known how to pick the right guy.

Am I My Mother?

A lot of time went to wishing a different life for myself. A different mom. A different mate. A different me. I fantasized about the good life I would have had if I'd been raised by my dad, or if I'd been able to just stay living with my aunts. I use to speak to my father over the phone every now and then throughout my time in college.

I enjoyed getting to know him, and I thought of him constantly during the many moments I sat in my truck alone. We lost touch with each other after I discovered I was pregnant. He would call me, and I purposely wouldn't answer. I was scared that if he found out I was pregnant, he would reject me just like my mother had done. I was avoiding my father because I feared he would hurt me.

I feared that he would break my heart. The same approach my mother had with Aunt Lia, I was having with my father. I was rejecting a person who wanted to love me because I was scared. Throughout my pondering, I considered contacting my father. In the back of my head, I knew he would accept me with open arms. But I just couldn't take that risk. No matter how much my heart knew he was a safe place for me, my brain understood that people disappointed, and I couldn't bear to reach out to being disappointed again.

Amidst all those thoughts and fantasies, I never dreamed about becoming rich or famous. I never wanted an expensive car or a job I could brag about. What I wanted was a family to love me. Freedom from pain. To be heard the correct way. And for at least one person in my life to know and understand me for who I really was. What I wanted the most couldn't be bought.

People take healthy, happy families for granted, whether it's the little sister who's annoying in how much she wants to emulate her older siblings, the mother who nags out of love and concern, or the father who is so tough on his children because he wants them to grow up to be strong and the best versions of themselves they can be.

People take these things and these people for granted. When anything becomes too familiar, human nature has a way of taking control and making you disregard what you're used to, even if what they're used to is lovely and wholesome and everything that someone else would do just about anything for. If only people could take each morning to appreciate the gold and gems they already have.

Someone with a loving and supportive family has it all. That person has all the love, potential, and future they could ever need, and they inherit so many beautiful perspectives on life in the process. If only people could be mindful of that.

Because you have young people like me who would do just about anything to have the kind of love they take for granted each and every day.

Other than my baby, nature was the only thing that kept me alive during this time, serving the same sustaining purpose it always did. There was the light peeping in through the bundles of trees, and the sounds of the creek and the fish that frolicked within it. There were the squirrels and the birds playing tag in the trees, or sometimes fighting with each other. There was the sound acorns make when falling from those tall trees I stared at constantly. And my favorite, the feeling I felt when a subtle breeze from the trees gently swept across my face filled with tears.

Nature is one of the most beautiful elements in life to me, and the way I see it, it has a close connection to love. Nature is self-love in one sense, since it nurtures itself. When it rains, it grows. When it hurts, it's only so that it becomes something much more gorgeous than before.

I soaked my pain in nature; I sunbathed in it. I would stay at a park for hours, just taking in the love. Every time a slight breeze would kiss my face, I would gently close my eyes and appreciate the kiss Mother Nature had for me. Out there, surrounded by nothing but trees and fields, rocks, streams and critters, I felt welcome.

I trusted them with all my feelings, emotions and secrets. If I was sad, I knew the natural sunlight would make me feel better. And I knew that nature would never judge me; it was never cruel. It was peace – the kind of peace I needed. Something that would never abandon me.

There were so many times I'd just sit on a grassy hill and think. It was nice out there. The apartment I shared with Vince's aunt and uncle was a cold, dreaded place that made me feel empty. I never felt welcome, and was reminded by Vince constantly that if I didn't like how he was treating me, I could leave once my baby was born, and leave my baby with him and his family. I had tried to express to him that I felt neglected and alone, and that I was getting nothing from him when he came home. Not help with a single grocery bag. Not a single, "How are you doing?" or "How are you feeling?" or "How is the baby doing?" Nothing.

I could never abandon my baby, and just the mere thought of it made me sick. So I began living in my truck most of the day, spending all my days and evenings driving around with my left leg, and gazing at happy families at the most peaceful of parks I could find. Vince's aunt and uncle were nurses who worked what seemed to be all day and all night. I would go back to the apartment in the middle of the night at times to sleep in their spare bedroom, and then leave right back out early in the morning.

I would park my car anywhere that had those tall trees and those playful squirrels. I chased the only peace I knew. I felt as though nature allowed my harsh circumstances to temporarily fade; it was my numbing medicine. My beautiful distraction.

My life, it appeared, had become a cycle, where I was coping with it as best as I could in the same ways I had as a child, even if I was dealing with much more grown-up issues. The truth was that I felt like I was that child all over again, trying to raise myself and failing at it no matter what I did. I wasn't prepared for the cruelty and pain of society. I wasn't taught how to survive on this man-made Earth. I was only taught how to perform, and do what I was told. All I could do now, was do my best.

I longed for something better though. There were dreams of independence and success in my head and heart. Dreams of freedom and hoping to one day become that girl who no one could hurt or break down ever again. Dreams of becoming strong and beautiful someday, since I felt anything but beautiful during those months.

When your self-esteem has been ruined, you feel your ugliest. I felt ugly. Inside and out, I felt horrid.

Realizations

I had many moments to think in my truck; nature had a way of making me deal with the pains I had tried so hard to hide in that small hidden place in the back of my mind - years of pain and unresolved issues. One included my relationship with my Aunt Valerie, and another, knowing that I wanted the best environment for my baby. I couldn't raise my baby in my truck, and I didn't want my baby around his abusive father. I wanted to be around my own family who loves me, and a family who could love him just the same. It took some time, but I sucked back all my feelings and called Aunt Valerie, begging her to let me stay with her after all. I had decided I couldn't take it anymore.

I was too embarrassed to tell her the actual reason. Too ashamed to tell her that I was in an abusive relationship with an unstable maniac. So I simply told her that I felt alone and wanted my own family around.

Half the truth, yes, but not the entire story by far.

As it turned out, I had sucked back all my feelings only to a certain extent. No matter how much I wanted to, I couldn't forget how my aunt had heard so many negative things about me and how her perception about me was tainted in the worst way possible. This woman I grew up around. This woman I loved immensely and who returned that same kind of love to me throughout my life. I felt as though maybe she didn't feel the same way about me anymore.

How could anyone love me after hearing all the horrible things my mother had said about me? That's why she couldn't be trusted. That's why I only worked up the nerve to ask her for physical shelter, not emotional refuge as well. I was still too scared to speak my truth. Still paralyzed with fear. So I guess I contributed to what she was tricked to think.

No matter what horrible things she did and didn't think about me, Aunt Valerie allowed me to move in that very day. I contacted Dan to help me move the little bit of things I owned. My stay with my two aunts was great at first, with both of them helping me. Just like that, I did start to feel love around me and for me again. I no longer had to struggle to carry grocery bags to my car, and Aunt Valerie would bring me food when it was time for dinner.

She was still in communication with my mother though, unfortunately. So there were numerous times when I sat in the house feeling like a cold criminal. They would be on the phone together, and I'd just sit there wondering about all the horrible things my mother was saying to her about me.

A good summary of this time with them while I waited to see my baby is this: Some days were good, and some days were rough. I was so broken and naive that most of the time, I felt as if I didn't even know who I was regardless.

But Aunt Lia did, it would seem. She had grown older and more fragile, even if she was still beautiful and poised as ever. Seeing her every day was a lovely experience even if other aspects of my life were less than perfect. I enjoyed her genuine spirit; her very presence sending so many memories rushing through my head and soul, making me feel like that hopeful little girl again.

Aunt Lia never judged me, as if she felt how brokenhearted I actually was. I didn't have the strength to let my sorrows pour out into her waiting hands. Yet somehow still understanding how wounded my soul had become over the years, she would try to comfort me, coming to my new bedroom and checking in on me all the time.

Every time she did, I fought back as many tears as I could, because no one had cared enough to do that for me in a very, very long time.

I remember joining her for dinner one evening, making my plate and sitting in the dining room chair next to her. She took one look at my plate and told me I didn't have enough food there for a pregnant woman. It made me laugh. Genuinely laugh. And then, since she was right, I got back up and got some more food.

Aunt Lia checked out my plate one more time before saying, "See? Now that's how a pregnant woman should eat."

This woman was the most amazing lady I knew for her outlook and capabilities. It seemed as though I forgot about all my shortcomings when she spoke.

One day, it stormed so badly that the power went out in the house, which was one of the worst things that could have happened, in my opinion. I hated the dark; I was terrified by it. All the spirits I'd seen as a child had come out at night. And as I got older, the darkness gave my anxiety a wide stage to perform on.

Knowing how I needed her calming presence without me having to say a word, Aunt Lia ignored her fragile frame and the pitch-blackness of the basement where my bedroom was. She was right there trying to find her way in the dark to check on me, even at the risk of her own safety.

Once she made it to my room, she asked me if I wanted to come into her room and sleep in the bed with her. I loved that she asked me, and I wanted to say yes so badly. I was definitely afraid, and I definitely wanted her love, her hugs, her concern, and her nurturing. But that same old protective wall kept me from admitting how badly I needed her, and that same old urge to decline help dominated my expression instead.

So what I did instead of saying what I wanted to say was smile and politely tell her, "No, thank you, Aunt Lia."

Since she apparently knew me so well, she must have also known that my smile was fake and my assurances were false. So while she let me give my "no" for an answer, she still asked if I wanted to walk upstairs together. And that was an offer I felt comfortable accepting.

Helping each other find our way up the stairs and in the dark, it was obvious we both had challenges. But through love, we helped each other through it.

That meant so much to me. Aunt Lia was just so selfless and beautiful. I wish I could have had the strength to pour my heart out and tell her my life. But I just wasn't spiritually ready yet.

That night, a neighbor came by to bring us some candles. And we sat at the dining room table, surrounded by darkness, yet comforted by the small glowing specks of light that illuminated from each candle. I remember just sitting there staring at her. I felt like that little girl again, in awe of my Aunt Lia's inner and outside beauty. In awe of how love comes so natural for her to express. Some moments went by and Aunt Lia's son Clyde came by the house to check on us. And during those moments, I could only think about how lucky her son was to have been raised by such a nurturing and loving mother. My Aunt Lia did a wonderful job with all of her children, and all I could do was wonder what my life would have been if my mother had done a wonderful job with me.

Back when I was much younger and still living with my mother, there were a few times when the lights went out due to a storm. I would tell my mother how scared of the dark I was, just for her to tell me I was only scared because I was evil and I did evil things. Then she would laugh.

Not my Aunt Lia, though; she never thought anything like that about me at all, and she never would have said such a thing to me either. She knew my soul and heart were in trouble. She knew it all because she felt it all, and knew firsthand how my mother treated people. Just like me, my aunt felt the pain of others without having to hear a word from their lips.

Wanting Better

I had begun my online classes again in order to get my bachelor's degree, I had a little bit of money left in the bank and decided to use a portion of it to try to finish school. My major was Behavioral Science, and I had begun to study about personality disorders for a class assignment. I found it extremely intriguing for one reason.

A lot of my research defined my mother.

I studied the material obsessively until I got it as familiar in my mind as I could, and as I did, I became captivated with the subject matter. The power of the human brain fascinated me. The disorders fascinated me. I considered some of them to be more of eccentric traits than disorders or diseases.

I considered them to be some of the optional ways the brain chose to work and process information. Besides, there were strengths in many of these so-called disorders right alongside the much more obvious weaknesses. That's when I began to realize that if someone were to master those strengths, they could be phenomenal – just like I had with my OCD as a child; a person could learn to master these brain patterns instead of allowing them to be the master. Back then, I was then able to use my OCD to be a creator. And now, I was exceptionally curious how trainable a mind could be if given the proper therapy and treatment.

My research, which had begun as the basis for a school paper, turned into an infatuation of mine. All those years, I had no idea that my OCD had a name or specific traits. I had always thought I was just weird and disliked because of that weirdness and the other eccentric traits I possessed. Once I was seeing the bigger picture, I was hooked and wanting to learn more. I wanted the full explanation for why I was the way I was.

It felt amazing to be able to put a name to something I had struggled with for so long.

For weeks straight, I must have read tons of material about OCD. After that, I dabbled in researching other personality conditions such as bipolar disorder, schizophrenia, and borderline personality disorder. It didn't take me long to realize that my mother exhibited most of the symptoms listed under that last category. The revelation didn't necessarily shock me; if anything, I was relieved.

Things began to make more and more sense with every sentence I read about children who grew up with borderline mothers. The similarities were staggering, and they moved me to tears to read about other people putting my pain into words so accurately.

Everything my mother has done and said. Her behavior and how she acted toward me and others. The way she reacted and responded to certain situations. Reading about BPD was like reading a biography about my mother's life and discovering the secrets to my childhood. All those years when I'd thought it was my fault somehow, when I felt as though I just wasn't good enough for love or good enough to be loved, and when I felt as though I deserved hate and mistreatment because I wasn't worthy of anything greater, it wasn't because of me - it was because of her.

Doing that research was such an eye-opener. I now understood and could confidently state that the mother I'd been born to had a personality disorder. A very severe one. One that can hurt people without her even knowing. And one that made any offspring feel exactly how I then felt.

On the other hand, it was a comfort and a blessing to discover all of that. But, it was still frightening reading about what BPD could do to the sufferer's loved ones, sometimes molding them into generationally cursed models.

I didn't want to end up that way. I didn't want my mother to ruin my life more than she already had. It was horrible just thinking of that possibility.

It was also complicated, filling me with mixed emotions. After discovering my mother's psychological profile, I'd be sad one moment and so very mad the next. Those same thoughts as before – the ones about what my life would be like if I'd had a different mother – came rushing back with a vengeance. I felt so bad for my younger self. And I found myself resenting every adult who did nothing about the situation my sister and I endured. Every adult who didn't want to listen to me. Every adult who ignored the real issue and labeled me as bad.

Struggling to mentally deal with it all, it wasn't uncommon for me to feel utterly lost and overwhelmed trying to sort through the long list of emotions that came with this information. Wanting a second opinion, I emailed parts of my research to my sister, wanting her response and opinions on the subject. I wanted to see if she saw it too.

She did. She definitely did. Latanya immediately phoned me, taken aback by what she'd just read and its correlation to our mother.

For the first time in a long time, I had answers to why we were raised how we were. And why we'd ended up with such an overwhelming amount of struggles to fight through.

There were reasons behind the paths I'd chosen in life. I was a mentally and emotionally abused child who grew up, went to college, and fell right back into the hellhole I was used to living in due to lack of love, knowledge and guidance.

As for my mother? She wasn't that way by choice. She was that way because her brain just couldn't help itself due to her own past abuse and neglect. Her outcome was damaged well before I ever came into the picture. Yes, it could have been avoided. She could have been helped. She could have been loved. But that just wasn't the case. Or at least it wasn't enough for her brain to react to in a positive way.

As a result, the ones who suffered the most might very well have been my sister and me. The children. Children always suffer the sins of their parents. They feel the resulting pain and despair.

We, the children, end up feeling the sadness, hopelessness, and anger that come out of these kinds of situations; as we age, our resentment ages along with us.

The weeks went by, and significant levels of added tension began to build up between Aunt Valerie and me. Because of all the horrid things my mother was whispering in her ear, she became stricter with me because she thought I was a problem child who had grown up to be a problematic adult. The way she saw me, I was disrespectful and going down the wrong path.

I couldn't really blame her when my mother was so good at lying and misleading people. But the lack of blame didn't mean my feelings weren't significantly hurt in the process.

Still, I kept silent.

I just couldn't open up to anyone about it. I couldn't ask for help. I couldn't jump into someone's arms and cry. My body, mind and mouth simply wouldn't allow any of that. Every time I saw Aunt Lia sitting there, gracefully enjoying life, I just wanted to hug her and tell her everything, all the pain I'd felt over the years and everything that happened. I wanted to just hold her and cry in her arms, but I couldn't gather up the nerve and courage to do it. Thanks to my mother and Vince, I was convinced that I'd only end up traumatized worse if I opened up. They'd both taught me that I'm safer when my feelings are kept to myself, and not expressed or shown to anyone. So being vulnerable was running a great risk.

Research was safe though, I thought. It was just between me and myself. Besides, there was still so much I wanted to know. So, after last speaking with my sister, I decided to do more research on how to get a parent professionally evaluated. My thought – my hope – was that if my mother heard she had a mental condition, then maybe she would get the help she needed. And if she got the help she needed, then maybe we could be that happy family I'd always wanted.

My research ended up pointing me to the courthouse, where I went in front of a judge to tell part of my story and pieces of how my mother behaved. This was a major moment for me, and I felt anything but empowered as I stood there in that courtroom.

I wasn't sure if this was the right thing to do or not.

I wasn't sure if this would help or make matters worse.

I was so nervous. My anxiety gave me flashbacks of my childhood days when I had to perform on those intimidating stages before those cold, calculating judges in those horrible audition rooms. Yet, sweating on the outside and literally panicking on the inside, I still managed to get up in front of the judge and tell as much of my story as I could.

As I spoke, I couldn't help but cry, which didn't do anything to make me feel more comfortable. But that small, sorry amount of hope I had left toward having a loving mother and a functional family kept me talking, telling details of my life to a man I didn't even know in hopes of reaching some sort of solution.

Deep down inside, I still wanted a real mom, and if getting her help was going to give me one, then help was what I was going to have to get her, no matter how it made me feel during the process.

After hearing what I had to say, the judge granted an order to force an evaluation for my mother. It wasn't until then I learned the details involved - how the police would be the ones to take her to the hospital.

I didn't want that. That sounded awful to me, and I asked them if I could just take her myself. But their answer was no. The proper protocol was for them to escort her there, they said, and no one else. The most I could do was be present when they arrived to her house to get her.

So that's what I did. They told me the time they'd be picking her up, and I waited in the parking lot outside of what used to be my house until they arrived, not knowing what to expect. My anxiety levels were wreaking havoc on my mind and body.

When they arrived, they proceeded to knock on the door. When she answered, dressed in her nightgown, they informed her why they were there.

Just like it had been in the face of so many other negative circumstances, her response was to laugh.

She laughed at me, and she laughed at the police, asking if we were joking. And when she finally understood it was not a joke, she was still chuckling while she told me specifically, "You weren't supposed to do this." She must have said that about three times, chuckling all the while.

The only way I could respond was, "I think you have BPD, and they're going to take you to go and get evaluated."

The police proceeded to handcuff my mother, which shocked both of us - her and me. I had no idea they would have to do that. It wasn't anything I wanted to see right then.

Despite everything, I still felt bad.

When I asked the police if she could at least put some decent clothes on, they told me that no, she couldn't. So I asked them if I could at least bring something for her to change into at whichever hospital they were taking her.

I got permission to do that and set right to my task, packing her a bag and finding her cell phone too so I could include that with her necessities. All the while, I tried to keep the bigger picture in my mind. I was doing this – I had instituted all of this – so that we could be a family, complete with a mother who cared enough to love me. That's what I wanted, and that made it worth it.

I naively thought that everything would change after the evaluation. The thought of how much better everything could be filled me with so much optimism, all of which was horrendously misplaced.

My mother went into that hospital, just as planned, but after that, it all fell apart. Being the practiced liar she was, she commenced to telling the staff about how bad and evil I was. According to her, the only reason I'd gone before the court and said what I'd said was because I was being spiteful and vindictive after she'd had to kick me out of the house.

That's what she told the nurses, and that's what they believed.

She also made them believe that everything I'd researched, learned and written about her abuse – both during my own hospital stay and as recorded in the court documents – was just random stuff I'd copied out of a book or word-for-word from the internet. I had fabricated the entire thing.

That's what she told the nurses, and that's what they believed.

She had done it again. How she managed to convince even mental health specialists that she wasn't in need of psychiatric treatment is bewildering. Yet she did nonetheless. The nurses took her side and, passing their manipulated understanding of the facts, persuaded the doctor doing the evaluation that she was there all because her daughter was mad at her.

That shouldn't have happened. It never should have happened. She should have gotten the treatment and guidance she needed to get better. To be better.

But I guess she was just that good at what she did. And with that final piece of proof piercing my heart, I gave up. So her story was the only one out there for people to listen to.

I didn't speak up against her accusations. I didn't tell anyone the truth. That paralyzing pain was back once again and for such overwhelming reasons. I was too paralyzed by pain to even think about trying. I looked all those people in the eyes and saw that it didn't matter what I had to say. They weren't going to believe me anyway. No one ever did.

During this whole ordeal, I found out a lot of side details I hadn't known before, such as the reason why my mother was still getting housing assistance after she'd kicked me out. Apparently, the government still thought I was living with her. Yet she had contacted our landlord and told him that I had willingly moved out and asked him if he could take my name off the lease, and he did, not knowing that my mother would never report that information to the housing assistance authority.

Leaving the hospital, I went back to my aunt's house, just to have a restraining order delivered to me two weeks later. According to the protective order, written up on my mother's testimony, I had shoved her and was overall abusive. It cited a date a few months back when we had, in fact, gotten into an argument right before she kicked me out. But during that fight, I never touched her. We just yelled at each other, which was what we usually did.

I knew the moment I read the details that she was seeking revenge for what I'd done. Only I was truthful and did it for love; all she was doing was her usual - spewing hateful lies.

After that, I had to face her in court over the allegations she'd leveled against me. I looked at her while she stood there before the judge, lying about how horrible and physically abusive I was. Me. A young woman, six-months pregnant, with that long-legged cast attached to my leg, and sitting in a wheelchair. I was abusive toward my mother.

I watched her as she lied about me, her movements and inflections and general words so familiar by now. I already knew the traits that came with her lies. They were as familiar to me by then as a loving mother's hugs would be to a loved child.

There was that nervous pitch in her voice that seemed to travel up and down. Her lack of eye contact, and her unsure expression while she proceeded to lay out new falsehoods on top of the old ones. I had gone into her home, she told the judge, despite knowing full-well about the restraining order. Moreover, I had stolen some of her things. Not my things. Hers.

That was another clever manipulation, since I had technically taken certain items from her house. Yet I hadn't gone there myself, and I hadn't taken anything that didn't belong to me. In actuality, I'd given a friend the spare key, asking him to collect the rest of my belongings that my mother had failed to throw out on that day she'd kicked me out of the house.

I couldn't afford new makeup and new bedding. I couldn't afford a new microwave and mini-fridge. So knowing I had a temporary restraining order on me, I thought I could have someone else gather my belongings for me. I even told him to get my pet cat Dan's sister had given me before leaving college. I had grown to love him, and I just wanted my little companion back.

Yet I didn't say any of that to the judge. I just sat in that courtroom, defeated before, during and after her performance. I didn't bother defending myself through the lies even though I know I should have.

After court, I quietly went back to my aunts', but Aunt Valerie was very upset with me and had been for a while. She thought it was horrible I'd sent my mother off to get evaluated, telling me that doing so was something you would only ever do to someone you hated. There was the added issue that my mother had been telling Aunt Valerie that I was stealing from her too. So my aunt gave me an ultimatum: tell her the truth or move out.

I chose to move out. I didn't tell her about my friend who'd collected my things because I felt as if I couldn't. I felt like I couldn't trust her. This woman I admired and loved, who had loved me more than my mother, and who I cared for so deeply. But I couldn't trust her because whatever I told her, I already knew would get passed on to my mother.

And I couldn't trust her at all.

By that point, I genuinely feared my mother and her ways. Her bitterness, her manipulation, and her lack of remorse were terrifying. Telling Aunt Valerie how I got my things would have been sending hell straight my way in the form of my mother's wrath. I wouldn't put it past her to have me flat-out jailed, pregnant and all.

Before I left that day, Aunt Lia looked at me with such sad eyes. They say the eyes are windows to the soul, but right then, I thought I could see straight to her heart, which was broken because of me. "I hate when you two fight," she told me.

Aunt Lia loved her family so very much, and always wanted us to be strong and stick together. She truly wanted love and unity between us all. So seeing her daughter and great niece not only fighting but actually coming to an impassable place in their relationship really hurt her. And watching her hurt face hurt me to the core. But I didn't think I had any other viable option, which was why I left and went back to my son's father's family.

Not fully though. Not completely. My stuff was at their apartment, but I still lived in my truck mostly. I couldn't trust them either. So I lived in my truck to protect myself from the abuse, with no one knowing. I cried every single day after that, alone.

Deja Vu

It's like I picked up right where I'd left off, spending my days in awe of other families. I went back to my old habits, watching other people, vicariously feeling happiness and joy through other people's lives. And also similarly, I found myself empathizing with their negative emotions as well - their jealousy and envy, regrets and resentment.

I suppose I should have been grateful that I was able to feel at all after everything I've been through.

That said, I still didn't hate my mother even if she was the destroyer of my happiness and the bringer of my pain. This woman who had birthed me was the worst person I'd ever met. And still, I didn't hate her. I blamed her, but I didn't hate her. No matter how much she had done to me, hate was something I could not genuinely produce. My body, mind and soul couldn't come up with the ingredients needed to hate.

So what was I when I moved out? I'd say sad.

Lonely and sad.

Filled with despair.

It was almost wrong how easily life fell back into the same old patterns that it did. Again, I looked to nature to console and love me. Again, I tried so hard every day not to have a nervous breakdown. Thoughts of how horrible my life was plagued my mind every single day. I spent most of my time trying to quiet those thoughts, but close to nothing was effective.

I would talk to my unborn child - who was now kicking in my stomach - crying to him and telling him that I didn't know what I was going to do. I would let him know that I loved him, assuring him that all I wanted was for everything to get better before he came into this world.

That didn't seem like it was going to happen though. Not when I'd gone right back to being emotionally and verbally abused by a man who would claim to love me one minute, then literally spit in my face the next. It was hell on Earth going back to his grasp, but I didn't think I had anywhere else to go.

I was still trying to get through school during this whole period. Earning my B.A. was the only way I could see out of the life I was living, so I would go to the library and study and submit my work to the professors from there. I was determined to change my life. I was determined to be independent. I was determined to be able to raise my child in an environment where no one would ever be able to hurt me or disown me again, and I had vowed to never ever be dependent on another human being for as long as I live.

It was getting closer and closer to my due date, and I knew I couldn't have my child living in the atmosphere I was subjected to. Again I thought, I couldn't raise him in my truck, or with his father and his father's family, being vulnerable to their wicked ways. The only place I could think of that I could afford and my child would be safe was back at home with my mother.

Yes, that would mean I'd have to endure personal pain and abuse from her, but at least my son would be safe in a home of some sorts.

There was no part of me that wanted to see my child have to struggle like I did. Every piece of my soul cringed away from the idea that he might end up enduring or inheriting the same abusive behavior as his father. I didn't want him growing up to believe that abusing women was okay.

It was true that I also didn't want my mother's unloving behavior to rub off on him either. But, oddly enough, I had seen her show love and affection to her other grandchildren. She was good at it with them, showing Latanya's children so much affection that she would even fail to discipline them when they needed it. I guess it was just her own children she couldn't love. Perhaps she was able to be a kind and loving grandma to make up for how horrible she was to us.

So while I was in something of a conundrum, I mostly knew she would love this new grandchild of hers as soon as she met him. My son would be fine; I just wouldn't be. But that part, I was fine with; I had no choice but to be fine when the health and well-being of this precious little life inside of me was on the line.

He was why I did it. Why I gathered up all the nerve I had left and asked my mother for my room back. I asked her for my home back. I didn't explain about the abuse I would continue suffering otherwise, not that she would have cared. I didn't go into detail about any of it. But she let me back in all the same.

My mother began to buy me things right away, like a new bedroom set - a really expensive one at that. I accepted it because I needed it; my old bed was uncomfortable and not in the greatest shape for a woman who was close to giving birth. I kept in mind that attached to my mother's gifts and generosity, is always a motive. My mother appeared nurturing towards me, and excited about her newest grandchild who would soon be making his debut. I was cautious with my mother; I never let my guard down, not for one single second. And on the other hand, I was relieved that my son would have a house and not a run-down truck to call home. For a moment, I could just put all of my despair behind, focusing on the positive thoughts and vibes I could transmit to my baby.

Soon I would learn that it was time for my mother to renew her housing assistance voucher, in order to determine if she was still eligible to receive rental assistance from the state. This renewal process demanded certain personal documents, along with handwritten answers to be reviewed by her caseworker. If my mother's income increased, or if her last dependent moved out over the past year, my mother would lose her housing assistance immediately. But if my mother kept me as a dependent and added my son as a second dependent living in her home, the state would then pay an even bigger portion of her rent than they initially had done before. She was even granted permission to move into a bigger house if my son and I continued residing with her.

Now her generous gestures began to make sense.

She needed me to stay.

She couldn't afford to have it any other way.

But again, I was cautious with my mother, so actions such as this didn't surprise me at all. I was more so concerned about getting my cast off before my baby boy arrived. I was about 7 ½ months pregnant when my doctor finally removed it. My leg was skinny and weak from everything it had undergone. All those months of not being able to use the muscles had left me with little to work with - not that I cared. I was just happy to get that thing off of me. And I figured that, after I gave birth, I could work on that area, along with the rest of my body, like eating right and exercising.

Vince was upset that I moved back in with my mother; he had lost his power to control me, and began voicing his distaste about my decision constantly. He made it clear of how stupid I was for my decision, all while sleeping with other women while I went through the rest of my pregnancy pretty much alone. He began hating my mother, and often said cruel things about her; he even went as far as threatening her life. Both he and my mother despised each other equally, which I found baffling since they shared the same abusive traits.

But I didn't care about what Vince had to say, nor did I care what he thought. I felt I made the best decision for my baby, and I was relieved to go from a Level 10 abuse back to a Level 8, as disturbing as that sounds. That's the way my last days up until my due date passed. And then my due date came. And then it went. My baby boy was taking his time arriving, so I proceeded to take my exams at the exam locations sites, even knowing that I could go into labor at any minute. That was just an issue I would have to deal with if it started mid-test. Until it did though, I was laser-focused on graduating and running away from the dysfunctional life I knew.

But it seemed as soon as I finished up with my exams, my baby was ready to come out and get acquainted with me and the rest of the world. I woke up one morning experiencing contractions; I was scared, anxious and excited all at one time. So I called my sister and explained to her the pains I was feeling and how far apart they lasted. With her having the experience of giving birth to my two nephews, she assured me that the pains I felt were the real deal and to go see my doctor, and I did. And sure enough, my baby boy was on his way!

The array of emotions that filled my mind was overwhelming. This was it. It wasn't comfortable and I knew full well it was going to get worse, but this was it!

The hospital admitted me that day and after more than twenty-four hours of labor, I gave birth to a beautiful baby boy, a child who had already survived so much. This little darling of mine was a fighter right from the start, having made it through all the things I had without breaking - without being anything less than perfect. He endured my leg operations, my depression, my heartbreak and my loneliness. And yet, he was still so lovely and sweet.

He came out with my big eyes, beautiful smile, a head full of hair, thick eyebrows and a baby mustache. To see this little, cute miracle with the same features as me tickled me so. It was love at first sight. I couldn't believe it really, but there I was. I was a mother.

Vince came home early from college in order to be present in the delivery room. And his parents and my mother were there too. The funny thing was that as soon as my son popped out, my mother appeared to be filled with joy. She even went so far as to kiss me on my forehead.

I didn't know how to take that. My mother hadn't kissed me or showed me a bit of genuine kindness in so many years. But I guess for once in her life, she was genuinely happy. It was the first time I'd ever seen any real emotion from her. I suppose that seeing her grandchild born was something beautiful, even to someone like her.

Really, I didn't dwell on that oddity very long, not when my main focus was on this beautiful being I'd just brought into this world.

Everything was utterly joyous until the day came time for me to fill out the paperwork to obtain my son's social security card and birth certificate.

Now, ever since I was three months pregnant, Vince and I had agreed on our baby's name. He had this great idea to blend both of our names together, an idea that I loved and found very creative. So he had come up with a particular combination, and I approved it; we chose to name him Lance. It was the name I used to speak to this little life ever since. For months and months, I'd been talking to my unborn child, my strength, and my companion. Sharing with him my deepest feelings, apologizing to him for all of the emotional pain, addressing him with this very name.

But when it was time to fill out this paperwork, Vince decided to change his mind. All of a sudden, he had a problem with it. He began to talk about how, in his Liberian culture, women didn't pick the name or even have a say in the naming process. He went on about his family's disapproval, and how our baby's name must be of African origin with a meaning - an African name I couldn't even pronounce.

He was hostile, controlling and belittling as he spoke to me, keeping a close eye on the social security and birth certificate forms the nurse held in her hand. And when I didn't agree, he became more aggressive, and then began demanding me to name our son after him instead. My thoughts and feelings on the subject were of no concern to him. And when the nurse handed me the necessary forms to fill out, that's when things got extremely ugly.

As I watched his climbing display of anger, all I could do was wonder why.

Why on earth would I do that?

Why would he think for a minute that I would name my son completely after him?

After my abuser? My tormentor?

This guy has abused me and treated me terribly throughout my entire pregnancy. Why would I make that additional connection between this innocent little life and someone with no morals, no respect and no integrity?

Vince's mother, I was certain, had put all of that nonsense into his head, as usual. That woman was just as manipulative and controlling as her son, and I had enough.

Enough of this guy treating me as if I owed him something.

Enough of this dysfunction he and his family tried to force on me.

This was the day I was putting my foot down, with no desire of lifting it back up.

I was not in agreement with his sudden change of mind, and I let him know that. I also let him know that this was our child, not his mother's child, and not his family's child. I wanted the name we had chosen months ago - the name we had both agreed on before his mother manipulated his mind to get her way.

Vince didn't take my resistance very well, throwing a rage-filled temper tantrum right there in the hospital room in front of the nurse and for everyone on that hospital floor to see and hear. Despite Vince's abusive and raging manner, the nurse who held the stack of birth certificate and social security forms to give to the families was still very there and present. She stood her ground and showed no signs of fear, and neither did I.

Not getting what he wanted from me, Vince snatched the form out of my hand and commenced to ripping it up, his face filled with all the immaturity and rage so familiar to me.

But me? I calmly turned to the nurse, who happened to have an entire stack of the very same forms in her hand. Smiling at her, I politely asked for another one, and she smiled right back at me. "Sure," she told me just as nicely as she handed over another packet for me to fill out.

Though polite in that exchange, the interaction was fiercely rife with emotions. Her smile was definitely one of pride. In me. She was so clearly proud that I'd stood my ground, and she was proud with how I handled it.

The thing was, so was I.

Together, we let Vince know that his tantrums were going to have no effect on anyone but himself. Plus, we were smiling because we couldn't believe a male of his age would act the way he did.

Realizing as much – that his actions weren't going to get him what he wanted or even get a rise out of me – he flew into an even bigger fit of rage. Continuing to curse and scream, he flailed his arms about like a bat out of hell. He paced back and forth in that hospital room, unwilling to control his emotions. And when that didn't get him anywhere either, he started screaming at the nurse, calling her a bitch and insulting her further.

She handled the situation beautifully though. That nurse just calmly contacted hospital security to have him escorted out of the building. And that was that.

This guy, this crazy person, had wasted no time at all acting foolishly all because he couldn't get his way. Our son wasn't even three days old yet, and he was acting so ridiculously. I smiled at the nurse that day, and I meant that smile. But overall, I was just so exhausted with his behavior and how he treated me. I was tired of his foolishness and his manipulative family members.

As such, I couldn't have cared less that he was out of that room when he should have been sharing a special moment with me. In my mind, our relationship had been way over a long time ago. I had no problem with him being kicked out of the hospital.

Vince's departure actually lifted a ton of weight off of my shoulders and I was able to relax in my hospital room and enjoy my new baby's beautiful presence without any distractions from Vince's abuse. When the day came to leave the hospital with my son, many feelings crossed my heart and mind. I was excited to be a new mother; the kind of love I had for my newborn was one I had never felt before. It was pure; Little Lance had my heart and my full attention. All I could do was think about creating a life for him where he would need and want for nothing. Here I was, a single mother - a single young mother. With no plan - just hopes of survival.

My first two weeks at home with my newborn baby, and not much help, was tough. I barely got sleep due to having to wake up every two hours to tend to his needs, whether it was the milk he cried for when hungry, the uncomfortable gas he felt when needing to be burped after a meal, or the cries he gave when needing a diaper change. This was all on top of the numerous doctors' appointments I traveled to for little Lance and myself. I had vaginal stitches and was in pain for quite some time, and every drive to the grocery store or doctor's office was always just as painful as the last.

Vince never came to see our baby, or call to inquire how he was doing. And despite the struggles of new single motherhood, I didn't mind it at all. I had struggled before without his help, and in my mind, I was confident enough to raise my son on my own.

I'd acquired a newfound strength that kept all of my energy on my son, and none on Vince and his dysfunction of a family. I wanted Vince to be gone for good, but also knew that in the back of my mind, that may not be a wish I could keep.

My Heartbreak

During this time of being a busy new mom was during the time my very first role model, Aunt Lia, began to fall ill. She was in the hospital, and it was one of the most heartbreaking and most uncomfortable situations I had to face. Because of the fact my Aunt Valerie and I weren't communicating during this time, my Aunt Lia never got the chance to meet little Lance. I went to visit Aunt Lia in her hospital room. At first, my feelings mentally poured. I hated seeing her like this, I hated seeing tubes down her throat and cords attached to her. I fought back tears as I usually would in heartbreaking circumstances. I stood there mentally telling her everything that was in my heart. How I felt. How I yearned for her to be well and pull through. How I had appreciated everything that made her wonderful in my eyes. During this moment, I was interrupted by what seemed to be Aunt Valerie's feelings, I stood there staring at her as she went on and on about how ashamed of myself I should be for not bringing Little Lance to come visit Aunt Lia before her falling so ill. And all I could do as Aunt Valerie spoke down to me was think of how it was more of her fault than it was mine. If Aunt Valerie wouldn't have been such a victim to my mother's manipulation and lies, if only we didn't allow her to destroy our relationship, I would have felt more than comfortable with bringing my new baby over to their home to visit. The sad part was that these words and feelings were exchanged in the intensive care unit, in my Aunt Lia's room, where Aunt Valerie and her two brothers surrounded Aunt Lia's bedside. And even though my Aunt Lia was sedated, I knew she heard the bickering, and I also knew how much it had hurt her in the past to hear us fight. So to avoid upsetting my Aunt Lia even further, and to avoid responding to my Aunt Valerie, I left the room.

I had intentionally stayed away from Aunt Valerie for a few months to avoid any more tension between the two of us. But in the midst of Aunt Valerie and my issues, Aunt Lia passed away.

The regret I felt over that fact and those conditions made her loss that much worse.

Aunt Lia was the first woman who gave me the perfect example of what a lady is, what she does, and how she should act. For years, I had studied her. I observed who she was as a person and her mannerisms. I was intrigued and inspired by her inner and outer beauty and grace. She was my inspiration of what kind of woman I wanted to become – what kind of lady I wanted to evolve into. And most of all, I loved loving her.

After she passed away, my mother started to show her true nature to Aunt Valerie, turning her back on her when she needed support the most. Really, my mother said some pretty horrible things throughout the time Aunt Lia was sick. I recall her nonchalantly telling me to get a black dress ready because it didn't look like Aunt Lia would pull through. It made me sick hearing her say it as if it didn't matter one bit that the woman who loved her enough to take her in and treat her as one of her own was falling ill. The rest of us were grieving about this wonderful woman who had positively impacted all our lives.

Yet there was my mother, letting her cold and nasty heart seep out of her chest.

We did go to see Aunt Lia in the hospital a few times. Each time I saw my mother being cold and distant. She would make sure to rush me during my visits with her so that I could take her shopping. The disrespect she showed her adopted mother and adopted siblings was the most foul thing I'd ever witnessed.

Then after a few short months, my Aunt Lia passed away. The woman who opened her heart and doors to anyone she cared for, had left us all. And as reality set in that Aunt Lia was no longer with us, my mother grew colder, and her behavior became stranger. At Aunt Lia's funeral, I recall her asking a relative if he would put together an end table for her while the immediate family was standing there waiting to be escorted into the church. I quickly turned to her with a "shush!" I had grown fed up with her lack of respect, and discourteous behavior towards the woman I had loved so dearly. She simply rolled her eyes in anger as if I'd interrupted her concentration.

She was concentrating on trying so hard to mask her true feelings about my aunt's passing. It seemed to be guilt. Guilt and sadness - both of which she masked with manufactured acts of nonchalant behavior. My mother showed no remorse on purpose.

But I knew better. There was no way she could escape her true thoughts and emotions, no matter how hard she tried.

She knew very well that she'd treated Aunt Lia horribly for many, many years. She had lied to her and about her, she hadn't appreciated her, and she'd treated her like a doormat. All my mother's life, she had treated the only woman willing to teach and love her like she didn't matter at all.

My mother's behavior was disgusting. I was just utterly and flat-out disgusted by it.

Aunt Lia had taken her in when no one else would. She had tried to teach her how to be a better woman and mother. She continued to show unconditional love for my mother no matter how ungrateful, evil, and selfish her biological niece became. Why and how could my mother then turn around and act so cold and unloving to her? How could she show no love or compassion? How could she abandon Aunt Valerie and her brothers the way that she did – the very same people who were more like siblings to her than anything else.

I was disgusted, but I wasn't surprised. Nothing really surprised me about my mother anymore. She was someone I tolerated, but not someone with whom I could form a genuine relationship.

After Aunt Lia's funeral, my mother cut all ties with Aunt Valerie completely. At the service, Aunt Valerie and her brothers had expected my mother to sit up in the front pew with them, where the immediate family would sit. But she behaved so strangely to them. They found her coldness and distance confusing and unsettling, as if this was a whole new person before them that they'd never met.

Yet that new person they'd just been introduced to was the same person I'd known all my life. This was my mother's true nature. The bitterness. The coldness. The vindictiveness. The selfishness. I was used to all that. So while they tried to make sense of this new taste of jealousy and envy that she doled out to them, I understood that they were simply seeing the latest example of a pattern - how my mother could turn on someone for absolutely no good reason at all.

As a result, Aunt Valerie began to realize things about her, an outcome over which I had many mixed feelings.

I hurt for her, knowing that she had to experience such treatment at the hands of someone who was supposed to be her friend and family member, and at such a time too. It was like my mother had just woken up one day and decided that Aunt Valerie was bad and that she wanted nothing to do with her. There my aunt was, suffering the loss of her mother -a great mother - and needing comfort and love, particularly from someone who should have been able to share her pain. She had her two brothers, yes, but she was Aunt Lia's only biological daughter and she wanted a sister's shoulder to lean on as well.

But my mother didn't have a shoulder to spare. She abandoned Aunt Valerie and left her to grieve. It was painful to watch those expectations dashed without an ounce of sympathy or tact.

Even so, I was disappointed that it had taken this long for Aunt Valerie to see who my mother really was. It hurts to have people you love look at you like you're this bad destructive person, and that's what I'd had to endure around her for years. And then there was also a sense of relief about the whole process; I was relieved that the truth was out there about my mother and that Aunt Valerie would finally understand exactly what I'd been going through for so many years.

You see, it's hard to put a person like my mother into words. It's difficult to come up with the appropriate definitions and descriptions to convey who she was and what she was like without the other party having suffered from her too – unless the other person had dealt with the same kind of dysfunction. Experience, no matter how painful, really is the best teacher.

You can try to explain something a million times to a person. You can use your best vocabulary to capture your feelings or the situation as perfectly as you can. But if the person you're telling can't emotionally relate, those efforts could very well turn out pointless.

This was certainly the case for me. Trying to explain and get someone to understand life at home with my mother was a daunting task in and of itself. It was complex and too painful for more innocent human minds to depict and understand, especially with how young and hurt my own mind was.

My mother turned on Aunt Valerie so quickly that it seemed like she erased their entire relationship, which had spanned more than thirty years. It had seen my aunt babysitting us kids, taking my mother places, and being there for her emotionally as well. It had involved being her confidant, even if what my mother confided in her was nothing more than malicious lies. Aunt Valerie didn't comprehend that, and so she did her best to be the sympathetic ear she thought my mother needed. And when my mother's father passed away a few years before, the whole family was there for her – Aunt Valerie, her brothers and Aunt Lia. They were right by her side like they knew she needed them to be.

My aunt did so much for my mother, for me, and for my sister. She never gave her any reason to behave the way she commenced to behave. Yet just like she always did whenever she wanted to justify her behavior, my mother began to make up lies to validate her heartless actions.

Aunt Valerie had trusted my mother. And in return, my mother turned on her. Again.

When I confronted my mother about her deteriorating relationship with my aunt, she only gave me excuses and ridiculous explanations. The reason why she'd cut her off, she told me, was because Aunt Valerie hadn't done a thing for her when her father passed away.

It was a lie. It was such a blatant, unapologetic, unmistakable lie. My mother had just lied in my face as if I hadn't even been there during my grandfather's passing. She spoke to me as if I didn't remember the first-hand help that Aunt Valerie, Aunt Lia, and my uncles offered her – and that she had accepted.

According to her now though, my grandfather hadn't had life insurance, which meant that my mother was expected to pay for the funeral costs herself. Fortunately, that didn't end up happening, since a family member from North Carolina stepped up and offered to pay for the entire service. But regardless, Aunt Valerie and kin hadn't offered to help out once with the funeral costs.

Maybe that small bit was true. However, if so, then my mother never asked them for any money. I doubt my aunts even knew my grandfather didn't have life insurance. How could anyone know what you need if you don't speak up to ask them or tell them?

I guess my mother expected everyone to read her mind and just start throwing hundred dollar bills at her like some of the strippers I use to work with. She couldn't have cared less about the support they gave her. The emotional and physical support meant nothing to her, and she didn't care to consider the fact that they'd missed days of pay from work to be there for her. The money they spent on the rental car and hotel rooms, and the fact that they picked up her daughters and grandchild and drove over six hours to North Carolina and back were insignificant details, according to my mother's narrative. All she was concerned with, for the purposes of her current argument, was that they hadn't given her any money.

In the middle of that drama – that mixed-up potion of sorrow, relief and disgust – I was figuring out how to be a mother. The first few months were rewarding and challenging all at the same time as I learned what my son needed and how to give it to him. Living back with my mother, she was sweet and humane to me for a little bit, acting all nurturing and concerned, as if nothing horrible between us had happened. She came across as downright helpful.

After that though, she went right back to her usual jealous and mean-spirited ways, none of which took me by surprise. With all the experience I had with her by then, I wasn't surprised at all. After familiarizing myself with her patterns for so many years, I knew what to expect when she appeared sweet and nurturing. Well-trained to her behavior, I knew better than to think her niceness would last long. And sure enough, it didn't.

Meanwhile, Vince was pretty much absent from the picture, still mad about how I hadn't gone with his name-switch back at the hospital. Too busy throwing his temper tantrum, he had only seen his own child a couple of times since then.

After I went home with my mother, while I was busy taking care of our son, he called to inform me that if I didn't do what he wanted in this regard, that he and I were over. It was a real threat on his part, I knew. But at that point, I really didn't care. I'd already given up on our relationship anyway. It was good and over this time; I was already convinced of it. So his ultimatum earned an easy and effortless response.

"Oh well," I told him. "Well, I guess we're broken up then."

That must have been the last thing he expected. However, it's the one I gave him all the same. And when he did his usual and threw yet another tantrum, it didn't change my response. So he kept his threat. He stayed away. And in so doing, he didn't just abandon me; he abandoned our newborn son as well. Since he couldn't get his way in this one ridiculous aspect of parenting, he chose not to be a father at all.

Was I surprised? No, not at all. He had showed me nothing but horrible behavior and judgment for months and months. Why would I be surprised that he'd turned into an overnight deadbeat? Sure, I wanted a family. But that desire wasn't worth the dysfunction and abuse involved in trying to achieve it with him.

As such, I did everything on my own. Doctor's appointments. The late-night feedings. Grocery-store runs. Every single thing that came with being a new parent, I did on my own. But it was okay because my son was worth it. He was such a feisty little fella and just as cute as he wanted to be with his head full of hair, thick eyebrows, big beautiful brown eyes, and big smile that could melt the ice from the heart of anyone. He was a joy to look at - a blessing to appreciate.

So while being a single mother – which I considered myself to be – was difficult, I loved being able to do what I could for my baby. Besides, all of that experience I'd gotten living in my car and having to fend for myself had, indeed, given me the strength to do the same for my newborn.

That's not to say I always felt strong. I would find myself crying at night often enough due to exhaustion.

For many months, his father didn't come by. He certainly didn't help me financially or physically, never once showing up to doctor's appointments or helping out in any other way. This is not to say he was completely out of touch.

It seemed as though the more independent I got, the more vindictive and abusive he grew with what he would say to me over the phone. He hated the fact that I didn't want to be with him anymore, and he really hated that I didn't seem to need him anymore either. His greatest weapon was growing weaker and weaker with every passing day. Before, he would keep me in place – in his place, not mine – by using my love for him against me. Yet, my love for my son became much stronger than any remaining feelings I had for his father, and there was no way I wanted his kind of abuse affecting my baby.

I began to recognize that he wanted me to struggle, and he wanted me to need him. He wanted me to pick up that phone and comply with all of his ridiculous demands with nothing in exchange except for the supposed pleasure of his company. He'd already been so angry when I moved back in with my mom. But I wasn't about to feed into his ridiculousness anymore; I began to fight back. I began to stand up for myself, calling the police or going to court when necessary. I began to demand respect instead of begging for it.

I still hated confrontation. I still felt uncomfortable being assertive, mainly because I lacked a necessary amount of confidence and self-esteem to do so while still feeling comfortable. I lacked the sufficient amount of self-love needed for a woman to be completely strong and fearless. This was new for me. Protecting myself and standing up for myself weren't areas of strength for me; they were deficiencies I fully recognized.

I knew very well that my fight needed work, but I fought back anyway, if for no one else's sake but my son's.

Finally, he disappeared altogether for a few months, and my emotions for my ex-boyfriend were reduced to annoyance and the modicum of tolerance I had to allow as the technical co-parent of my son. But then he would return, trying to be a part of our lives again, blaming me for his absence and behavior as usual. Worse yet, he began lying to everyone, telling whomever he could that I was denying him access to his child.

That right there solidified in my mind that something was indeed wrong with him. How could someone disappear from his child's life, with no calls, no texts, no emails, nothing, and then turn around and blame the mother for his disappearing act? And no, I don't think he was just saying whatever he could to make me look bad. I think there was more to it than that. The way he argued with me about the subject and the way he spoke was as if somewhere in that twisted mind of his, he truly believed his ridiculous lie.

I suppose he also truly believed that there was a chance he could get me back into his abusive clutches, because he stepped up his game in time with mine. The more confident I became and the more comfortable I appeared without him, the more he tried to break me. He tried to break my reputation, and he tried to break my spirit. He hated that I was coming into my own. He resented me for leaving him in an attempt to be happy.

He hated me for trying to love myself.

Throughout all this, I was deliberately meeting new people and creating an identity for myself – a foundation I could call my own. I found myself networking, branching out and exploring my world, figuring myself out, and forming new relationships. All of those efforts led me into a local music studio, where I got paid to sing some hooks for certain artists in my area.

Yet my struggle for redemption – for growth and health and healing – was far from over. I was still naïve, so meeting new people could be a dangerous thing for me when I had no idea how to decipher between positive individuals and negative individuals.

As such, freshly out of an abusive relationship, if a man was nice to me, I treated it like it was the greatest gift in the world. Because, to me, it kind of was. I just wasn't used to being respected and shown common decency. Clearly, there was still a lot of room for improvement.

My mother babysat for me whenever I was out and about. It simply amazed me how much love she had for her grandchildren when she had such contempt for my sister and me. I continued to constantly wonder if that same love could be applied to the relationship she had with her own offspring, and whether she was trying to right her wrongs through our children. It was exceptionally weird regardless. She would disrespect my sister and me, showing us all the hate in the world, only to turn around and become "grandmother of the year" afterward.

Then again, for once, her vindictive behavior benefitted me. The older she got, the more bridges she burned, so she never went anywhere and never really left the house. When I was younger, she used to go out to places often enough. But she began secluding herself away from her larger family and the larger world to just stay in the house, which made her a very reliable babysitter.

That meant I was able to go out and network with people in order to create more and better opportunities for myself. My main goal was to be successful enough to be able to separate myself from my mother and my ex. I had dreams of becoming independent enough that I didn't need anyone or anything from anybody.

I just wanted for my son and me to live comfortably, with peace all around us. That was my goal. And the more hate those two certain people showed me, the more I pushed to become something for myself.

I would be with my son all day, then leave to go to work at a makeup store in the evening, then work part-time in the studio whenever someone wanted to hire me for a hook. Somehow, with that very busy schedule, I even managed to go on a few dates, which were overall nice and refreshing experiences. And always – always – the more confident I became, the more I wanted for me and my son.

As a mother, you learn as you go, in general, asking those you respect for advice along the way. For me, in particular, I didn't have anyone to talk to back when I was pregnant, so I bought a book about what to expect. And once my son was there and growing right in front of my eyes, I once again wasn't sure where to turn. Since my Aunt Lia had passed away, I began to realize more and more that she had been my only easily accessible example of a good mother. I knew if she was still with us, I could have asked her anything if I'd only gathered the nerve to do so. If I'd needed advice about discipline, learning strategies, home remedies, or anything else about motherhood, Aunt Lia would have opened her heart up to give me the best advice and help a young mother could ever want.

With that in mind, I found myself thinking a lot about everything I wanted to say to her, as if I was ready to open up and let my words escape my emotions. Knowing that it was too late for any such thing, I'd sit back and visualize the bond Aunt Lia had with her children whenever I felt lost, overwhelmed, or even just worried.

That was especially true as I began to realize how my son's behavior, compared to other children's, was more difficult to manage. He was much more hyper, aggressive and defiant, and his tantrums were much more intense as if he had absolutely no control over his behavior. It had gotten to the point where I needed my mother to babysit him just so I could go to the grocery store. Although I wanted to take him with me, I knew I wouldn't be able to get my errands done due to all the correcting, disciplining, and repeating I'd have to do just to keep him in line. I'd even considered buying one of those child leashes before to help rein him in. That's how hyper my son was.

But overall, I honestly took my son's behavior as being just a phase he was going through, and figured that there were areas I just needed to work on with him.

There was another aspect of my life that I knew needed some work, and that was my job. At times, I felt like a modern-day slave working for retail. I would bust my butt in that store, working hard, doing menial chores and tolerating tedious people, all for a small check every two weeks. Plus, I had to pay to park my car every day, so half of my money went straight to that, while the other half barely covered my car insurance.

Working in the studio could get me much better pay than selling makeup to a bunch of rude, superficial customers, I knew. That's why I determined that I just had to focus harder and do as many hooks as I could to make that goal a reality.

The little bit of money I was bringing in for a job I couldn't stand just wasn't worth it to me. I wanted something bigger. Something better. This is exactly what I started working toward, doing more networking, reading books about marketing and the music industry, and reading books about business in general.

I educated myself so that I wouldn't feel like such a guppy in a tank full of sharks.

Even so, I was very worried about my future. I still had no financial aid, yet I still had classes to finish before earning my degree. Yes, I had this dream and this talent that had nothing to do with a behavioral science degree. But I couldn't take too many risks in the music industry when I was a young single mother with no physical or financial help from my son's father.

Once again, I was trying to figure everything out alone. What was my purpose in life? Was I making the right decisions? I didn't know, but with so few other choices, I leaned on my own understanding. Sometimes it seemed to get me closer to where I wanted to go; sometimes it led in the opposite direction.

Depending on the understanding you have, it can potentially leave you more hurt and more accessible to failure. It can lead you straight down a blinded, muted path, where you're confident at being blind and deaf, hearing and seeing nothing, as if you're walking and breathing with your mind halfway functioning. As if you're partially unconscious.

No one can grow or survive that way. Growth comes from knowledge, experience, loving yourself and guidance. But some experiences are too damaging to recover from, leaving you beaten and feeling destroyed. These unhealthy experiences can eradicate you, leaving you with no path to return back to, because you simply can't find your way.

And the only element you're left with is this dark, plaguing fog that affects your senses, direction and stunts your personal and spiritual growth. Those are the risks that leaning on your own understanding involves, so it's a foolish choice to make when you don't have to go that route. But in my situation, depending on what I knew was all I had.

Looking back at that period, I know I made mistakes. I wanted so bad to find someone who could see so much spark within me that they'd dedicate their time and everything they knew to helping me grow, build, and manifest into the beautiful flames they knew I could become. And since I was already looking there, I made the mistake of thinking that someone like this could be found in the music industry. I was still that little girl yearning for a parental figure and desiring guidance.

But in an industry filled with greed, manipulative role models and sin, sometimes you lose your way. When all you can focus on is what you're so desperate to achieve, you end up wanting a certain lifestyle so badly – a new reality you can escape into – that you lose sight of what's really important, which is you. You end up abusing yourself trying to escape your horrible reality.

The people who run the entertainment industry know this very well, and they take full advantage of it. They take advantage of poor young kids with the most beautiful talent. They take advantage of the girl who's been abused and doesn't have a loving family of her own. They take advantage of the youth who need confirmation badly enough that they'll do anything to get it.

If you're misguided coming into this industry, you will die inside.

Perhaps I forgot that for a little bit, because I began to confide in certain individuals and groups that I apparently shouldn't have looked to as confidants.

Insane Producer

There were many times I was an apprentice to certain people in the industry in hopes of perfecting my craft and gaining some kind of exposure. I had a schedule where I would take care of my walking and talking toddler baby boy during the day, go to work at the studio getting paid to do hooks in the evenings, and on the weekends, learn from this one famous producer who was introduced to me by my sister. My mother was still my babysitter, which allowed for me to be a mommy and work on my career at the same time. I was green, and in a way, my producer loved the idea of a naive artist he could mold and control. He would help develop my sound while educating me about the certain things that occur in the industry I wanted to get into. He took the job of molding me seriously, and would assure me constantly that I could trust him with any and everything. He went by the name Chico, and he was a great influence musically. He was very talented and highly respected by fellow musicians and producers; he could play almost any instrument and was responsible for writing and producing a few hit records that won many awards. But the more time I spent with him, the more I realized how insane he actually was.

He was mean, cold and selfish. And called every woman he crossed paths with a "bitch," as if we all had that degrading name stamped on our birth certificates. During our first few visits with one another, I'd watch him get angry every time a college commercial played on TV; it was as if he regretted all the Grammy's he'd earned in the industry I so desperately wanted to be apart of. I would just sit down on the couch across from him flabbergasted by his chain smoking, use of language and sudden mood changes.

And although he was a bit mad, he was a genius at what he did. He would teach me about melodies and lyrical techniques, and the more I worked with him, the better I became. And the drunker we got, the more I accepted his musical insanity. I can recall a few times dozing off on the couch after an all-nighter as I usually would, just to catch him sitting down beside me, slowly caressing my face with his fingertips as if I was his newly-prized pet pooch.

And because of how afraid I was of his sporadic behavior, I didn't dare open my eyes or say one word. I just lay there, hoping that his gentle forehead strokes wouldn't turn into some sick psychopathic love scene.

One night, during one of our many songwriting sessions, I'd experienced my first case of writer's block, and with Chico being the kind of person you don't want to disappoint, I was more than terrified of his reaction.

But instead of scolding me as I assumed he would, he became interested in wanting to know why my mind drew blank at the topic. But in the back of that very same mind, I knew he already made his presumptions from studying what kind of broken individual I was since the first day we met.

But I entertained his curiosity anyway, and I began to tell him a brief summary of my life's story. And surprisingly, he was understanding and attentive the entire time; he even opened up about some of his own life experiences as well. And as I continued to learn from him, moments like this happened often, with him trying to seem relatable to me. But of course this gentle side of him didn't last long, as he proceeded to reel me in emotionally, just to torment me for the sake of creating better music.

This toxic relationship went uninterrupted until the day it ended with his hands around my neck. He finally allowed his anger to get the best of him, and strangled me until I passed out. I woke up to him caressing my face in the palm of his hand all while apologizing repeatedly for what he had done.

After that, I wanted out and I wanted to get far away from him, and that's what I did. He made attempts to get back in my good graces after that incident, but I was completely done with him. I was disgusted with myself for even allowing this person to treat me the way he did for so long. I felt foolish for not learning from my past abuse. I wanted a better life for my son and me so badly that I took the mistreatment and covered it up completely with this perspective of the bigger picture.

My son was still in his toddler stages, getting into any and everything, exploring his world, pushing his limits and learning as he went along. And so was I. I realized that the music industry was filled with nothing more than deceitful, greedy people who'd been traumatized by the people before them. Abusers from past abusers, traumatized by certain situations and affected by the mistreatment of an industry that could never love them back.

I had my share of run-ins with horrible managers and artists, and after my last situation with Chico, I was done trying to learn the industry through the eyes of anyone else. I made a decision to just do things on my own, learning the hard way as I went, as I was so used to doing.

It's painful living life by one golden rule.

To trust no one.

Because no one will care about you; they may act like it…

But no one will love you

You are as valuable as what you can offer, and when your spark goes out in this ever-changing business ran by an ever-changing society, selling your soul may be the only thing that may revive your opportunities. Desperate for the money and addicted to the need of feeling accepted by people you don't even know, or those who don't give a damn about you, people may view you as a jester and nothing more.

And the greater your rejection, and the more intense the cruelty you receive becomes, the more you feel obligated to prove your critics wrong. In your heart, you believe you will never be good enough for anyone. Not good enough to be sincerely loved and not good enough to be genuinely liked. The pressure will eat your soul alive until you barely recognize the individual mocking you in the mirror.

I've felt this way my entire life and I've subconsciously returned back to the mistreatment I was so used to getting. It's a constant internal pressure, and there's no peace from the verbal assault, no peace from envious and judgmental people who know nothing about you, and no peace from the unhealthy motives of others.

These industry people made me scared to leave the house and network; the trust issues I already had got worse. I felt vulnerable and I hated it. So I got accustomed to networking online and over the phone. I never worked with people in the studio one-on-one. I would do my set of tasks separately from everyone else and electronically send my clients my work so that I would never have to be in the presence of anyone except my engineer who I was comfortable being around. I wanted away from these horrible personalities and put great effort in doing so. With everything I'd already been through in life, why in the world would I want to subject myself to more of that?

Challenges

Back at home, the older my son got, the more his behavioral issues became apparent, making me weep too many times over. I would look at him while he slept, and I would cry. He was coming out of his toddler stages and facing many difficulties and the more I tried to make sense of it, the more I wept. I would caress his cute little face and just cry, worrying about my child's mental development. I would sit there and just cry seeing the beauty that had been created by so much pain. Reflecting on my pregnancy, I asked myself if his conduct had anything to do with how I was treated and what I had been through when I was pregnant. If my situation had been any different, would my son still be struggling the way he was?

That question was a powerful one, and I began to obsess over this better life that I knew I wanted for the two of us.

I began studying little Lance's behavior and keeping track of all of his behavioral patterns, so every time we visited his primary physician, I could discuss with her what I've been noticing, and what she's been noticing as well. Both his doctor and I kept close watch of Lance's behavioral changes in hopes he was just going through a phase he would eventually grow out of.

And as I continued being a single mom, I resumed to overwork myself, staying up all hours of the day and night trying to change our circumstances. I would take Lance to school and then continue to work. I was a machine, putting in hours non-stop, disregarding my pleading body when it was tired and wanting to stop. I was obsessed with the thought of a healthier and wealthier life. I was obsessed with the thought of me and my son trading in the life we had for a better one.

Naturally, with that busy schedule, I didn't get much sleep and found myself taking naps that I really didn't want to be taking in the middle of the day. I wanted a better life financially for us so badly that I neglected the most important elements of life: love, health, spirituality, integrity and peace. I neglected myself, I neglected my soul. I couldn't value peace, because I didn't know what that was. I couldn't value love, because I hadn't received much of it and I most certainly couldn't value the importance of family because I didn't have a healthy one.

I love my son immensely, but do I love myself as well?

I take care of my son all day everyday, but do I take care of myself too?

Do I love myself enough to take care of my emotional and spiritual well-being?

Life leads with love, and it ends the same way. What you put out into the universe is what you will get back. This I didn't know, my perspectives weren't that well put together. I gave my Universe anger, despair, sadness, confusion and an unhealthy lifestyle.

In return, my Universe gave it back.

I wasn't fulfilling the purpose God had planned for me, I couldn't even love myself enough to hear God's words, to speak to him, or to take and appreciate his guidance. My pain and struggles were meant for something greater.

But this I didn't know.

So I continued to live life, lost.

Tired Soul

During this time, Vince began to leap in and out of our lives for all of the wrong reasons. He never wanted to co-parent civilly, and his main concern was to torment me; it was never to be a good dad to our son. He would come around just to bring his wickedness in my direction, causing conflict over issues that shouldn't require any. The more confident I seemed to become without him, the more he would try to win me back in order to destroy me all over again, as if he needed me to be at my lowest of lows at the hands of him only.

Every time he came to the realization that I wasn't interested in having a personal relationship with him any longer, he would grow angrier still. The more I showed him that all I wanted was a co-parenting relationship, the more vindictive and bitter he became.

With no thought of the potential consequences, he would try to harm me physically and emotionally, never once stopping to consider how it could affect my ability to take care of our child. He just didn't care. Full of such rage, he didn't like it when other people liked me or complimented me; you could see the anger that slowly covered his face every time someone was nice to me in front of him, or favored something about me, or liked what I wore. With every compliment that came my way, his cheekbones and temples would pulsate with rage as if he was trying hard to hold himself together, as if he could self-combust into flames at any given moment.

That's one thing he couldn't hide, at least not from me. His rage. He struggled with that more often than not as if it took too much energy to hold up his charming facade for such a long period of time. He was unpredictable. And the worst part about it was that he never saw his behavior as being wrong or abusive at all.

He would do horrible things to me, and then lie to me and everyone else about ever doing it at all. He acted as if I'd ruined our family and relationship. He went about life hating me and hurting me because I wanted out of his abusive control. Because I wanted out, I had to suffer. Because I didn't want to take his cruelty, he had the right to try to make my life miserable. He was a sociopath, a toxic individual who created his own reality of his innocence in his head, while causing pain in the lives of others.

Abusers – they'll manipulate and they'll lie to you. And when you no longer give them that power, they'll try to manipulate your family or the people close to you instead. I'd seen it before so many times over with my mom, and now I got to see another human being display such reprehensible traits, trying to alter how other people saw me.

Abusers want everyone to hate you just as much as they do. It's sick. Their lack of morals and integrity is sick. The amount of hate they harbor in their hearts is sick, as are their psychopathic or sociopathic traits. He was doing his best to brutalize and harass me all because I'd left him because he didn't treat me right.

Attempting to ruin my self-esteem and the potential I saw in myself seemed to be his only goal in life. It was like he gained pleasure from making me suffer, along with making my life as a mother hard. He absolutely enjoyed himself at my expense. Of that, I have no doubt.

During his so-called visits to see our son, it was very clear that he couldn't or wouldn't control his rage around me. He would scream in my face, telling me that no one would ever like or love me but him. He would tell me I was pathetic, doing and saying everything he could to try to tear my confidence apart and convince me that I was nothing more than the pitiful soul I once thought I was.

He tried as hard as he could.

But something was changing in me. I was recognizing that those hateful words and his hateful behavior should have no place in my reality anymore. I had broken free, and I deserved to stay that way. Moreover, I was going to stay that way.

Being around people other than him, broadening my social horizons even just a little bit, allowed me to see my worth, my talents, and what I was capable of doing. I was able to see how grateful people were to be in my presence, that they actually enjoyed my company. They liked me and considered me a worthwhile person to be around, which made this ex of mine - and his opinion - in the minority. He could not determine who I was anymore.

So one day, when he decided to come by my house again under the excuse of seeing our son, I let him know all of that in an extremely clear manner. By then, he had already begun voicing his opinions of just how horrible a person I was. Reciting his same old lines of abuse, he tried pushing all my buttons in order to get a hurtful reaction out of me.

But on that particular, beautiful day, the only reaction he received was one of confidence.

When he looked me up and down with disgust and said, "Look at you," I just twirled around with a big grin on my face, flipped my hair and replied, "Yeah, LOOK AT ME," with all the confidence I'd gathered back within myself since leaving his side.

I felt it too. I felt the appreciation I had for myself. It was powerful!

He felt it too; I could tell. And boy was he angry about it.

Yet I hadn't said what I did to make him angry. And whether he liked it or not didn't bother me. My reaction was for myself and my spirit, not his.

Seeing my smile shining on my face with my newfound self-esteem brought about an intensely different reaction from him. You could see the lividness on his face and feel the hate in his soul. He left after that, but not without throwing a tantrum, which involved him flinging juice all over my mother's living room floor. As if that wasn't immature enough, on his way out, he kicked our son's stroller and spat in my face.

I know what he wanted me to do in response. He wanted some kind of an emotional outpouring, tears or apologies, or better yet, me begging him to take me home with him. But I didn't do any of it. Instead, I calmly called the police, starting off a chain of restraining orders and court visits, which would eventually end up with me gaining full custody of my son, although I had already been taking care of him full-time anyway. But there was a lot that happened in between. A whole lot.

He didn't take that very well. Then again, I didn't expect him to. I was simply doing the mature, responsible thing in light of his irrational, childish behavior.

Admittedly, I never expected him to go as far as he did.

He kept texting me, trying to break me down through his written words until I got sick of the abuse and told him I was just done. I didn't want to be with him, I explained, and then I let him know why. I told him that he treated me horribly, and the only thing I wanted out of him was a co-parent. That was it and nothing more. I was as direct as I'd ever been that he didn't then and never would have another chance with me. I just wasn't interested in being degraded anymore.

To that, he texted back to tell me that he didn't like the situation and that he was going to do something about it. Then that is precisely what he did.

Vince ran off to the commissioner's office, where he wrote a false report about how I'd assaulted and tried to kill him, which resulted in a warrant for my arrest. This disgusting vessel of a person actually got me thrown into jail with his deliberate lies and tenacious bitterness, all because I didn't want to be with him. This was the beginning of many false reports and orders Vince would write up in hopes of getting my son taken away from me, or in hopes of me being thrown in jail.

Apparently, it did not occur to him that he'd left his own son temporarily motherless in the process. Collateral damage. He really just didn't care.

Sitting in jail, I found myself crying and thinking about my son. Thank God he was at home with my mother and not with his other babysitter that day. Because my ex went driving around to my various family members' homes, looking for my son to take him away from me. Every single one of them refused to tell him anything, since they knew what kind of person he was, either having seen him abusing me or hearing about it. Either way, even if my child was with any of them, they would never have allowed him to take my baby boy.

There's no good reason for him to have tried to do what he did. He only wanted to hurt me, and he didn't care who he had to hurt in the process to do it, even his own child. He'd already shown as much, though this latest example of his depravity was the lowest he'd sunk so far.

After all, this was the son he didn't mind abandoning because he couldn't get his name changed. A son he'd once left stranded at the grocery store with his mother after he stole her keys and threw them outside during one of his many tantrums. A son he was "supporting" with $84 a month in child support. And when I told him that wasn't enough to make much of a difference, he told his entire family that I was a gold digger.

This person didn't care about my son or me. All he cared about was getting back at me for leaving.

I did get out of jail, but only on the condition of being placed on house arrest until the trial. It was something I intended to fight, and I clearly needed a lawyer in order to do that.

During this time, somehow, my mother and biological father began to reunite over the phone. Really, it appeared to happen overnight. And so it was my biological father who ended up paying for my legal counsel.

All the charges ended up being dropped before too long, but not because my lawyer beat it. My ex made it quite clear that the only way he would drop the charges was if I stayed with him – if I begged him to take me back, in fact. Scared about the possibility of a future where I was in jail, separated from my child, I caved. I did it. I begged.

I cried while I did too. Not because I actually wanted a relationship with him again, of course. I cried because I felt trapped right back into a life of torment, where getting out had just been made impossible.

He had me physically, but nothing more. I no longer loved this abuser I was tied to. I despised every evil little piece that made up his foul soul. If his aura could speak, it would probably kill with words alone. I agreed verbally, but in my heart, mind, body, and soul, I wasn't in a relationship with him and never wanted to be.

Saved from a prison sentence, yes, I'd still managed to go right back to another form of confinement. A form of slavery, even. I continued to live at my mother's house, but I was scared that if I tried to break up with him again, he would press false charges again and, this time, he wouldn't retract them. I lived in abject fear of what he might do next, thinking about my son's future the entire time. Every moment when I could actually gather up the nerve to leave this man, I would end up thinking about my child, about how he needed his mother with him, not in jail. And then I'd lose my will to fight all over again.

I couldn't comprehend why this ex of mine would want to keep me around as some kind of prisoner. Why hold me captive like this? Why not find someone else and leave me the hell alone?

Caught in this kind of cage, I felt unsafe all the time. For a while there, I had no one to really protect me from this lunatic – which he knew. I'm sure he enjoyed it too. All the while, knowing how he was a coward who was scared of other men even while he didn't mind abusing women, I would dream of a relationship with some tough man who could save me from this hell I was living in.

This is when I started to learn the extent of the abuse Vince's mother went through at the hands of her father, bringing me more and more clarity in the process. Every single thing about what had happened to me ever since this man walked into my life began to make sense. And the more it did, the more I wanted my son to be far, far away from it.

I recall how, one time, Vince's mother sat me down and told me that I shouldn't be with someone who treated me the way her son did. She actually went so far as to try convincing me to leave him, not knowing that I'd tried a dozen times. Despite this, I honestly never felt as if she cared about me or my well-being. She said what she did in order to keep her son out of jail and out of trouble.

She knew he was abusive and immature, with severe anger problems. And she would, on occasion, express her worries for his mental state. But that was it. She never actually did anything about it. Overall, she was his enabler, advising him on how to weasel his way out of the destruction he kept causing instead of correcting it. And the thought of her influencing my son next, either directly or through her own son, was terrifying.

I didn't want him growing up thinking it was okay to roam this earth hurting people - hurting women specifically - or robbing people at gunpoint for their cars, which was something his father had done before.

I didn't want my son thinking it was okay to spit in a woman's face simply because she'd expressed an opinion. Or push a woman up against a car so hard that the resulting bruise on her arm was over a foot long.

I didn't want my son to end up like his father. I wanted him to experience a life without abuse. I wanted him to have something I'd never had - a peaceful, stable life, with loving people constantly surrounding him. I wanted him to understand that, yes, there was a dark side to this world, but he didn't have to live among all that negativity. He would need to know it was there, of course - to know it was bad. He could even learn to feel the pain that side of life could offer by listening to me and my stories. But baby boy, don't you ever in a million years go into that life of darkness through your own poor actions and decisions.

I wanted my son to know and fully understand that there was so much better awaiting him.

What Love?

Through all of this, I constantly had another impediment in my way as I tried to build a better life. And that would be my own mother.

I watched as she competed for my own son's love. Jealous as always, she wanted any and everyone to love her more than they loved me – something I never understood. Yet that was how she operated with all of her grandchildren. Moreover, her way of doing that was by taking discipline out of the equation altogether, making my sister and me look like the bad guys when we did have to discipline our children.

As a parent, I can say this without hesitation: If a child does something wrong or dangerous, you correct them immediately. You don't allow him or her to continue thinking those negative actions are appropriate and okay to execute. A lack of discipline turns into an array of bad habits. Those bad habits can then turn into a lack of morals. And a lack of morals too often turns into a generational curse that can be passed down from father to son and mother to daughter.

When you allow a child to lie, hit and yell at adults, that's not love. Yet this was just a few of the many things my mother would let her grandchildren get away with, especially my son.

That kind of leniency teaches children to fall into immoral and even criminal mindsets. If Lance thinks it's okay to yell at and hit adults as an adolescent, what else will he find appropriate when he's an adult?

My mother couldn't see that kind of logic and nurturing mentality though. All she could see were her goals of gaining favoritism over her grandchildren's mothers. To my knowledge, not one time did she take into consideration the damage her behavior could cause to my son and nephews mentally.

She didn't want to be a part of the village they say it takes to raise a child; she wanted to be in competition with it. When she was around, I would see my nephews misbehave terribly and get away with every single mischievous action they thought up. She would even go so far as to whisper in their ears how horrible, unfair, and mean my sister and I were when we attempted to discipline them in front of her. She went out of her way to plant bad seeds into our own children about life and about their mothers.

Not surprisingly, this caused an even bigger rift between she and her daughters. We both stood up to her, openly and verbally fixing the wrong she was causing when it came to these precious, growing lives. It felt like a never-ending battle, where we constantly had to correct them in front of her, telling them how wrong she was for allowing them to misbehave the way they did, and that there was no way they would grow up to be respectable men listening to our mother's nonsense.

I passionately and determinedly wanted what was best for my child. My son. The love of my life. He was the greatest thing I'd ever created, and looking at him, I felt like Picasso admiring the beauty of my work. This was true love.

Every night, I'd go into his room and bombard his cute little cheeks with as many kisses as my lips could allow. He made me overprotective, nurturing, and so proud and excited when he learned qualities I hardly learned from my mother. They were my own by instinct. Always curious to know what was on his mind and how he felt, I wanted to know how his days were in school and if there was anything bothering him that he wanted to get off his mind. I wanted him to tell me everything so that I could help him when he couldn't solve a problem for himself. And I would create strategies to strengthen his thought process so that, as he got older, he could analyze issues more efficiently on his own.

Essentially, I wanted the best for him. I wanted him to have the best and be the best. When my son was born, that was when I understood love fully.

But as usual, wherever love and I coincided, my mother was rarely too far behind in a mission to destroy it with her manipulating ways.

As such, I would discipline my son after he'd done something wrong, sending him to his room for a timeout. After I had lectured him on his behavior and got his young mind to open up to new perspectives so that he could learn to see more clearly, after I'd made sure to tell my son why he was wrong while making him understand the consequences of his actions, she would go into his room too and attempt to undo every single piece of integrity and morality that I'd just worked so hard to instill.

I would hear her telling him that nothing was his fault, that the faults were all mine. She would continue with how wrong I was and how much nicer she was than me. My innocent son was becoming a victim to my mother's sick mind. And that, I wasn't going to tolerate.

So I'd go back in myself to confront her about what she was saying and doing. This created many arguments between the two of us, naturally. I wanted to instill structure and knowledge within my son. I wanted him to walk and speak with morals. I wanted him to know right from wrong and how to conduct himself appropriately as he grew up. And all my mother wanted to do was destroy those important lessons. She was willing to destroy my relationship with my own son just to feel special.

My son would break things, smear his feces all over the carpet, yell, and talk back to adults. He was a bit defiant, and he needed structure – and I knew it. But every time I tried to give him that structure, or every time I had to pop him on the mouth or hand for disrespecting me or some other adult – even my mother, at times – she would run into his room and say the most horrible things to him about how I was a bad mother and that, if it were up to her, he wouldn't get in trouble at all.

She'd be smiling the whole time too.

This became a cycle I had to deal with constantly. And the harder I fought to correct her words, the harder she manipulated and the meaner she was to me.

Judging by her past behavior and what I already knew about her, not to mention how she grinned whenever she saw how upset I'd get, she enjoyed my frustrations. She enjoyed watching me struggle to discipline my son and clean up her messes.

Between Vince and my mother's impaired judgment, my son was at risk of having little to no morals at all – at risk of being another unconscious young black man. I knew I needed to separate him and myself from all these negative influences. I knew I needed nothing but good, positive, spiritually connected people around us.

Still held in some sick kind of captivity by Vince, I decided that the only way I was going to be able to break free was to date and find a good man who actually treated my son and me the way we deserved to be treated. There was one giant problem to that plan though.

I was scared to death.

I was scared of picking another wrong guy. I was afraid of being sent back in time to a place where I was even more imprisoned and being abused, misused, and mistreated like I had been before. I was mentally drained and, honestly, had grown to despise men. I viewed them as horrible, lying, manipulating, disloyal creatures. Every single one of them. It wasn't right, but I was going off of too many harsh lessons I'd learned in life.

Unfortunately, I was also going off of too many harsh lessons learned when it came to picking a new man. I knew nothing about creating and maintaining a healthy relationship, or what to expect from it. In a way, I was brainwashed to be attracted to unhealthy relationships, having been told one too many times that abuse is love, and love is abuse.

Imagine being a dog for a moment. A dog only knows dog food until you introduce him to table fare. If his master never gives him scraps of steak and potato from time to time, then – in his mind and in his world – all he knows and all he's aware of when it comes to culinary options is his dog food. That's all there is. That means that, when he's hungry, he's conditioned to salivate and think about his dog food. Because he just can't visualize the taste of something he's never had.

This is how I was while trying to identify the good men vs. the bad ones. I hadn't yet had the pleasure of tasting steak and potatoes. All I'd ever had was dog food.

Trying to Escape

There was this guy who eased into my life amid all of this dysfunction between my mother and my son's father. He was a DJ I met through networking. At the time, I was more than ready to be done with the abuse, and I wanted to put my fears aside and try my hand at dating. This was while Vince was still around, still occupied by trying to keep me captive by cruelty that took my self-esteem right back down to being low, brittle, and damaged. I was vulnerable, and it was very evident.

An abused woman is an obvious woman. You can sense the lack of value she has for herself, which makes her an easy target for more abuse.

At the time, I was a tired single mother to a cute but rowdy boy. And this DJ was a charming New Yorker with a fitted hat, Timberland boots and the baggy jeans to match. His name was Tyrone and I met him at the bar during an event, and we were together every day after that.

There was a lot to like about him. He was family-oriented and had many kids of his own. While I was rather looking for a new relationship to keep me safe from the current one, it was Tyrone's family-oriented approach to everything that really got me interested. Family was important to him, and bonds were too. So I really did think that this could be the right relationship for me when he loved my son and treated him as his own, acting very protective of the both of us. After years of feeling unsafe, that protection he provided felt like something we needed.

Ten years older than me, he would encourage me to be myself – to find myself. He encouraged my creativity, no matter how much of an amateur I might have been. Under his guidance, I began to live life and discover new things about myself. This man opened my mind to my creativity as an individual, spurring me to play around with makeup, clothes, and new looks.

Little by little, my self-esteem began to mend from all the abuse that my mother and Vince had done to me all those years. Plus, we had lots of fun together. So much fun. He would bring his daughter, and I would bring my son, and it felt good. He was giving me that family structure I'd always wanted.

And as long as I was with this man, Vince didn't have the courage to harass me anymore. For once in my life, Vince left me alone. I felt safe with him, even safe from my mother.

This new boyfriend of mine personally witnessed how my mother treated me and even had some choice words for her in response. Naturally, she hated Tyrone because of that, which resulted in her trying to sabotage my relationship with him many times over.

She called him on the phone to leave obnoxious and irrational voicemails, and she did the same thing with texts, trying to create as much ruckus and chaos as possible in hopes that he'd get fed up and leave me. But the more she tried to break us up, the crazier she appeared. Moreover, he didn't leave me.

I began to live life and get out more - both Lance and me. We went to museums, restaurants, beaches and hotel getaways. Tyrone traveled a lot for jobs and he always wanted us to come along with him. I loved it that way, because it meant I barely had to see my mother – and neither did my son. I appeared happy, and my son was having a great time.

The sad thing was that over time, Tyrone wasn't as great as he appeared to be. He had many flaws that just couldn't be ignored, and trust me, I tried in order to preserve our family-oriented lifestyle.

He was a pathological liar who would fib about any and everything. And he would cheat on me constantly whenever he went out of town without me. One evening after experiencing women's intuition, I went through his phone, finding all sorts of vulgar text messages he'd had with other women throughout the course of our relationship. He had cheated on me with about six different women within a six-month period alone.

It was a devastating realization. I felt as if my world had crashed down on me. The heart I was brave enough to give him after years of abuse - he took it and brutalized it. I felt as though he crushed my happiness and the possibilities for more of it.

I was loyal, loving, faithful and open. I kept thinking, how could a person gather up such nerve to betray someone who is so good to them - someone who did nothing but try to love them?

I drove all the way home in the middle of the night for two hours crying non-stop when I found out about his infidelity, thinking along the way what I could have done wrong for him to do this to me.

I was feeling as if maybe I wasn't good enough of a girlfriend. When I got home, I went straight into my room to cry and think some more.

Despite trying to suppress my whimper into my bedroom pillows, my mother still heard the cries. She opened up my room door and caught me sobbing and distraught. Looking pitiful, drowning in a face full of my own tears. She stood at my doorway watching for a little while before she asked me what was wrong, and while my mind was reluctant to answer, my emotions weren't. I began to tell her a snippet of what happened, as our house phone began to ring off the hook with Tyrone on the other end.

And once she got the details, my mother answered the next time it rang, happily informing him to never call again. She then looked me in the eyes and said, "You should get checked out."

After that comment, I asked her to leave.

I gave her a snippet because deep down, I knew there wasn't going to be an "I'm so sorry." No trying to wipe away my tears. No giving me the "you're a great young woman and you deserve better" speech. I also knew that what I had just confided in her would come back to haunt me the second she got angry with me. But as I always did, I hoped for some compassion from her anyway.

Of course, my phone continued to ring throughout the week, which led into months of him trying to explain everything away and rationalize it. Sometimes I would pick up the phone just to hear what he had to say. It was as if my brain and heart were battling each word and phrase that came out of his mouth, knowing what I shouldn't do but having the urge to disregard my gut instincts anyway. And of course, it didn't take long for my mother to throw my break-up in my face during one of our many arguments. She yelled at me, "That's why you lost your man," which gave me another reason why I should never confide in her ever again.

This time apart from Tyrone made me think.

I thought about the family setting we'd built.

I thought about how my son would feel losing his father figure and me losing a protector.

I was scared to lose the safest situation I thought I had at the time, as if the options for a better man didn't exist for me.

I had been abused so bad and for so long, that this situation is something I would consider safe. I fooled my own mind, playing the happy moments that we shared together over and over in my head, while blocking out the possibility that all of our happy moments were most likely shared with other women.

So I ended up giving this relationship one more try.

Not for love, but for the sake of my constructed environment.

I stayed for the family setting I had always dreamt about.

Soon after a while, his cheating didn't bother me anymore; he had already broken my heart so there was nothing else left for him to break. We continued enjoying our beautiful facade and didn't think much of it.

I even started going on dates with other men, and deep down I knew Tyrone knew it, but he couldn't dare speak on something he also did himself.

And soon, tables began to turn and I was the one appearing to be committed, while dating on the side.

And it felt great.

I felt free and empowered.

The more free spirited I became, the more he tried to get back into my good graces. And the more confident I became, the more his insecurities grew.

I began to change as a person, turning cold and unconcerned of his feelings. I saw Tyrone as my handbag and nothing more. I wasn't that young girl he could continue to hurt anymore; I was now a kitty on a prowl.

Our relationship continued like this for about another year. Until one day, I just decided I was done. I had lost so much respect for this man that I couldn't even stand to be anywhere near him. We weren't even intimate anymore. We were living a lie, holding on tight to what we both wanted - family structure.

We wanted it, but ruined our chances of it.

And now all we had to show for it were these facades.

I ended up hurt and angry; I compromised my integrity and ignored what I really desired out of life.

I didn't really want boyfriends outside of our relationship. I wanted a healthy relationship and a family of my own. That's what I craved so very much. But my bitterness, disappointment, and heartbreak took control of my emotions and my judgment, letting anger change me.

Perspectives

Tyrone knew of my background of abuse and mistreatment. He knew how difficult it was for me to open up to him, and he knew he'd initially brought me to a place of trust. Yet, he did what he did anyway, and then refused to change his extremely bad habits. Oh, he would protect me from anyone and everything else, but not himself. That was asking too much, apparently.

Recognizing his good qualities, I asked myself time after time whether I should just settle for what I had - a man who halfway showed me that he loved me.

For my part though, I made sure to be far less invested. If you protect your feelings well enough, you can survive in any relationship. That's the way I viewed it at least, and so I made sure to keep a good part of my emotions out of the equation. I figured that if I just kept the love I had for my son and myself, I would never feel the pain of a broken heart ever again.

There were plenty of times during this phase where I'd simply sit down and think about what love actually was. Watching other couples around me, I would focus on the woman in particular, asking myself if she'd perhaps gone through the same thing as me. I wondered whether she loved someone who acted on the ability to break her heart into bits and pieces, just to pick them up and try to mend them back together again.

But anyone who looks at life realistically and maturely can tell you that mending only goes so far. The altered object or person is never really the same as it was before. No matter what tools or strategies one tries to use to fix the damage, it will never be the same.

There might be pieces that are lost. Other parts might be too broken to repair. There could be cracks that still show through whatever materials you used to try to cover up the imperfections created from the break. And the more something breaks or the more pieces you lose, the more difficult it becomes to repair until repairing is no longer an option at all.

Nobody wants to feel like a fool for loving someone. Yet this was the third significant relationship where I was left feeling that way after trying so hard to let someone love me. Yes, my mother fits solidly onto that list. With three solid examples, I figured that it wasn't worth it to fully love anyone. Why open up my heart for more of that kind of pain? Why risk my feelings?

By the time I finally left this man for good, the truest part of me still wanted a real relationship, but the hardened part of me was convinced that men were nothing but liars and cheaters. Trusting one of them, I was convinced, was the most foolish thing a woman could ever do.

That was my viewpoint, and I was sticking to it. I stuck to it for quite some time too. Whenever my eyes settled on a man, I'd see a taker; I'd see a soul-snatcher like some kind of creature that crawled from the abyss with one evil purpose in mind. I walked around believing that all men would eventually rob you of your compassion, good judgment, and everything that made you a loving human being, leaving you empty, bitter and dry.

Obviously, I was very jaded. Looking back now, I can see that I began entertaining men who were no good for me since, deep down inside, I didn't want it to work out. I wanted a reason to escape before I was too emotionally invested.

Relationships became like a drug for me, where one was never enough to satisfy my cravings. Addicted to synthetic love, I'd search it out like a seasoned addict, taking in a taste of what someone else thought was love. And then, when the relationship became distasteful, I'd take the nearest exit, leaving them begging me to come back through emails and phone messages.

Sometimes I cared, and sometimes I didn't. Either way, I knew they were no-good males in the first place. I was too smart to not recognize that on some level. And I was too smart to let that kind of man get a real hold on me again. I just wasn't smart enough to give real love a try. Not yet. Not when my past attempts at real love had hurt so badly.

Basically, my heart was scared, and so I chose to stay ignorant – ignorant to everything and everyone that was real love or had real love. As a result, I was turning into my mother, hurting and hurting others with little to no remorse.

The cycle was clearly continuing.

Control

Every day, my dearest mother would treat my son nicely and treat me like dirt. She would leave the house every morning saying "I love you" and "have a great and blessed day" to every living creature in the house except for me. She would specifically call each name out so that they didn't feel excluded, and then she would just as specifically not call mine.

At that time, it was only her, my son, our two pet cats and me.

We continued to fight about her attempts to manipulate my child against me. Every other day, it seemed as though a new fight over the old issues would occur. To retaliate against my disapproval, she would purposely slam doors and leave her TV on really loud in the morning before she left in order to disturb my sleep or simply irritate me. I might very well be up all night working at my music or marketing efforts, which she'd very well know, but that would give her one more reason or opportunity to be cruel.

She continued to tell me I was nothing because I'd lost my man and my looks. She told me that nothing great would ever come out of my music. And since she and my father were speaking more often, she would call him to tell him that I was never going to make it as an artist – that I was destined to continuously fail in life because I wasn't being nice to her and that's the reason God was punishing me.

I would stand by to hear her speak lies about me to my own father, bashing every inch of what makes me as she laughed and giggled from her own cruel entertainment. And the first thing that would cross my mind was why my father would continue to sit on that phone with her and entertain her bashing his own daughter.

I became numb; the anger I'd developed, transformed into not feeling anything at all.

As her levels of abuse grew, so did my tolerance for it.

After a while, I would sit back and listen to her try to manipulate my father into not liking me or loving me anymore, and I would smile as I cared less and less for them both. And when she attempted to antagonize me further, taunting me with hurtful words, taunting me with the better relationship she appeared to have with my father, I would look at her and that disgusting grin she'd have plastered on her face, and simply would tell her to "Shut the fuck up."

The amusing part to my response was her shocked and puzzled reaction. Putting her hand on her chest, where her cold dark heart would be, as she quickly turned herself into victim of the year. She would then call me evil, a demon and the devil as she had always done. She really acted as if I was supposed to continue to allow her to treat me the way she had all of these years. She would then continue her charade by calling up my father and giving him more one-sided details about what had just happened. She would explain the situation as if I had just come into her room and verbally attacked her with no cause or reason. And as she told her lies over the phone, I would yell the truth at the top of my lungs for the both of my so-called parents to hear. I would yell about how she went out of her way to hit me subliminally. I would yell about all of her overtly belittling comments. I screamed about her urge to antagonize me until I snapped. I felt as if years of bottled up emotions came fizzing up to the top of my head until I verbally exploded.

I made sure they both knew that they could kiss my ass at any given moment. I had grown tired; I was tired of allowing people to treat me any kind of way. And I was mostly tired of the feelings I had to feel after being abused.

The more me and my son stayed there, the more I worked towards earning enough money for us to finally be able to move. I knew full well that she was letting me stay there for two reasons and two reasons only – her grandson and the fact that she would lose her Housing Opportunities Commission voucher and the food stamp money I was getting if I moved out. I was becoming much, much more savvy about her situation.

At first, I began educating myself on business-related matters because I never wanted to get screwed over in the industry I was working so hard to make it in. As such, I took great interest in anything pertaining to contracts. But one thing usually leads to another, and so it did in this particular situation.

Knowing how she was on the HOC aid list, I began to research how housing assistance worked. That's how I discovered that, if HOC found out that I moved out with my son, she would lose that entire voucher that very same day. And then she'd be forced to pay the entire rent portion on the townhouse we were living in at the time.

As soon as I discovered that detail, I let her know I was aware of it. I refused to allow her to kick us out; that was not something I planned on letting happen. So I told her that if she ever tried to compromise our living situation, I would report her to HOC.

Naturally, she hated that, and she tried to get me back by acting as rude and nasty as possible to any friend I happened to invite into the house. She'd say that she didn't want me to have any company because I was disrespectful. She used any and every excuse she had to deny my friends from coming over, as if she couldn't stand the sight and sound of another person taking any liking to me. Here I was having to speak up and out to protect my son's mental and emotional growth, and to protect myself from her constantly, and she had the nerve to consider me the disrespectful one. She was just as delusional as Vince. Two abusers in a pod, ready to destroy any person who spoke up and out against their cruelty.

She wanted to control who liked me and who loved me, as if stopping these people from entering her house would destroy my friendships. My mother would go through extreme, desperate lengths to run people away from me, but all it ever did was make her look more like a nutcase each and every time.

Many times, I even offered to help pay the rent; I would watch as her eyes lit up like a Christmas tree, and then see them quickly diminish after her hearing my terms. I told her that if I was to start paying rent, she would have to allow me to have company over every once in a while. I explained to her how unfair it would be, my paying a portion of the rent while still getting denied visitations as if being held captive in some dungeon ruled by an evil warlock.

And many times, she refused by replying, "Oh no. I don't think so. That's okay." Really though, she should have simply come out and stated that she never wanted me to be around people who loved or cared about me. It was as if she had a prayer of dictating such things around the clock.

Everything about her began to repulse me - her laugh, her cough, even her presence disgusted me. As soon as she came home from work, I'd fix my son dinner, kiss him a bunch of times, and I would leave the house or go straight to my room. I did this everyday, taking care of my son all day and avoiding my mother all night.

Sick of the Sick

The more numb I became, the more receptive I grew to become. My mother's signals continued to disgust me. She treated me like the love of her life when she needed a favor or a ride to the store. I grew sarcastic and dismissive towards her, viewing her as less than a human being and more like a dangerous dog you don't want to get close to. I was more quickly to call her out on her shit when she needed something from me, making fun of how phony and deceptive she was to her face. I was laughing at her, but not with her.

I began to challenge her ridiculous theories openly. She was a person with no educated thoughts, a person who would disguise her ignorance as valuable life lessons. I grew to realize that she was a person who wanted to appear knowledgeable without putting any real work to actually becoming it. I would overhear her teaching my son something that had no validity to it at all, and I would quickly intervene, correcting her narrow-minded lectures with real education and facts. I didn't want my son growing up uneducated about life like Latanya and me. I didn't want my son having to learn the hard way because my mother taught him wrong.

I made sure that everyday, my son gained more clarity and common sense to counteract my mother's negative influence. I taught little Lance how to read in less than two weeks so whenever he questioned anything anyone had to say, he had the necessary skills to research and read the truth for himself. I grew obsessed with introducing him to new things and new information.

And as our explorations continued, my mother had no choice but to sit and watch from the sideline. Why? Because she didn't have it in her to teach anyone anything of substance. After a while, the lessons I supplied for Lance were so comprehensive that if she wanted to add her two cents in, she would have to educate herself first, and I knew this was something she'd never do.

I began to have flashbacks of my childhood, focusing more on all of the neglect I'd been through. I began to acknowledge that teaching my son was something that made me happy, it made me proud, and I did it because I wanted to do it. I wanted to teach Lance things for his own benefit, not my own. It was a maternal instinct - actions from being a nurturer. I caught myself questioning why my mother could never do the same. What was missing from her DNA to make her not want to teach my sister and me when we were growing up?

Drowning

It seemed as though the colder I grew towards my mother, the more my son's father would creep out of his hole in the wall to harass me. I no longer had my protective New Yorker boyfriend to protect me from him, and somehow Vince knew this. He would text me the most foul, awful things, calling me every horrible name ever created by sinners themselves. The harassment became non-stop. Every morning, I would wake up to a handful of hurtful and degrading texts from him, and every night, he made sure to send me more horrible comments before I fell asleep. Vince would belittle me and my parenting, he would try to convince me that I was some awful person and mother who deserved no one and nothing spectacular. He made it his duty to tear me down, little by little, every single day. And just like my mother, if I responded in frustration and anger, he appeared to love it and dish it out even more.

I spent many moments attempting to trick my mind into believing that his words didn't affect me as they once used to.

But that was a lie.

They did affect me; they hurt me.

I would subconsciously replay his hurtful comments in my mind all day, and no matter what I did, those horrible words always came back to haunt me. Those words created doubts in my mind about myself. Both my mother and Vince took turns chipping at my self-esteem and confidence. Every corner I turned was a person who was supposed to love me, yet was hurting me.

I was already numb, and already cold with negative perceptions on what love is.

I became completely dark; I gave up.

And I began to drink more again. As soon as my mother came home from work, I would still make sure my son had his dinner and shower. But instead of going out to work or network as I usually did, I would go upstairs with a fifth of liquor in my hand and lock myself up in my tiny room that could barely fit my bed. It got so bad that I literally began to live in my room when my mother was home. I tried avoiding her at all costs. Sometimes, I would even turn my TV up really loud or wear headphones so I wouldn't have to hear her hurtful comments from inside my small room.

My bottle and my music became my vacation away from the realities of my pain as if I was living in my own country song. I would drink so much, I'd get sick. I would just sit on my floor and cry. I was so depressed, and inside, I felt so lonely and incomplete. It seemed as if my life was in shambles, surrounded by too many people who were either focused on bringing me down or didn't care if that was a side effect of their actions. I couldn't get away from the world, so I locked myself in an alternative one as I drank to escape every little bit of pain I had left to feel.

Having friends didn't matter to me anymore.

Having a life outside of my room didn't matter either.

I always felt like a homebody who was forced to have to leave the house, so I didn't mind it at all. I felt alone anyway, feeling like no one could ever understand me or what I was going through. So what difference would it make to try to create new friendships or keep the ones I had?

I lost interest in living.

I lost interest in feelings.

I was depressed, feeling like more of a zombie than a human being.

Taking care of my son and managing his challenging behavior on my own while numb from years of pain made me a prisoner of my own anguish. I was someone who couldn't fight anymore because I was too occupied with hating myself, someone who denied that happiness exists. I wanted to escape permanently, and the only being that kept me here on this Earth was my son. I'd daydream about the two of us living happily in a beautiful house surrounded by lakes and trees. I'd imagine us bothered by no one cruel, with maybe a pet dog or two - just us, and knowing what happiness is and what it feels like. No longer drowning in pain, but swimming in a lake of peace. This is all I wanted for the both of us.

Dealing with depression, I also began hating music. I felt mandated to continue, and thought about all the countless long hours I had put into making my dream a reality in hopes of creating a better life.

I felt as though it was no longer worth it; the industry was just as deceitful and abusive as the abusers I had in my personal life. And the more attention my musical identity received, the more I heard how much of a loser I was from my mother and Vince. The both of them spoke the same language, as they made attempts to halt my rising confidence and self-esteem in its tracks. According to my mother, my beauty was fading and I would never amount to anything. According to Vince, I was an embarrassment to co-parent with and I was stupid and foolish. These two were so busy trying to destroy me that they failed to realize I was too busy destroying myself.

Still drinking heavily and alone in my room at night, depressed and hopeless, I cried every night, that same quiet cry I wept in my closet as a young girl. As a grown woman, these tears felt more toxic, as though they were melting my flesh slowly but surely, drip by drip. And with every tear, I felt the subtle tears that seemed to rip through my heart like a freshly handmade Hattori Hanzo sword.

I was at my lowest.

And I believed in nothing good ever happening to me.

Trust Not Even My Father

My father and my mother continued to speak more frequently, and I continued to want nothing to do with neither one of them. In my eyes, any person that could sit on the phone with someone as they bash your own child is someone I can't trust. And from what I continued to hear, their conversations appeared to be back-and-forth gossiping. I viewed him as pathetic for allowing my mother to manipulate him well enough to turn on the daughter he'd wanted to build a relationship with for all these years. It was as if he never had his own experiences dealing with my mother, her lies, manipulation and hurtful and selfish ways. And because of this, I considered both my parents to be fools.

He would ring my phone sometimes, but my hurt always stopped me from answering. I lost all interest in getting to know the man I used to daydream about running away to. And the more my mother walked past my room, loudly gossiping about me to him over the phone, I would stay uninterested.

After my mother managed to ruin any hopes of building a relationship with my father, her relationship with him began to develop trust. I began to notice my mother talking to him about life insurance. One evening, she had all my father's life insurance policies spread out on her bed, while discussing them with him. She was managing them for him with the same kind of fraudulent love, attention and concern she'd use on me as a child after a successful audition.

As it turned out, since they were still legally married, my father had made my mother the beneficiary to his policies.

Finding that out, I was utterly disgusted, knowing exactly what was going on. This new situation my mother finagled herself into was a great opportunity for her, because my father had many health problems. He was in the hospital constantly and took many medications everyday for his issues. He wasn't in the best of shape. He was a strong man, but beneath the surface, he was falling apart. He was an amputee, having lost his leg from an infection that set in from a horrible accident during his days as a fisherman on the skylark boat.

In my mother's eyes, I guess that all equaled up to one money-making opportunity, because she definitely seized on it. For all intents and purposes, it appeared that she'd done it again; she had landed yet another gig to pimp someone out of their finances into a beneficial situation for herself. If I wasn't fully disgusted by her before, I certainly was at this point.

The anger I held towards my father turned into emotions of pity. I started to feel bad for him. He was probably thinking he had some chance to repair his marriage, and all he ended up with was getting taken advantage of. I thought about warning him plenty of times, but I also thought about how important it was for me to not get too emotionally invested in this man I barely knew. I was in a dark place already and didn't need another human being destroying me deeper.

It took me some time to gather up the nerve to confront this man. I waited weeks for the perfect time to finally answer the phone when he called. I hesitated at first, contemplating all the negative ways our conversation could go. But my anxiety turned into adrenaline, and then one day I answered. He sounded surprised that I finally decided to pick up the phone.

He didn't waste any time asking me why I had ignored him for so long, and I wasted no time explaining to him my reasons why.

I told him how I didn't appreciate the gossiping he engaged in with my mother, and how I thought it was sick of him to entertain it. He then tried to assure me that he was mainly just listening and trying to figure out what was going on. I allowed for everything he told me to go into one ear and out the other.

He continued to speak, and changed the conversation about my mother. Slowly but surely, my father and I began to understand that the lies my mother had told us about each other were just that - lies. We began to discuss her in depth, uncovering everything she'd done to me and everything she'd done to him - the same abuse, mistreatment, selfishness, lies and manipulation. She had hurt us all, negatively impacting all our lives with both her carelessness and carefulness.

I spoke to him about how she treated me as a child, and how she was continuing to treat me.

I told him about the conflicts she created every time I provided structure and discipline for my son, and every time I confronted her about this, she would tell me she could do whatever she wants because it was her house I was living in and she paid all the bills, despite my many attempts at offering her rent money. I allowed for him to catch a glimpse of my reality.

I wanted him to feel it.

Because feeling my pain through my words was the only way he would have understood.

That's the only way people ever understand; they have to relate. It has to spark a nerve within them to feel the circumstances of others.

After that conversation, we spoke every night, getting to know each other more and more each day. The more I got to know him, the more I got to know myself. I got so many of my personal questions answered in the process. He gave me what I needed to clear away so many misconceptions my mother had planted in my head about the man who had sired me. I got to hear about his family, and discover how similar I was to them as well. It was so nice having that connection, even if it was just a psychological and spiritual bond, even if I didn't know any of them outside of my father's words.

The more my father and I spoke over the phone, the more irritated my mother began to appear. She would creep up to my door and eavesdrop on the conversations I'd have with him, carlessly allowing her shadow and creaks from the wooden floor by her tip-toeing to give her away.

She turned paranoid in wondering what the both of us knew about her, and made it her duty trying to find it out.

This entire time, I learned that my mother had been giving my father false hopes of fixing their marriage. She told him that they would eventually move back in with each other and love each other the way they should have for all these years. Yet, I would hear differently from her, as she spoke negatively about my father to someone on her cell phone, explaining in amusement how she and him are nothing more than just friends and that's all she desired for them to be, despite how he felt. My father even disclosed to me how my mother wouldn't give him her cell phone number, and that he was only allowed to have our home phone number to reach her. If my mother was out and needing to speak with him, she would block her number when calling him. I recall on several occasions where my mother made jokes about that, making statements such as "I don't want him bugging me."

After my father confided in me with this tidbit of information, I felt it necessary to talk to him about his life insurance policy, explaining how he should reconsider allowing my mother to be his beneficiary. I told him of how her behavior reminded me of the countless times she'd manipulate me as a child.

Overwhelmed with facts and information about my mother and how I grew up, he continued to speak with her over the phone, but it had become short and straight to the point. He never said too much, as if he had built his own quick fortress in between their relationship. And every time my mother tried to get him to engage in gossip about me, he would get off of the phone by politely telling her he had to phone her back later.

Wanting Positivity

Still keeping a close eye on my son's behaviors with his primary care physician, I'd often find myself amazed more and more each day by how brilliant and amazing of a child he was becoming. He developed his own special character and voice. He was into bugs, science, football, philosophy and nature. My little Lance liked to learn about how things worked and how things were made. He could retain tons of information – fast – and remember it forever. If you taught him something one time, he'd think it over, come to his own conclusions, and then go and teach other adults and kids at his pre-school. This child of mine was becoming such a brilliant, bubbly, inquisitive, and loving child.

He would talk to everyone, lighting up the faces of every adult around him with his beautiful character and cute face.

I saw a lot of myself in my son, yet I also noticed other things as well. This included how his attention span wasn't as strong as perhaps it needed to be. And while he aced anything academic that came his way, he had some difficulty with common-sense tasks. He also seemed to get irritated and frustrated very easily.

At a young age, I focused on training him up to be a man of integrity – an effort my mother kept battling me about. That was a given, it seemed. A constant. Yet it was something I refused to take for granted. She was not going to influence his life the way she'd influenced mine. And I refused to allow my son to develop into an abusive sociopath like his father. I battled everyday to not allow the negative influences from my mother and his father to effect him.

I continued to work hard at disciplining and teaching him about right from wrong, despite my mother's tactics and his father's bad behavior. I couldn't allow my son to be disrespectful. There were times that he would talk back and even scream at adults, his teachers relayed. And he slapped, choked and hit both adults and kids. My son had a temper; he had a problem with rage and he needed to learn how to control it for his own sake, if not for those around him. Yet my mother continued to tell him that any bad behavior on his part wasn't his fault at all; it was mine.

The more passionate I was about his well-being and the more I tried to make her see the errors in her ways, the less agreeable she was. The less agreeable she was on the subject, the angrier I got. And the angrier I got, the more she antagonized me. She would tell my son things like, "You don't want to be a loser in a career that's not getting you anywhere like your mother," or "I want you to actually finish college, because your mother didn't." They were all subliminal jabs meant for me to hear.

No, I hadn't finished getting my B.A. because my financial aid ran out. And yes, I was still struggling to make it in the music industry. I was facing challenges, but I was working hard to overcome them. And it didn't matter how hard I tried; I knew for many years that I could never be good enough – never enough to her liking. Something was always wrong with me. Always. I was bad. I was evil. I was this. I was that. And she would say all of this to my child, the one person I love the most.

I couldn't even raise my child in peace; I wanted positive role models around my son. I would constantly get these beautiful flashbacks of the time I used to live with my two aunts. I would sit on the edge of my bed and just smile, remembering how happy I was. This is what I wanted for Lance. I wanted him to experience healthy and loving people, not people like my mother or like his father.

I would cry thinking about my Aunt Lia and how she didn't even get the chance to see Lance when he was born. I would break down, wishing she were still here to love us both. I missed her so much. And I missed the relationship I had with Aunt Valerie before the pain and manipulation my mother had caused. And although Aunt Valerie and I were working on repairing our relationship, it was still a challenge. The both of us are very empathic people; we sense and feel every emotion. And when we were in the same room together, we would sense the discomfort from each other, knowing that the both of us wanted to just break down and express our feelings entirely, along with what had happened over the years, but we were just too scared to do it.

This occurred for a little while, but we continued our healing process the best we could. Just as we did when I was a kid, we began to go out to festivals, events and family functions together. I loved it. And most of all, I was happy that Lance was now able to experience these joys with us. It was great! It would be Lance, Latanya, my nephews, my cousin Omar my Aunt Valerie and me. We all valued the positivity and the sincere love we gave to one another, and we appreciated Aunt Valerie for continuing to be a great influence in all our lives.

And soon, my aunt and I started to open up more about what happened between us. Just like I had opened up to my dad, I began confiding in her as well, disclosing to her everything I had been through with my mother for the past couple of decades. It broke my aunt's heart hearing things that happened to me as a child that seemed to happen right under her nose. I could hear how upset she was by the tone in her voice, and I noticed her fighting back tears as she told me how sorry she was that I had to go through the things I did. Just like my father, my aunt and I began exchanging information about my mother, uncovering the lies and deceit that negatively affected us for so many years. We both felt bamboozled, as if we were robbed of the happy times we could have been spending together as a family.

Wool Over Sheep's Eyes

    As for our extended family, word began to travel about my mother's behavior. She was still burning bridges with people who cared about her, and isolating herself from her friends and family.

    It seemed as soon as the relationship with my aunt began to mend itself, the one between my sister and I began to deteriorate. Surprisingly, Latanya and my mother began to speak on the phone, often. And it wasn't a coincidence that shortly after their reuniting, the bond we once had began to suffer.

    The one and only girl who could know my exact trauma - since it was identical to her own – began to turn on me. Damaged as she was, Latanya was the type of person to do and say anything to get our mother to love her; she always wanted her approval, and the more our mother wouldn't give it to her, the more she craved it.

    She may have found the will to move out all those years ago, but she hadn't found the strength to move on. It was like some sick competition she had with me that I wasn't even aware of for the longest time, started and encouraged by my mother. Naturally.

    My sister apparently held onto the fact that, when we were kids, our mother treated me better. But Latanya never realized that it was really because I was making money for her and she wasn't.

    Since our mother made sure to never tell her oldest daughter that fact, as my sister grew, so did her jealousy. She would try to impress our mother time and time again, only for those efforts to fall flat every time, leaving her to run off crying. Like any other abused child, she just couldn't understand for the life of her why her own mother couldn't be proud of her. And I suppose she never was able to grasp that it was simply never going to happen.

There's just something about a mother's love that you're always going to want; we're born to need it.

In my case, I still wanted that love too, but I knew better than to expect it from her. And sadly, my relationship with Latanya remained broken.

As He Grows

My son's situation, for one, hadn't changed. He was still excelling academically, yet still having serious behavioral problems. There were so many mood swings. He was growing more hyper, not less, and more unaware of the dangerous actions he committed against himself and others. His defiance levels were rising too, and he hadn't stopped struggling with simple, everyday common-sense tasks.

I remember taking him to parks and carefully observing how he interacted with the other kids. I would notice his aggression and over-excitability when playing.

My son clearly didn't understand the concept of limits. He never knew when a kid didn't like something that he did, and he never knew when to stop. It went beyond being inconsiderate. You could tell that he just couldn't help it. He was extremely impulsive and repetitive. At times, he would say the same thing over and over again, and a lot of his actions annoyed the other children.

This was heartbreaking for me to watch. I would have to sit there and watch my son get rejected by his peers, looking at his sad expression and the bewilderment in his eyes.

To counteract all that, I began to coach him, roleplaying in an attempt to develop his social skills. He was a visual learner, so I made sure to apply techniques that would keep him visually engaged and focused.

It was hard work. I can't properly describe what hard work it was. Not in mere words. Many times, he knew what to do or what not to do, yet his brain would make him do the total opposite. For example, I tried to teach him how to ride a bike and rollerblade, but he was more interested in pretending to fall than staying upright.

It seemed like he was never interested in regular child's play. Not when there were gadgets to tinker with and subjects to study. Recognizing this, I tried out another parenting technique. If he had a fascination with something, I just followed his lead.

First it was bugs. Then animals. Dinosaurs came next, followed by sports, the universe, and cooking. Whatever the topic, I allowed his mind to get what it wanted and apparently needed too, either getting him science kits or books, doing Google searches with him or going out on walks in the woods. Every fascination that came along, I made sure that he was able to learn about it until there was no more information left to be taught. And the results were so encouraging. Under that guidance, he became so much more at ease and less rebellious. It appeared that, when he was given free rein to apply himself, he could be great at anything. My child was a little genius, and I couldn't be more proud of him.

But he was still a little genius with a rage problem. I couldn't be with him all of the time, of course. He couldn't satiate his hunger for learning twenty-four seven. So there were plenty of times where he became abnormally frustrated for a child his age. It was a problem that seemed to get worse as he got older too. One minute, he'd be this sweet little pleasant boy, and the next that child was gone and, in his place, was a complete stranger.

I do need to state at this point that I was very blessed to have Aunt Valerie officially back in my life and back on my side. She definitely helped provide an understanding of moral and social structure in Lance's life. And it was also nice to have my father on my side. Recognizing more and more how his separated spouse hadn't changed at all over the years, he stopped speaking to her nearly so frequently. Being the God-fearing man that he became, he would still check in to make sure she was alright. But that was it; he made it clear that he didn't approve of how she treated me, or how she constantly undermined the structure and discipline I worked hard to provide for Lance.

For that matter, so did my mother's best friend. Between the two of them confronting her on this subject, she decided one day that she'd had enough of the valid criticism, and stopped speaking to them altogether.

That lasted until she needed a ride somewhere or some money sent to her bank account. Then she'd contact them.

To her own detriment, the older my mother got, the less she was able to hide who she really was.

Change

Thinking back, what probably hurt me most about my family situation was how, once upon a time, I really had genuinely loved my mother and my son's father - the two people who seemed so set on utterly destroying me now. And it did seem as if they were succeeding when I was rotting away in so many forms under their careful applications.

My father was worried about me. I know he was because he said so many, many times during our long conversations. Those were now happening every night, and I talked to him about almost everything. He never judged me for what I said or how I felt. He just listened when I needed to be heard, and he taught me about God when it was his turn to speak. For all the years we'd missed not being with each other, we tried to make up for them over the phone.

We really would talk for hours, which meant that he had plenty of time to hear the pain in my voice. As much as he tried to hold it in and be strong for me, I know my situation made him hurt too.

Sometimes I would lie in my bed or on my floor and imagine what a world without my presence would look like. Would it be better? Would anyone miss me? How would my funeral be?

I was clearly depressed and bordering on suicidal. Every time I looked in the mirror, I disliked what I saw. I hated the girl that stared back at me. She was weak, frail, and hungover. Sometimes lightheaded, too. My world felt so dark that, at times, I would get dizzy with my mind rushing in unnatural patterns. I worried constantly and would combust into a million tears, trying to wipe them away with my hot, clammy hands.

I would tell my dad about how I was feeling and the thoughts I was having, to which he did make me feel a little bit better. And knowing how much he wanted to be able to take me out of my current situation – knowing that he was there and he cared – was important too. He really was so helpful on explaining so many aspects about who I was and what I face. He even gave a name to those rushes of negative emotions I would get. Anxiety. He knew because he got that way too. As it turned out, it was a family trait.

I honestly felt like anxiety was one of the worst battles I had to face. Sometimes it made me angry, sometimes scared, and sometimes just damn-near crazy.

During this time, my sister and I attempted to form a real relationship. But it was always so weird and very fake. It was as if we barely knew each other, and in a way, we really didn't. Ten years apart, she left our mother's home when I was just a young girl. Ever since then, despite the occasional interactions, she had her life and I had mine. We couldn't help but notice how that made things difficult. Her jealousy and the fact that she was letting our mother trash talk me didn't help, of course.

But even more than that, we were both uncomfortable with substantial feelings. Any kind of real emotion that came up between us made us feel uncomfortable or, as our mother would say, weak. We had a difficult time expressing ourselves with strangers, acquaintances or anyone we weren't intimately close with in an emotional sense. In a word, we were both damaged.

And yet our damages showed themselves in different ways. For my part, I appeared hardcore and tough on the outside. For hers, she was the girl who was so desperate for love that she got herself openly and willingly taken advantage of by men and everyone else around her. She would disrespect her entire being in a desperate attempt to get a guy to love and marry her, while the very sight of a wedding dress would make me want to hurl.

We were opposites who couldn't help each other become better women because we were too intimidated of real-life feelings and situations.

To be honest, we were two lost girls under the same spell - a spell that hurt us and made us hurt others because we were hurt. It was a spell of dark magic, of chains that wanted to not only envelop and hold us back from our own potential but also bind those we came into contact with. I saw the damage our mother had done to our lives, our hearts, and our minds. And I knew I would fight tooth and nail before I'd let that happen to my child or nephews next.

The more and more I started to realize exactly how horrible my upbringing really was, the more and more I wanted to improve my surroundings for my own child's sake. I wanted to better develop my child, my thought processes, and myself. I wanted to eliminate all negativity. I wanted to be surrounded by people who loved me, and I wanted to not be surrounded by my mother's constant attempts to cut me off from everything good this life had to offer.

I was always a spiritual person. Ever since I was a little girl, I knew there was more to us than what we could tangibly grasp. But I needed to get my spiritual roots back. I knew that. It was just so very difficult to find room for positivity.

So when an opportunity came around to get away for a short while, I took it. An old friend of mine reached out to invite me to one of our old college pal's house to catch up like old times. These people were part of that small group of genuine friends I'd formed bonds with while in school; in fact, I can honestly say they were the only genuine friends I had on campus. As the years went on, we'd just kind of lost touch and went our separate ways, so I hadn't seen them in about a decade. But they were always positive people who made the best out of life.

I needed that. I missed them and what they offered. So I said, what the heck. Why not get out of the house for a while and have a little fun? Anything would be better than being cooped up in my room, hearing more of my mother's nonsense.

It was such a relief when my friend Daniel came to pick me up, and off we went. Being there among that small but special crowd was so great, and I realized how much I'd missed these eccentric people. All the good times just came rushing to my head as we took shots and cheered about all the good times we'd shared when we were younger and dumber. It seemed like we picked up right where we left off, like no time had passed by at all. It was a great night until it ended, and it ended pretty terribly.

Driving back, Daniel ended up falling asleep at the wheel. I looked up from checking my phone messages, and all I could see was this winding road that looked like it was fighting with the car.

The car lost control, flipping over about five or six times, tumbling on top of huge boulders that decorated the sides of it's dark narrow road. I remember trying my hardest to fight against the force of it to stay alive. I didn't want my head to go out of the broken window and the car to land on my head.

That didn't happen, but we did land upside down in a crushed and mangled wreck, looking at each other in shock and panic as the fumes filled the car making us black-out continuously. Fading in and out of consciousness, every time we woke up, we would frantically try to escape the crushed vehicle. But we couldn't. Both of the doors were embedded into the ground, making it hard to escape, plus we were extremely weak.

It seemed like this was the end for the two of us. We were going to die.

I kept thinking about my son, my family, and the time I had wasted focusing on misery, realizing how I could have done so much more with my life! I thought about my struggles and how my son was going to end up without his mom. I want to say that he gave me a reason to fight – to survive. And I suppose he did. But it was a struggle.

I fought with myself; one part of me really wanted to die just to end all my pain. My son should be okay, that side of me reasoned. He had family who loved him; he wouldn't even remember me. Even so, I did hope that, one day, he would hear the truth about me instead of the lies his dad and grandmother would keep telling.

It got to the point where I was ready to die. I was waiting for the car to blow up, wondering where I'd go - hell or heaven?

Then, seemingly out of nowhere, we were ripped from our seats and thrown into the grass away from the smoking vehicle. As I looked around, I realized there were policemen and firefighters everywhere. We'd faded in and out of consciousness so much that we didn't even see them there before.

The stretch we lost control on was a dark shortcut of a road with barely any lights illuminating it and barely any other reason for other cars to be using it at that time of night. It was narrow and haunting. The only reason the EMTs, firefighters, and police knew to come was because of the two men in the car behind us who called in the accident. Those two strangers saved our lives.

As the firefighters were spraying down the car we were in, I laid in the grass, confused and unable to really think straight, I absently moved my tongue against my gum-line. It was a movement that immediately set me screaming when my gums were all out of place. They felt like a solid, squiggly line.

As it turned out, my jaw was broken; my gums were deformed and out of place. I had lost teeth and some were even loose. I knew instantly that something was horribly, disturbingly wrong.

Staring at Daniel, I screamed at him like I'd never done before. I screamed that I hated him. "Look at my face," I yelled. "Look what you did to me, I hate you!"

And proceeded to giving him a facial beating with the little bit of energy I had left. I beat him like Keisha did Meth in the Belly movie, until he finally caught my hands and held them captive. Looking in his eyes, I could tell he was utterly heartbroken. But I didn't care in that moment; I was too angry, scared, and shocked to care about anything but my immediate self.

In a panic, I tried to get up to run toward the medics. I just wanted to run. Yet that wasn't an option, which was made very clear to me right away. As soon as I made an attempt to get up, every police officer and EMT was yelling at me to stay where I was, lying down on the ground.

Sure enough, the second I tried to take a step, my body just collapsed. I couldn't walk. It was so banged up that a single step gave me the most excruciating pain I'd ever felt even while my mouth, jaw, and entire face hurt so badly that I thought everything in it was broken. All I could do was crawl.

Daniel tried to come after me right away. Seeing all the blood coming out of my mouth, he thought I had punctured an organ and was hemorrhaging inside. The EMTs were rushing over too. Putting me on a gurney, they slid me into one of the waiting ambulances and raced me away from the scene. During the drive, I was still woozy and still disoriented while they tried asking me questions to see if I had any brain damage along with my more obvious injuries. But I was in so much shock, I kept screaming. I don't remember making much sense at all.

I remember the ambulance speeding through streets, around traffic and past cars. The speed gave me panic attacks, making it feel as if we were on the road forever. Then finally, we were there, and I recall lots of lights as I was rushed through the hospital halls. I remember the nurses and doctors setting up gadgets around me and the murmurs of medical terms mixed in with the urgency to move me from one ward to the next.

They strapped me down for MRIs and X-rays, and hooked me up to IVs. I remember hearing that I had facial fractures and that my organs were leaking, plus I was coughing up dark blood periodically.

Getting the news, Aunt Valerie rushed to the hospital, terrified. I got to see her long enough to understand how scared she was. This was the first time I'd ever noticed her anxious, and I suppose with good reason. She was with me when the doctors told her that my organs were leaking and that they might need to do surgery. I had to watch her face and heart drop as she heard and processed that news.

I, however, could only think about how I was alive. How I had prepared to die, and yet I hadn't. How I still had to deal with life when it would have been so much easier not to. I was so disappointed.

I'd been ready to go. I had said my goodbyes. And now, sitting there alive, I didn't know what to think about it. I wasn't sure how to feel, not even after the next MRI and the news that my damaged organs were clotting up on their own.

Those first few hours, I was too drunk for them to give me any morphine for my pain. But that alcohol had more than enough time to leave my body, since I stayed in that hospital for about a week. During that time, I was in pain from the teeth I'd lost, my broken jaw, a split disc in my back and severely bruised hips. That said, I didn't mind being there; I actually enjoyed it.

It was my first peaceful experience in a long time, where I was once again in a compassionate and caring environment. In light of that, my injuries didn't matter. My physical self may have been exceptionally damaged, but my soul was getting fed. And it felt amazing. Being away from the music industry, away from my mother outside of the times she came to visit, and away from my son's father was amazing. I got to enjoy rest and love. I got to experience hope and a reminder that being surrounded by genuine compassion was an actual possibility after all.

Just as with my last hospital stay, I sat in my room and reflected on everything about my life, trying to make sense of everything that had happened in my short years of living. I wanted to understand my life. I wanted to understand my situations and my consequences.

After almost dying, I wanted to escape my negative environment even more. I wanted to be free of everything that felt like captivity to me, and so it wasn't too long before I spoke to Jesus intimately. I talked to him as if there was no one else in this universe but Him and me. And while I didn't ask him anything, just shared, I knew I wanted a clear head. I wanted a chance.

Later that evening, while I was still lying on my hospital bed, I saw something that I'd never seen before. There were two orbs, one black and one white, floating in my room, one in front of the other. Staring at them both, I found that I wasn't afraid. I felt calm. I felt safe. I did wonder who they were, but overall I just embraced the company.

They stayed there awhile until one of the nurses came to check on me. Then they both slowly faded out, leaving me smiling in their wake.

Admittedly, their disappearance did make me even more curious about what they were exactly and what they wanted. Maybe they were just there to inspire some more thinking. I wasn't sure.

Nevertheless, I did think some more. I did realize that I had no real life. I'd been living my life wrong with no actual purpose despite how much potential God had given me. I was therefore disrespecting him by not utilizing the gifts, mind, power, and very existence he gave me to fulfill something greater than what I could accomplish on my own. I'd been living an unrighteous life and was weakening my seven chakras in the process.

My life could be better if my actions, reactions, and thought processes were better. I could become a person who embraced love. I could be a woman who worked for the good guys while loving God as much as he loves me. I realized I'd been playing for the wrong team for so long, and that my ways were not God's ways.

How can you have a better life with an undisciplined soul? I was making music that polluted people's minds, lyrics that supported violence and lust. I was damaging the youth, planting negative perspectives in my community all the while allowing similar levels of negativity to overwhelm me. I made it comfortable for that pessimism to dwell beside and inside me. My current purpose was a lie; it was smoke and mirrors to distract me from my ultimate purpose while I went around hurting, hurting myself, and dating hurt and hurtful men. I was using my intelligence and gifts to play for the other side, and it was damaging me from the inside out.

Basically, I needed a better relationship with God. I needed Him like my lungs needed air.

The doctors and nurses were extremely surprised at how my friend and I made it out of that car crash alive and un-paralyzed. They said we were exceptionally lucky.

We weren't lucky though; we were blessed. Hearing all the details, I became more and more convinced of it. With all the details still so fresh, it hit me how Daniel and I kept our bodies so close together during the accident while we were flipping. Despite the unnatural and terrifying force of that car being tossed apart and bashed in, there was another force involved that was even stronger – stronger than anything I'd ever felt before. How we kept together like that was nothing but the work of God.

There was also my chain to consider. I had a physical chain on that night that was wrapped twice around my neck, yet it somehow came off during the accident. I cannot give you a concrete non-supernatural reason why. Yet when my friend went to go see the damaged car in the compound, he found that my necklace had never broken. It had simply been removed, embedded into a small crack of the front windshield. He had to literally break the chain just to get it out.

If that chain would have stayed around my neck, I would have choked to death in the car. As many times as I lost consciousness, that chain could have strangled me in my sleep.

We weren't meant to die that night. My purpose was so much greater than what I was then doing with my life. The more these epiphanies and perspectives set in, the more I began to think those orbs in my room were a confirmation.

Throughout my time in the hospital, Daniel, along with my other good friends and family members, came to the hospital to lend their support. And those gestures meant the world to me. And after seeing how hurt and distraught Daniel was for causing the accident, my anger towards him quickly melted.

Before the accident, I had a dream that I died. While stuck between dimensions, I felt this strong sense of resentment and anger for not accomplishing more and for not being more mentally and spiritually focused.

I was mad at what little healing I had contributed to the world and to myself. My mother might not have taught me to do much of anything in a mature or godly manner, but that didn't mean I wasn't capable of it. That didn't mean I wasn't meant for more.

Slowly but surely, my visualizations of what I wanted in life and what I needed to do took solid shape; they became more understandable and realistic to me. I wanted a life with purity, genuineness, and the guidance and love from God. I wanted to do His work and be the best mother I could be.

All of my materialistic and selfish desires began to fade as I drew closer to God, and my understanding of who I was and who I needed to be grew stronger. I felt like a child just waking from an extremely long nap.

Going back home after my week-long hospital stay, I didn't return to my old drinking habits. That no longer interested me; It no longer seemed like a solution. Instead, I took up smoking ganja, which led to some of the most intense reality slaps I'd ever been through. Every time I smoked weed, I began to relive my worst moments, the mistakes I'd made and how I must have made people feel because of my actions. I began to piece together my life that had led to where I was now. I began to understand. I began to see.

Marijuana opened up another side of my brain that problem-solved my entire life. It gave me the insight to make better decisions. Marijuana was my therapy, even though I cried many nights while coming to all these realizations. They hurt so badly. But my soul was being repaired, and I most certainly felt that too. I was on a mission to regain who I'd been created to be before the abuse, trauma, negative influences, and the effects of my own ego.

I felt rebirthed. And now, I wanted to go to church.

Of course, I had a long road to recovery ahead of me, and not just spiritually. Physically, I had a slew of surgeries up ahead of me to repair my jaw and teeth. Due to my back injury especially, I had to be in therapy for months. But thanks to my newfound perspective, I didn't complain or sulk, and I wasn't depressed. Calm and focused, I looked at this stage of my life as a stepping stone.

I did have to rely on some temporary makeshift teeth for a little over a year. So going out to eat or attending any social setting where food was involved was extremely uncomfortable for me. Honestly, I tried to avoid those altogether, letting people who cared about me come visit instead. My true friends wanted to show their support, stopping by to give me the love and affection they knew I needed to get through this latest trial. And I was more than willing to embrace all the positive actions and feelings they offered.

Since my mother had stopped being kind and considerate after the two-week mark, she didn't always appreciate their visits. I recall my friend Edward coming over after he had gotten off of work, and us just standing in the kitchen talking for a while. It was a good interaction until my mother arrived and made it clear that he was not welcome in her house. Yelling at him, she called him a "thing" and threatened to call the police if he didn't leave.

His presence, she claimed, was bothering her peace.

Now, this was a woman who stayed in her room eighty-nine percent of the time. She would come home, take a shower – which was located upstairs in her room – come out to make a plate of food to take to her room, and then just stay in bed in her room watching TV all evening. Therefore, I couldn't take her claims seriously when my friend and I were simply hanging out downstairs.

I knew what was really going on. It was a common enough theme by then. My mother resented any male who stopped by during my recovery. Honestly, she never wanted them visiting me before the accident either. Any guy who might possibly have even the smallest of crushes on me was a threat to her, as if the thought of someone loving me through my hard times was intolerable.

This time around, she went so far as to threaten him with the police, which I refused to let her get away with. Standing up for my friend, I ended up telling her a thing or two about her behavior and herself as well.

To start with, I pointed out how the man she was verbally accosting had never done anything to her; he'd been nothing but a gentleman to us both. And then I addressed the root of the problem, confronting her on how she was always trying to sabotage my relationships with people who I loved and who loved me. I told her that it didn't matter what she did; I would never let her actions and tactics make me alone and bitter like she wanted me to be. Misery loves company, and I wasn't going to be riding on that misery train with her.

The whole time, my friend just stood there, looking at her as if she had lost her damn mind, understandably so.

That talk, deserved as it was, didn't make a dent in my mother's viewpoint. She simply went upstairs to make good on her threat and call the police, so my friend gave me a hug and left. I couldn't have apologized enough, but he made it clear he didn't blame me for the interaction. He thought she was insane.

This, to some degree, wasn't untrue.

As soon as I stopped drinking, and as soon as I declared my love for God and began going to church again, my life began to change because my state of mind did. I had applied for my own HOC voucher back when I was pregnant and living in my car, and out of nowhere, years later I received it. Which meant I was finally able to move out of my mother's house and away from her. The relief I felt at that separation was overwhelming, and the act itself further changed my life in so many worthwhile and necessary ways. I was able to foster a positive environment for myself and my child without my mother interfering and ripping it to shreds. I was able to teach my son the way I wanted and he needed. I was able to love him the way I wanted and he needed. I was able to more easily raise him right.

It felt so wonderful to have that ability.

Unfortunately, when you release yourself from one negative entity, another might very well try to sneak up on you in its place and wreak havoc. That's precisely what happened at my new apartment, where my son's father began to lurk around. He began to text more and try harder to appear as friendly as possible. Since I hadn't forgotten the years of abuse he'd put me through, I was very cautious. You could even say that I viewed him and his latest attempts to get me back like a science project before me, waiting for him to fall back into his old patterns.

Plus, after so many years, I just wanted to know why. Why the abuse, and why the mistreatment? Why the cruelty?

Of course he went on about how he wanted his family back, along with some other sick rehearsed lines. He would try – and try hard – to get us back, blaming all of his past actions on his past immaturity. He'd changed, he told me. And I believed none of it.

I would have been a fool to believe anything that came out of his mouth. He was a liar - a con-artist who was good at tricking himself and others. But, not me. Not even while I gave him the opportunity to prove me wrong.

I allowed him to come around more, and would listen when he felt comfortable enough to confide in me about his problems with his family. Just like I did with my mother, I studied every single thing that made up his wicked little soul. With every action he performed I felt as if I was an audience member at a poorly rehearsed play. This examination continued for a few months, and after a while I was able to stay ten steps ahead of my abuser, successfully predicting his every move. It felt like a much needed game of chess.

I realized his poor choices stemmed from the inability to think and process things logically. He was impulsive, and his natural instinct was always to be cruel and to resort to violence as his solution for almost everything, with anyone. Vince struggled with social skills, and didn't have the skill to convert his anger into words in order to develop healthy communication between his family and peers. And when he appeared to do something nice for you, it always seemed forced and too complicated for him to do innately.

So not only was he cruel to me, he was cruel to many others and was unable to control it. I studied him like a list of cheat codes to my favorite video game. Because just like with my mother, I knew I had to understand his crazy in order to protect myself.

Then soon enough, his facade wore off completely. He snapped. It was after a phone conversation where I mentioned the three thousand dollars worth of child support he owed me. I guess he figured if he remained nice enough, I wouldn't feel comfortable confronting his "nice ass" about this issue. Well, he was wrong. The child support that he owed me was increasing each month.

Instead of talking to me about it and telling the truth, he hung up on me. I immediately texted him, telling him not to come by my apartment like I was sure he wanted to. At the time I was recovering from hernia surgery and the last thing I wanted to deal with was a grown persons temper tantrum. But twenty minutes later, he literally came and kicked my door in while our son was in school.

Screaming and flailing his arms, he proceeded to throw my lamp and decor pieces across the apartment like some kind of drugged up maniac, punching doors and displaying the exact kind of person he was trying so hard to keep hidden from me. I threatened to call the police several times if he didn't leave, but it was like talking to a brick wall. It didn't matter what I said, and it didn't matter how I said it or how helpless I looked. Nothing seemed to get through to his brain receptors well enough for him to comprehend that he needed to leave.

I didn't want him breaking my things or putting his hands on me. Especially since I couldn't defend myself because I was still in recovery from my surgery, something he knew of, but clearly didn't care anything about. This was what the old me had to deal with; it wasn't what I was supposed to be handling now. Yet it was still happening right in front of me. After the third time, I told him to go. He snatched my phone away, and then shoved me down onto the couch. Every time I tried to get up, he would push me back down. And I began to feel the pain in my abdomen from where the surgeon made the incision.

So there I sat, not wanting to bust my stitches, watching him trash my apartment as he continued to scream like a wild banshee. I kept sitting there until he moved away from me, starting toward the kitchen. That was when I made my own move.

Getting up, I grabbed the Taser he'd bought me out of my room, and then calmly walked back toward him. At the sound of the device charging, his aggressive demeanor changed of course. Just like that.

It was like he woke up from a trance, as if his brain and physical body were in two different dimensions one moment, only to be suddenly joined back together by the sound of my high voltage taser.

He begged me not to tase him, and I replied that I wouldn't under two conditions: he gave me my phone back and he left. He did as he was told, taking off running like a bat out of hell, leaving me to finally speak to the police. Because what he failed to realize, is that before he snatched my phone from me, I had already dialed 911, leaving the operator to hear the entire thing.

I felt like it was a bad case of déjà vu. But the only difference is, I fought back, and outsmarted my abuser. And for the first time, I felt as if I had gained control over my life. I found that I truly wanted to stand up for myself and fight back properly. I needed to set a good example for my son and myself, showing how no man should treat a woman so poorly. No person should take such mistreatment and abuse. And with that being said, I pressed charges and got a restraining order. I protected myself and, in court, I spoke up and verbally related my ordeal. I expressed my pain and my need for help and protection against this male who'd been horrible to me practically the entire time I'd known him. This person was a bad influence in my life, and I made sure the judge heard that.

I was fighting back, and it felt damn good. It felt damn right. It felt like something I was supposed to have done a long time ago.

It's sad, though hardly surprising, that he never once saw the wrong in his actions throughout this process. During our court fights, he continued trying to manipulate my child into thinking I was to blame for his actions, saying that it was my fault he'd ended up in jail and then on probation. The fact that he could be such a tyrant, then turn around and point the finger back at his victims so consistently and unrepentantly still boggles my mind.

Fortunately, my son was getting older and wiser despite his persistent struggles. I had been working hard to instill morals and integrity in him, and they seemed to be doing some good. He even asked his father why he'd come to our home and broken our door and our things, to which Vince responded "Be quiet Lance" as if Lance was wrong for wanting to know why his own father would do such a thing.

Once again, reality had struck my son's father. Due to his behavior and irrational thinking, he would never get his family back. He had lost every opportunity at trying.

After this incident, we moved again. We didn't want that man knowing where we lived. We wanted peace, and a paranoia-free existence where we didn't have to wonder when he was going to kick down our door again, or even yet, be found lurking in a bush somewhere. It got to the point, where my son would pace the hallways of our new place in the middle of the night, wanting to make sure that I was safe and in my room. It would be three o'clock in the morning, and I would catch him creeping into my room to check on me. No matter how much reassurance I gave him that his mommy was okay and would continue to be okay, he couldn't stop worrying.

It was horrible and heartbreaking to witness. I wanted my child to worry about nothing more than being a kid and getting his homework done. And for my part, I wanted to just focus on living my life in peace and being a good mother. But instead, it felt as though we were both too occupied trying to relieve ourselves of the drama and chaos that was his father.

I decided to get my son the professional help he needed, not just because of his loony bin of a father, but because of continuing challenges my son was still dealing with. My bright, young boy was full of life, knowledge and love, but his struggles were taking a toll on us both. So I took him back to his doctor to explain all the issues we were still facing. That's when his primary physician suggested taking him to see a psychiatrist and to seek out a therapist as well.

And with her guidance, I was able to find a psychiatrist and therapist located in the same facility, and immediately filled out all the necessary paperwork, only to find out that the waiting list could be six-months long. Moreover, my application was lost in the mail then, forcing me to go to the outpatient clinic in order to fill out another application to hand in right then and there.

As it turned out, that additional stress was actually a godsend, since the receptionist there was so nice and observant. Recognizing that I was going through hell trying to manage the situation myself, I admittedly looked a mess - exhausted, worried, and like I'd given up on life itself. I was fighting back tears while I spoke to him and handed over the application papers, with my son in the background looking like he just couldn't control himself. I knew he was trying hard to behave. I knew he was. Yet he was still fidgeting in his seat, making strange noises and facial expressions, and not following directions.

I suppose it was obvious I had my hands full. And I also suppose that receptionist had already seen it all, but he still managed to move that six-month waiting list down to two weeks. He was such a blessing!

Between the second move and my son's clear and rising anxiety, I was exhausted, especially when the older he became, the more complex his issues seemed to get. I was stressed trying to manage his fits of defiance, impulsivity and rage. I was overwhelmed with his lack of comprehension and hyper tendencies. Sometimes, honestly, I felt as if I was raising ten children on my own instead of one.

I was tired of getting the phone calls from his school. I was tired of worrying about what dangerous things he would do to himself and others next. And I was tired of seeing him sad and confused because he just didn't understand why he couldn't control himself or make friends. My son's confidence and self-esteem were at risk as a result of all this.

During our first few visits with Lances new therapist and psychiatrist, it didn't take long for them to discover that my son suffered from a mood disorder, yes. But there was more to it than that. He had symptoms of about five other disorders as well. ADHD, OCD, ODD, anxiety.

On the one hand, it was good to get a professional opinion. But, it increased my anxiety levels significantly. I found myself worrying about him constantly: his feelings, his future, his current and future successes, his health, and his wellbeing. It appeared he was facing and would have to continue facing challenges that might be foreign to other children.

His psychiatrist began to talk to me about different medication options to consider, and it took me a while to study each one enough to move forward with a treatment plan. But I finally agreed to one, granting permission for my son to take mood stabilizers to control his rage. This helped round out one issue but completely ignored the other ones. And when I tried pointing that out to his psychiatrist, he became irritated and rude, making it obvious that he didn't want to hear anything I had to say.

If my observations from past visits were correct though, he was like that with most women. He definitely treated his female staff badly. Fortunately, my son's therapist listened, both to my concerns and the concerns of his school. She also had her own interactions with him to go off of, so she was able to see the big picture, going so far as to recommend I take him to be tested at the autism testing department located not too far from the psychiatric outpatient center we were going to. It took three rounds of testing, but we did get the confirmation eventually. My son had everything we'd suspected this entire time: ADHD, OCD, ODD, and anxiety. But all of his challenges boiled down to one diagnosis, which was autism.

So here my child is with all these issues, which took a toll on the both of us. At times, his anxiety would get so bad that he'd leave scratches on my wooden dining room table from picking at it with his nails, not even knowing what he was doing. He would swing on shower rods and towel rods, and he killed his pet fish by squeezing them to death. My son would talk obsessively about the same things over and over again, and many times throughout the day he would even talk compulsively to himself.

I found myself exhausted and barely eating. I was running from therapist to psychiatrist, doctor to doctor. Test to test.

My main goal, of course, was to help him get better - to help him be able to live a fulfilled life with morals and responsibility. I wanted him mentally healthy, and I wanted him to be able to use his eccentricities for something good. I would encourage him constantly, reminding him of how smart he was and how much potential he had. We just had to get him on the right track, I explained.

Once he started taking the psychiatrist-prescribed medication, his behavior didn't change until we upped his dosage. Then it did start improving, which was a relief. However, the work wasn't done yet. He needed a team of professionals who had experience helping children with complex mental issues. I needed that team to actually listen to me - to join with me in a common goal - to help my son manage in life better.

In order to achieve that, we had to change clinics. Because I just couldn't take it anymore. I used to leave the original psychiatrist's office in tears and with no hope that anything was going to get better when it came to my son's condition. Between his attitude and lack of results, that man had my anxiety spiking to levels I had no idea it could reach. The worst feeling in the world is to think that no one in the world can help your child. It's the scariest and most heartbreaking feeling a mother could ever experience.

So Lance and I started to see a new psychiatrist and therapist at another clinic, which turned out to be everything we needed. It was a team effort, complete with compassion; and my son and I automatically felt comfortable with them.

I began to express to Lance's therapist my concerns, explaining how it broke my heart to see him go through so many challenges, especially at such a young age. A mother's worry for her child is one of the strongest, most intense feelings you could ever experience. And it is one of the strongest motivations on this planet. As such, I got used to observing my son's every move, facial expression and reaction. I made it my ultimate duty to understand him completely. And whenever he had problems understanding himself, I made sure that I was always right there to help him figure out all the wonderful and eccentric things that made up who he was.

I began to study more about his mental conditions. This led me to create customized learning strategies so he could learn what other kids learned without him ever falling behind due to his impairments. And little by little, I began to notice all my hard work paying off. All of these doctors' appointments, countless hours researching, school meetings, and strategies started to positively become apparent in my son's behavior. He began making friends and thriving in areas he lacked in before. And I kept great communication with Lance's therapist and psychiatrist to insure his progress.

I also began to develop a great relationship with the staff at his school. They all loved him; they saw the same greatness and potential that I could see in him, and they continued to help us with strategies, accommodations and support. That place was amazing. You could tell that everyone there truly enjoyed helping children, and I appreciated them immensely.

Throughout all these challenges, Lance kept such a beautiful heart; he continued to be such a wonderful soul. I'd constantly encourage him that, no matter what pain or hurt he might experience due to other people's negligence, he should work hard to never ever lose his ability to love; that is one of the best and most beautiful qualities he had.

My son was turning into the most compassionate, observant, and caring young boy I knew he could become. I realized this more and more each day. He would automatically know if I was having a bad day or if I was hurt. There wasn't a single feeling I could hide from him. Whenever I'd pick him up from school after a rough and grueling day, the first thing he'd ask me was, "Are you okay, Mommy?" That would then be followed up by "How was your day?" and "Did you eat?" And if the answer to that last one was no, he'd lecture me about how I needed to take better care of myself.

He loved his mommy, and I loved him too so very, very much. My son - the first and only true love of my life. I sacrificed and dedicated myself for one goal only: to see him flourish. It was to allow him to reach the very maximum of his full potential and to see him grow up happy, healthy, and a positive, peace-filled adult.

Our chase for positivity and peace was challenging, yet rewarding nonetheless. There were many moments where I felt too exhausted to continue, but I did, because the bigger picture was a beautiful one. I had many epiphanies throughout this transformation, but out of them all, there were some more powerful than others.

Awake

This is what I realized.

It seemed as though the moment I made a vow to live better, to love better, and to do better, negativity came in and tried to break me or keep me from fulfilling what I'd said I'd do. My life had been nothing but a battle of souls, with the spiritual attacks coming hard and fast whenever I seemed to make a breakthrough.

The better of a mother I became, the more behavioral issues my child would inevitably face. The better of a woman I became, the more emotional challenges I had to take on. And the more I separated myself from negative people, the more those negative people tried to claw their way back in and attack me with their tactics.

It was hard. There is no way to describe how hard it is without some shared context. But I will say that, the more I drew closer to God, the more blatant and obvious the attacks became. I got clarity on how petty they were. They became openly wrong and ridiculous. The shorter the grass got, the more apparent the snakes hiding out there became.

God was giving me the vision, knowledge and mental power to fight my battles righteously. He was giving me the power and discipline to be the bigger person and ignore people who attempted to hurt me or do me wrong. My only goal during this time was to love; I never wanted to hate again. I had hated for far too long. I had resented for far too long. I had been through so much pain throughout my life, but I finally had the courage to change and love.

This was the first time in my whole life that I wanted my mark on this world to be that of a servant of God. A child of God. I wanted Him to use me to help and love others. I wanted Him to use me to heal corrupted and misguided minds. I saw my culture dying and struggling. I saw the beautiful black queens and kings around me misrepresenting themselves and turning into something they were never meant to be. I saw the youth stumbling through life, not realizing that they can do and be so much better. Black men were disrespecting black women, and there was such a divide within our culture that was tearing apart our families, morals, and chances of knowing real peace. My people were brainwashed puppets, focusing on things that were never made to matter. I saw slavery all over again – just in a different form this time – where my people went through life ignorant of how we once ruled the planet. Ignorant to the strength and leadership in our very own DNA.

I had opened my eyes. And now, I wanted to forever put being part of those problems behind me. I wanted to become part of the solution instead.

We were created to be strong, mindful and benevolent. We were created to love and rule under God. This world has taken our accomplishments and power. We as a people have been manipulated into hating each other and tricked into believing that hate is love. Our oppressors want us to glorify immoral behavior so they can destroy our beautiful essence and our potential to be great like we were once before. They plague our mind with frivolousness to distract us from our spiritual destiny.

And it's to such disappointment that we allow it to happen.

When these epiphanies came to me, they came on strong. They hit hard, challenging me mentally, emotionally and spiritually. To wake up one day and become this spiritual blossom - this lover of life and love – an advocate for positive change? It was a tough assignment to take on, yet it was so refreshing at the same time.

It meant that I no longer related to the people I once related to. My state of mind was different. It had expanded. It allowed me to recognize how I knew things I'd never known I knew. It was like I had the experiential insight of a woman who had lived a hundred and twelve years, with all that time to process life and think it over. Many times, this new perspective confused me. I baffled myself. I fought with myself.

One moment, I'd be proud of my current state and the next I'd be so disappointed in my past decisions.

I was saying goodbye to how I used to be – to who I was. I told my old self that once I left it, it needed to be gone and never be able to return again. I would remember my past as lessons learned and nothing more.

I was turning into a spiritual warrior - more nurturing, more patient, and more protective of myself and the ones I loved. Taking all of this in and changing a little more day by day, I began to discover my gift for counseling and my way with words. Contrary to how I'd felt so often in the past, I was blessed with the ability to communicate. At times, yes, my anxiety made me feel as if reaching people through my voice was impossible. But that was a lie I simply needed to push through to the best of my ability.

I was blessed with the words and knowledge necessary to nurture and minister to the ones I truly cared about, making people feel something more than perhaps they'd allowed themselves to feel and opening minds to brighter perspectives. More and more, I knew this was my purpose. My calling.

With my words, I have the ability to help people see what you need to see. I take ego out of the equation, allowing those listening to see so much deeper inside themselves or their situations instead. With my words, I can create empathy and true-life solutions to problems.

For those who have suffered so much already, I can say that I've felt how you've felt, and seen what you saw. There doesn't have to be any judgment at all; only eye-opening understanding.

I have seen minds open up in front of me, and I've been so blessed to watch the pain melt away from a person's face when I was done. I've enjoyed helping people who lost their way just as I once did.

And here's an even deeper level of beauty that comes out of this process of conveying words. Once a brighter perspective is formed for one person, others follow up that same path, with each one being more conscious and brighter than the one before.

I can't tell you where I get these words from or how I'm able to put them together so that feelings can meet understanding in the mind of whomever I'm speaking to. I have no secret formula for it at all. This is God's gift to me; this is what I was meant to do.

I was designed to help heal many - many hearts, families, and souls. My calling is to help bring about a positive change in this wicked and corrupt world we're forced to call home. This world in which we must physically exist. This world we call society. In this world, my tongue has become a weapon for the greater good, and my mind has become my armor. The fog cleared from my eyes and left nothing but beautiful streams of clarity that are so beautiful, they could be melodic. Like a rainbow after a thunderstorm.

After rebirthing as a child of God – a servant of God – your old surroundings seem like deadly, dark paths you fear to ever re-enter again. And more often than not, you find yourself wondering so many questions, possibly even berating yourself over them.

What have I done? Why did I do those things to others or myself? How could I have done those things better? How could I have allowed such disrespect? Where was my respect for myself throughout this entire ordeal?

You beat yourself up about the morals you lacked and the love you didn't give and have. I know because I have and I did. I'm telling you this from personal experience. And so please take this following statement the same way as well…

Don't mentally and spiritually torment yourself trying to figure out your stability from before you were saved. There's a very high chance that you simply won't be able to understand it. And besides, what does your past matter now that you're following the grace of God? You're now saved from that fog you were once living in. Your pain and self-destruction are over! And that old you is now an entity you wouldn't even want to be in the same room with anymore.

So instead of focusing on all that disappointment, bring light to your newly found being. Embrace the beautiful colors of your newly developed aura. Bathe in the fact that you made it out alive.

The devil wants us to dwell on the past - to be sick and depressed with how we once were. We have to stand up and recognize that the devil is a liar, which means your past was nothing more than a series of lessons to be learned and opportunities to build your character. Understand that you had to go through hell and high water in order to serve your purpose, so that you would survive and help others with their own journeys – their own battles.

We all have destinies. But what's a dream worth when we don't have to fight for it? Our pain, and our trials and tribulations are that fight to become greater and better.

No matter the subject you're studying, you have to be a great student first in order to become a great leader and teacher. You have to follow your professor's guidance and study the modules any teacher's aides hand out to you. When it comes to life, your professor is God and your teacher's aide is your life experience. And while those life experiences can be rough – so exceptionally agonizing at times – you often have to go through pain yourself in order to help release it in others.

A soul that has been through nothing won't have the spiritual strength to run the demons away in others. I can say that with utmost confidence because I've been through the kind of mental, emotional and psychological torture that would make most people insane. And I'm still fighting because I refuse to give up after all the fighting I've already had to do. I'm not going to let those lessons learned go to waste. My trials and tribulations will not go in vain.

The thing about being abused all your life is that you're somehow unaware of how you're living in an environment that's trying to harm you. Or maybe you recognize the harm to some degree, but won't or can't see how bad it really is. You may think you're really okay, or you might assume that, maybe, in the future, you're going to be okay. Your mind and soul are besieged by a heavy, dense, dark fog; you aren't able to see the severity of the abuse. Not until that fog begins to clear. That was the case for me. All my life, I had dealt with abuse. Abuse from my mother, from other kids, from my son's father. All my life, I had lived in a broken world. And as such, I was sadly accustomed to it.

So don't be scared or feel ashamed to talk to someone who loves you, or seek a therapist, because attempting to get out of your conditioned life isn't always as easy as it should be. Everyone needs healthy guidance, no matter what age.

When I set up my first appointment with my therapist, I was so nervous. I had never talked too much about what had happened to me to anyone before, not even to my aunts. Even when it came to my father, I kept certain information to myself, unwilling or unable to let anyone else share the burden. What I didn't share, I buried away deep down inside for no one else to see. For that matter, I learned to bury it so well that, when I went out in public or interacted with friends and extended family, I could usually put on a great show that life was pleasant and filled with hope, when in actuality, I was dying inside.

As such, my first appointment with my therapist was out of my comfort zone, which I think she recognized. I suppose she had to considering how high my anxiety was and the obvious fact that I was fighting back tears before I even sat down in her chair. But she was very sweet and soft-spoken with me. She was compassionate and non-judgmental. She had so much love and so many nurturing qualities about her that, for once in my life, I felt safe enough to open up about my real life. That's not to say I wasn't a mess trying to express it all. In all honesty, I could barely hold it together while I spoke with her.

My therapist's face said so much while she let me talk. She looked as if she just wanted to hug me and show me what love was really about, and when she did say something, she told me how impressed she was that I was still living, walking, and breathing after so much abuse.

It was such a relief to get confirmation and assurance that I hadn't deserved what was done to me. I was a fighter and so I could keep fighting still.

I continued to see her every week after that, resulting in one revelation after another. Now, these didn't come easy. I would sit in her office and pour my heart out, crying until my eyes were puffed up and red as I detailed events and painful milestones and old wounds. Each time, I tried so hard to suppress those tears, but my soul just wouldn't allow it. Apparently, it knew better than me how much I needed to release in a safe and caring environment.

The more I saw her, the more I realized that what I'd been through was a truly traumatizing experience, one that had shaped my worldview into something skewed, twisted and unhealthy. The more I spoke to her, the more I learned about myself and about the beauty that had created me. The real me. The me I was beginning to figure out, and the me who God intended me to be.

The moment I asked God to give me the support I needed for my son and me, amazing people and resources began to surface. My therapist gave me the strength to speak and the platform to be heard. She nurtured me back to health, helping me to see that I'd been wrong for so long about staying quiet and protecting my abusers. I guess I felt like if I stayed quiet and took the abuse, the next bad thing they'd do to me wouldn't be that bad.

In other words, I was fearful. I allowed bullies to run my life and break me down. I'd allowed these people to tell me I was worthless, to cripple my growth and my value. The more I saw of my therapist, the more I saw in myself. It was like being alive for the first time, just in adult form. Under her careful guidance, my perspective changed ever more until I was ready for nothing less than peace and happiness for myself, my son, and the family and friends that truly loved us.

Vince was ordered by the court to stay away from me, and I only communicated with his parents regarding Lance. I also set strict boundaries with my mother, allowing her to see Lance in a supervised setting to prevent her negativity from rubbing off on him, but my relationship with her was over. My relationship with anyone toxic was over.

I began working hard to create a positive and peace-filled existence for us.

It's simple, certain people belong in your life, and certain people don't.

My conscience continued to become stronger and stronger, as I allowed God to alter my being more and more, which in turn, helped me to see my goals more realistically. I felt empowered to achieve those goals.

I became more assertive, showing every negative element that tried to disrupt our peace know that its behavior and thought processes were not welcome or tolerated. I genuinely felt like my own construction crew as I went about demolishing the ugly elements in our lives and renovating it into something much more beautiful.

The dark generational chains that had been wrapped around my son and me needed to be broken. They needed to be unlocked. We needed to be free of them, and not only for our sakes but also for those of generations to come. This was my legacy at stake. So everything I was doing? All my efforts? They were going to save my family for years and years to come.

God was giving me – and still continues to give me – the knowledge, strength, patience, people, and resources I needed to break the bonds that had been passed down from my mother's parents, to my mother, to me, and on to my son. However long it had been going on, it had to stop here. And God was helping me day by day to make sure that happened.

He is so amazing. He'll do things for you in your life that will have you feeling and knowing that it was Him and no one else. The more I love God, the more I cherish Him and the more I thank Him for keeping me alive and giving me what I needed to raise myself. Looking back on my life, I can see that I was never really ever alone; he was always right there looking out for me, guiding me, and loving me.

God gave me everything my mother could or would not. He made me strong, and he made my son intelligent and special. He gave us gifts to use to do his work. God molded me to be one of his many soldiers in a world that is so sickened from pain and despair. There are too many factors out there that unintentionally or deliberately try to put us to spiritual sleep, and for a while there, I let them. I was a hopeless zombie controlled by something downright dangerous. But when I woke up, I realized with astounding clarity that the only things that should and did matter to me was God, family, love, knowledge, wisdom and peace.

I did everything I could to keep that focus – to retain that truth – throughout my everyday schedule.

No More Chains

My mother and Vince had held me back for so many years, but that was my past. The moment I freed myself from their torment is the moment I began to live. It's the moment when everything began to make sense. It's the moment I finally heard what God had been trying to tell me the entire time. The only thing that had held me back from embracing my true nature and everything my aunts had instilled in me was pain.

I could now see the gifts and strength and abilities God had given me to be able to really live and to love – both myself and others. I became more humane and more passionate about helping others. My life was no longer about just me and mine. I had goals to help others, especially young girls who were just as lost as I was, who had been mistreated and abused to the point where they couldn't see anything positive about themselves or around them anymore either.

I finally woke up and began to fulfill my destiny - becoming more and more like God's child each and every day. I began to tap into the knowledge and wisdom he had always supplied to me. I found myself challenging others to grow. I became the teacher who never wants to stop being the student.

All those truly traumatic events I'd endured growing up became lessons of strength and knowledge instead. Everything began to make sense - my life, my pain, and my purpose. I was no longer that lost girl; I was slowly, but effectively, finding and learning my way.

Music was no longer my ambition. My ambitions had turned into something much greater - being a voice for young girls who, due to trauma, haven't developed theirs yet. I wanted to birth queens. I wanted to heal princesses so that they could someday help and guide other hurt young girls, to turn their pain into strength and give them the love they could only dream about.

What it came down to was that I wanted to do God's work. I wanted to make Him proud. He'd saved me and trained me into becoming a mental, emotional and spiritual warrior, and now I was ready to fight. That meant that, in addition to providing support and protection for the little lives around me, nobody was going to hurt my son or me again. And whoever tried to would meet this newly trained but powerful warrior God had created out of me.

Because I had a purpose now. I had a life filled with the love and guidance that I always yearned for. And no amount of evil was going to succeed in ripping it away from me. I was and am God's child. There was nothing else standing in my way – no matter how hard they tried.

My actions were not as they used to be. Instead, I was utilizing my words to fight my battles in constructive ways. I was using my faith and my prayers. I began to take the time to think.

When you have a purpose and a strong relationship with God, you will get spiritually attacked. You are so important that the devil will try his hardest to take you out of the game. He will try to send negative people disguised as spiritually-connected people to invade your space. He will try to destroy your happiness and peace. And most of all, he will try to throw you off your mission.

In this man made society, you will go through battles, and at times you will feel discomfort and possibly even pain. I can't promise Heaven on this Earth. But when you have faith in God through your many journeys, your battles will already be won.

You'll stop wondering why your life is such a struggle, asking yourself , "Why me?" and "When's it going to end?" You'll realize you were asking the wrong questions and depending on the wrong person or people to help. I know it's tough to get out of that mindset. Left to emotionally, mentally, and physically fend for yourself, to bathe and almost drown in your own ignorance. Not being able to hear our Heavenly Father because you refuse to listen.

I know all too well, because for years, I ignored Him myself. For years, I tried to manage without Him. And so I had to shoulder my burdens all by myself as a result.

But because you're a true warrior of God, that evil won't ever be able to truly knock you out. As long as you keep fulfilling your purpose, talking to God, and asking him for the things you need to keep standing and to keep going, nothing will be able to keep you down for long. This was a lesson I kept finding out over and over again. And now, this is a lesson I'm sharing with you.

Maintain

Our light is a gift from God. He created us with it and gives us so many wonderful qualities and characteristics in order to fulfill the purposes we're designed to fulfill. I genuinely don't know where I would be without Him. To look back at my life and remember those times when I wasn't actively walking with Him is one of the scariest things my mind can fathom. To walk without His guidance and love – to walk blindly, unprotected by His grace – is to walk straight toward destruction.

We all have a purpose, yet too many of us lose our way. When that happens, it's because we're either too hurt to see clearly or too scared to pursue what we know we should.

Your pain and every single traumatic experience you've ever gone through are skills and lessons to make you strong enough to survive and help others. The more experience you have, the more valuable you can be. But in order to understand the pain you've gone through and turn it into something useful, constructive, and beautiful – even if that pain is something as strong as a generational curse that's held your parents and grandparents back and is now seeking to hold you and your children back as well – you have to wake up and understand that the trials and tribulations you've gone through can now be your armor in a battle that is way bigger than yourself.

But what you shouldn't do is let pain defeat you. Pain can make you stronger. It can make you resilient and strategic. It can create character. Pain can either forge you into something powerful, or destroy the potential you know you have.

Which choice will you embrace?

This man-made world is tough, I know. It can be so very tough, and there are so many deceptive concepts and so much deceptive content so readily available. But as you gain wisdom, you begin to realize how unhealthy those choices are, whether they come in the form of food, entertainment or people. They have nothing but more pain to offer, so they're automatically stuff that you don't need.

As for the pain you've already experienced or can't avoid going forward, never let it turn you into something horrible. Never be that person who can't stand to really look at himself or herself in the mirror. Everyone has a past, yet our purposes and destinies are more than enough to triumph over all of that. Our trauma and life experiences can be turned into things that can help and educate our world. We just need to learn how to decipher between the trash and the gold. And to do that, we need to let God be our guides through life. Once we do, we'll realize that He's the only guide we'll ever need.

We are greater than what we think we want to be. You are greater than what you think you want to be. So don't settle for mediocrity. Don't settle for less than what you're worth. You need to tap into who you really are and ask God for the guidance to find your way. Don't be trapped in a lifestyle that cannot love you back or bring you peace. Don't be conditioned into thinking that what you're doing now is all you can do or all you can become.

Open your closed mind and step beyond the walls others have tried to place around you or you've tried to place around yourself. Walk out from that supposedly protective enclosure in order to really see life: what it is, what it means, and what it can be.

You weren't made to struggle; you were created to thrive. You were meant to be the best version of yourself - not the best version of your ego - but the best version of who God created you to be. If you would only strip yourself of what you thought you knew and deleted all the man-made influences from your memory, if you took away what people think of you and your worry about what impressions you make in front of others, and if you gave back all your social and professional titles...

What would be left?

And who would you be?

That, my friend, is a question worth asking. Because the real you is a person worth pursuing.

Made in the USA
Columbia, SC
26 July 2018